Critical Theories, Radical Pedagogies, and Social Education

EDUCATIONAL FUTURES
RETHINKING THEORY AND PRACTICE
Volume 45

Series Editors
Michael A. Peters
University of Illinois at Urbana-Champaign, USA

Editorial Board

Michael Apple, *University of Wisconsin-Madison, USA*
Miriam David, *Institute of Education, London University, UK*
Cushla Kapitzke, *Queensland University of Technology, Australia*
Simon Marginson, *University of Melbourne, Australia*
Mark Olssen, *University of Surrey, UK*
Fazal Rizvi, *University of Illinois at Urbana-Champaign, USA*
Linda Tuahwai Smith, *University of Waikato, New Zealand*
Susan Robertson, *University of Bristol, UK*

Scope
This series maps the emergent field of educational futures. It will commission books on the futures of education in relation to the question of globalisation and knowledge economy. It seeks authors who can demonstrate their understanding of discourses of the knowledge and learning economies. It aspires to build a consistent approach to educational futures in terms of traditional methods, including scenario planning and foresight, as well as imaginative narratives, and it will examine examples of futures research in education, pedagogical experiments, new utopian thinking, and educational policy futures with a strong accent on actual policies and examples.

Critical Theories, Radical Pedagogies, and Social Education

New Perspectives for Social Studies Education

Edited by

Abraham P. DeLeon
University of Texas, San Antonio, USA

E. Wayne Ross
University of British Columbia, Canada

SENSE PUBLISHERS
ROTTERDAM/BOSTON/TAIPEI

A C.I.P. record for this book is available from the Library of Congress.

ISBN: 978-94-6091-276-4 (paperback)
ISBN: 978-94-6091-277-1 (hardback)
ISBN: 978-94-6091-278-8 (e-book)

Published by: Sense Publishers,
P.O. Box 21858,
3001 AW Rotterdam,
The Netherlands
http://www.sensepublishers.com

Printed on acid-free paper

All Rights Reserved © 2010 Sense Publishers

No part of this work may be reproduced, stored in a retrieval system, or transmitted in any form or by any means, electronic, mechanical, photocopying, microfilming, recording or otherwise, without written permission from the Publisher, with the exception of any material supplied specifically for the purpose of being entered and executed on a computer system, for exclusive use by the purchaser of the work.

TABLE OF CONTENTS

Acknowledgement: Through Collaboration, All Things are Possible vii

Introduction: On the Edge of History: Towards a New Vision of Social Studies Education ix
Abraham P. DeLeon and E. Wayne Ross

1. Anarchism, Sabotage, and the Spirit of Revolt: Injecting the Social Studies with Anarchist Potentialities 1
Abraham P. DeLeon

2. Embattled Pedagogies: Deconstructing Terror from a Transnational Feminist Disability Studies Perspective 13
Nirmala Erevelles

3. Ecojustice, Community-based Learning, and Social Studies Education 25
Rebecca A. Martusewicz and Gary R. Schnakenberg

4. Why have School?: An Inquiry through Dialectical Materialism 43
Rich Gibson

5. Gumbo and Menudo and the Scraps of Citizenship: Interest Convergence and Citizen-making for African Americans and Mexican Americans in U.S. Education 65
Anthony Brown and Luis Urrieta, Jr.

6. "The Concrete Inversion of Life": Guy Debord, the Spectacle, and Critical Social Studies Education 85
Kevin D. Vinson, E. Wayne Ross and Melissa B. Wilson

7. Critically Examining the Past and the "Society of the Spectacle": Social Studies Education as a Site of Critique, Resistance, and Transformation 115
Brad J. Porfilio and Michael Watz

8. The Long Emergency: Educating for Democracy and Sustainability during Our Global Crisis 139
David Hursh

9. Building Democracy through Education: Human Rights and Civic Engagement 151
William T. Armaline

TABLE OF CONTENTS

10. Critical Reflection in the Classroom: Consciousness, Praxis, and Relative Autonomy in Social Studies Education 163
    Wayne Au

11. The Radical and Theoretical in Social Studies 183
    Stephen C. Fleury

ACKNOWLEDGEMENT

Through Collaboration, All Things are Possible

Although a bit cliché, the statement above best reflects what this project has meant for us. Emailing Wayne on a whim after being inspired by the collection he put together for *The Social Studies Curriculum: Purposes, Problems and Possibilities, 3rd ed.* (State University of New York Press, 2006), he was, to my amazement, interested in the project of a young and hungry scholar. We pitched the book to Sense Publishers and they saw promise in our ideas and offered us a contract. We hope this book adds to their impressive library of critical books in education.

Through our collaborative work, we assembled a wide variety of talented scholars that have reaffirmed the importance that radical ways of knowing and critical theories can have in social studies education. As this book fruitfully demonstrates, traditional status quo social studies education reproduces problematic assumptions about the world around us. In a direct way, these scholars challenge this notion and offer us possibilities for something different. This book features new and familiar voices that refuse to accept the status quo in their teaching and scholarship. We want to extend our deepest gratitude for their hard work and patience with us during the editing process. In addition, we would like to thank Youmna Dbouk for her work editing the manuscript. We hope this collection inspires you to ask questions, take action, and create new possibilities for your praxis.

Abraham P. DeLeon: For Stephanie: thank you for your patience and love. For Mr. Bad Ass: thank you for your enduring companionship. For my family and friends: you have my heart. For my intellectual mentors: I extend a deep thank you for helping me see the world differently. For the rebels, malcontents, weirdos, anarchists, punks, and social visionaries: *infiltrate*.

E. Wayne Ross: The highlight of this project for me, both personally and intellectually, was the opportunity to collaborate with and learn from Abe. He is a principled, activist-scholar with bold and fresh ideas that push hard against the established boundaries of the field, which can only benefit from the insights and challenges his work produces. I continue to gain much from my longtime intellectual partnerships and friendships with Kevin Vinson, Rich Gibson, Perry Marker, Steve Fleury, and David Hursh. My most important collaborator is my soul mate, Sandra Mathison, words cannot express what she means to me.

INTRODUCTION

ON THE EDGE OF HISTORY

Towards a New Vision of Social Studies Education

> *Savages, while differing from civilized men in the methods that they use and in the results that they reach, still deal with causes. They think themselves surrounded by occult influences and mysterious powers ... at the opposite pole of thought are the conceptions of unity, law, and order, which constitute the core of modern science and philosophy.*
>
> B. A. Hinsdale, *How to Study and Teach History* 1894, p. 102

Historical study has a long tradition within public education and B. A. Hinsdale's work was one of the founding texts in developing what we consider today to be "social studies". Although "social studies" as a disciplinary mechanism within public schools did not formally emerge until the end of the 19th century (or the official 1916 NEA report that established the scope of social studies education), the teaching of history was a staple in most public schools as a vital and important component of a liberal education that introduced students to the classics of Western culture (Ross, 2006b; Thornton, 1996). Steeped in a Eurocentric framework as Hinsdale's comments reflect, public schools in the United States developed their curriculum and standards around these narrow conceptions. "Stereotypic images, carefully constructed and equally carefully defined, are, therefore, mechanisms of control linked to structures in the society which provide stability, power and status" (Mangan, 1993, p. 8). With the rise of neoliberal capitalism and intensification of industry over the past century since Hinsdale penned his comments, public education has slowly shifted towards a framework rooted in high-stakes testing and the discourse of "accountability" (Gabbard & Ross, 2008; Mathison & Ross, 2008; Ross & Gibson, 2007). This is, of course, also influenced by the larger epistemological trend that places quantitative, empirically based forms of research and knowledge as some of the only legitimate forms of understanding the world. However, with the rise of *No Child Left Behind* (NCLB) and its narrow understandings of reading, math, and science, social studies and the arts have virtually disappeared as time is now spent on test preparation and these other academic areas (Au, 2009; McGuire, 2007). We, of course, understand that this is a larger trend of modernity, but it is also how these particular content areas help reproduce a highly militarized, hierarchical, and industrialized State (Saltman & Gabbard, 2010). It is not an accident that schools help reproduce the prevailing status quo that is steeped in a politics of exclusion that seeks to marginalize, displace, oppress, silence and stifle dissent against the prevailing social order. Schooling is implicated within this hegemonic system and traditional social studies education helps reproduce this reality through its detached narratives of

INTRODUCTION

progress, modernization, and empty promises of political participation (Ross, 2000). Hinsdale's comments also demonstrate the pervasive nature of systemic racism that permeated early conceptions of indigenous peoples and historically oppressed communities of color. These racialized, classed and gendered ideologies were wholly inscribed into Westernized epistemologies from the rampant colonialism that existed during this time period as well.

The curriculum and pedagogy of social studies education has, unfortunately, primarily been a mechanism that helps (re)produce dominant conceptions of our social world, while at the same time silencing and marginalizing localized, indigenous, and other ways of knowing that falls outside the linear and Grand Narrative of Western history. The recent debate over the Texas social studies curriculum is also alarming as the conservative board that oversees curriculum has decided to omit certain facts, personalities, and realities from an already skewed historical interpretation (Foner, 2010; McKinley, 2010). Vinson and Ross (2001) argue that the paradox of social studies curriculum and practice is that it is marked by both the appearance of diversity (e.g., the various "traditions" or aims proposed for social studies curriculum and instruction) and the appearance of uniformity (e.g., stable curricular scope and sequence and entrenched patterns of instruction).

For example, it has been variously argued that the aim of social studies education should be: (1) cultural transmission; (2) understanding history and the social sciences disciplines; (3) reflective inquiry on social issues; (4) personal development; or (5) informed social criticism (among others), which gives the field an appearance of pedagogical and curricular diversity. Despite the historical debates about the purposes of social studies, the classroom reality—past and present—is that social studies aims to conserve dominant cultural perspectives by uncritically transmitting information from corporate textbooks and government syllabi, while socializing students to enter adult life without a ripple of discontent or change.

Well before conceptualisation and enactment of the current standards-based approach to education reform, the most durable and common pattern of social studies teaching was the uncritical transmission of information. Cuban (1991) found that social studies teachers in the 1980s taught much like their counterparts in the 1940s:

> the vast majority of teachers [employ] teacher-centered instruction. The pattern includes activities using the textbook and teacher as sources of information for assignments, recitation ... tests, and individual seatwork. Talking by the teacher ... exceeds talking by students, whose responses are generally confined to answering the teacher's questions. Occasional use of films, videos, and other devices supplements these activities. This core pattern is most frequently enacted when the entire class is taught as a group. Infrequently at the high school level, but with slightly more frequency at the elementary level, small-group work is a vehicle for classroom activities. (p. 204)

Social studies teachers have also consistently relied on textbooks as a primary source of information. These patterns of instruction in conjunction with content analyses of social studies textbooks—which illustrate that many texts are marred by an embarrassing combination of blind patriotism, mindless optimism, sheer misinformation, and outright lies (e.g., Leahey, 2010)—add to the evidence supporting conservative cultural continuity as the dominant pattern of social studies education. NCLB and the standards-based education reform movement in general have intensified these patterns of instruction and in many cases reduced the content of social studies to what is on government-mandated tests, while social studies has all but disappeared from many elementary schools, which may in fact be a blessing in disguise.

In addition to the considerable uniformity in the pedagogical practices of social studies teachers over the decades, evidence from large-scale studies indicates that there has long been at least superficial uniformity in the social studies curriculum, e.g., basic topics, sequences, course titles, and textbook contents (Vinson & Ross, 2001). Ironically, studies of teacher decision-making indicate that the cultural beliefs of teachers are also the basis of teachers' mediation of curricular topics, sequence, textbooks contents, and other learning assignments, which made the enacted curriculum quite diverse—at least in the past.[1] The use of high stakes testing and other reductive accountability systems[2], linked as they are to curriculum standards — seriously threatens the diversity that has existed within the formal curriculum, and, more importantly, it threatens potential for diversity in the enacted social studies curriculum.

Fortunately there has been resistance to these dominant conceptions both in activist politics and within the academic milieu. Academics and social activists continue to debate whether and how scholarship and research should be tied to an agenda for social change and justice. Though a central topic in many academic disciplines, this debate is especially salient for educators, who are explicitly or implicitly charged with facilitating the intellectual growth of future generations and the general public. Further, as suggested by educational philosophers such as John Dewey (1916) and Paulo Freire (1970), educators in a presumably democratic society are similarly charged with facilitating a critically engaged public and providing empowering educational experiences for their students. To wit, there is a well-established presence in the more current academic literature that supports building a democratic, critical, and anti-oppressive pedagogy dedicated to cultural, economic, and political critique and the creation of an egalitarian and democratic civil society (Darder et al., 2009).

In recent years, education scholars have proffered critical theories that seriously questioned capitalist, racist, sexist, ableist, speciesist, and other oppressive ideologies and argued for critical literacy and cultural critique (see Darder et al., 2009; Andrzejewski et al., 2009). Such critical pedagogies have been used to challenge educational practices and theories that are mired in domination. Social studies education can engage these social problems in very critical and direct ways because of the interdisciplinary nature of the content, its focus on building civic understanding and participation in students, plus its implicit and explicit inclusion of a historical framework. These foundational principles of social studies allow the integration of more critical approaches.

This book grows out of—and attempts to challenge the limits of—what has been described as the tradition of "informed social criticism" within social studies education (Martorella, 1996). This approach to social studies is rooted in the work of social

INTRODUCTION

reconstructionists (Brameld, 1956; Counts, 1932) and related to the more recent work of "socialization-countersocialization" theorists (Engle & Ochoa, 1988), critical pedagogues (e.g., Freire 1970; McLaren, 1998) as well as critical sociologists and anthropologists of education (e.g., Anyon 1980; Bowles & Gintis 1976; Willis 1977). This literature explores themes such as the hidden curriculum, socio-cultural transformation, and the nature and meaning of knowledge and truth. The work of Jack Nelson (e.g., 1985; Nelson & Ochoa, 1987; Nelson & Pang, 2006: Stanley & Nelson, 1986), Stanley (1985), and more recently Hursh and Ross (2000), Ross (2006), and Segall, Heilman, and Cherryholmes (2006) perhaps best represent the current status of this tradition.

From the standpoint of informed social criticism, the purpose of social studies education is providing students with opportunities for an examination, critique, and revision of past traditions, existing social practices, and modes of problem solving. Social studies content in this tradition challenges the injustices of the status quo. It counters knowledge that is: (1) generated by and supportive of society's elites; (2) rooted in rationalistic and oppressive forms of logical positivism; and (3) consistent with social reproduction and the replication of a society that is classist, sexist, racist, ableist, etc. While the means and ends are specific to individual classroom settings and students, it can include, for example, redressing the needs of the disadvantaged, transforming human rights and ecological conditions. Moreover, teachers and students may claim their own knowledges—their content, their individual and cultural experiences—as legitimate bases for action. Instructional methods in this tradition are situational, but are shy away from lecture and information transmission and toward such processes as "reflective thinking" and the dialogical method (Shor & Freire, 1987), socio-cultural criticism, textual analysis/deconstruction (Cherryholmes, 1999), problem-solving, critical thinking, and social action (Stanley & Nelson, 1986).

Building upon the informed social criticism tradition within social studies scholarship and practice this volume attempts to fill a gap in the current literature that exists relative to more radical forms of theory and pedagogy in and outside of academia. This book aims to open the possibility for the inclusion of a wider milieu of radical theories in social studies education (critical race theory, neo-Marxism, anarchism, human rights, disability studies, etc.), while offering alternatives to classroom practice rooted in these same theories of liberation.

In recent political struggles throughout the world, emergent radical (as opposed to liberal reformist) approaches to social change have become a powerful presence in such struggles as the "anti-globalization movement," grassroots activism over resources, indigenous struggles, and others that increasingly employ a human rights framework to address social problems. This book begins with the assertion that such emergent and provocative theories and practices should at least enter our ongoing discursive forums on social studies education in the 21st century. The "Battle of Seattle," autonomous actions by the Animal Liberation Front and Earth Liberation Front, and other global protests have demonstrated the success that radical actions can have in resisting rigid state hierarchies and oppressive regimes. Anarchists, eco-activists, feminists, critical race theorists, queer theorists, and other marginalized perspectives should be included as viable alternatives to the current neo-conservative

ON THE EDGE OF HISTORY

and neoliberal agendas expressed by such educational policies like *No Child Left Behind* and high stakes testing. The social studies, with its interdisciplinarity and historical based inquiry, allow us to engage in critical social inquiry and progressive ideas can be introduced into the traditional classroom. In sum, this book is designed to include and address radical theories in the conversation on social studies education, as they exist (discussed or not) in the praxis of many contemporary global (and local) political struggles.

OVERVIEW OF THE BOOK

This collection of chapters focuses upon this notion of struggle and social justice. Each author has taken a different theoretical framework and applied it to the context of social studies education. In Chapter 1, Abraham DeLeon explores anarchist theory and how as a tradition it combines theory with praxis, situating our research and classroom practices as acts of resistance to the current statue quo. In this chapter, he advocates for a *politics of infiltration* that is rooted in radicals placing themselves within established institutions and practicing acts of epistemological and ideological subversion and sabotage. According to DeLeon, anarchist theory provides a link currently missing in critical pedagogy when rethinking the notion of autonomous direct action and its ties to political action inside and outside of the classroom.

Chapter 2, takes us to a "transnational, feminist and disability studies" framework that examines two key historical events: Hurricane Katrina and the current wars in Iraq and Afghanistan. Through these two historical cases, Nirmala Erevelles attempts to explore the ways in which race, class, gender and disability is lived in the United States and the "Third World" through the concept of *invisibility*.

Rebecca Martusewicz and Gary Schnakenberg, in Chapter 3, examine social studies education through the lens of ecojustice education and both authors explore classrooms where these principles are being lived by teachers who infuse their pedagogies with these ideals. Ecojustice education examines cultural assumptions that help legitimate and justify ecological and cultural destruction worldwide as well as exploring how various communities are resisting these hegemonic neoliberal forces.

In Chapter 4, Rich Gibson asks "Why have school?" as a means of exploring dialectical and historical materialism and asserts that these approaches help reveal the interrelated nature of various forms of oppression and how these can be transformed. Gibson's chapter illustrates how dialectical materialism can be employed as an "action-research" approach that supports equality and justice in the social studies classroom.

In Chapter 5, Anthony Brown and Luis Urrieta, Jr. engage social studies education through critical race theory. More specifically they examine how the discourse of race frames the notion of citizenship within the context of the United States and the discipline of social studies. Through an examination of contemporary and historical examples of Latin@ and African American experiences, the authors highlight ways these groups have challenged the way "citizen" was conceived.

The concept of *the spectacle*, plays a key role in the analyses offered in Chapters 6 and 7. Kevin D. Vinson, E. Wayne Ross, and Melissa Wilson explore the work of Guy Debord (particularly his book *The Society of the Specatcle*) and

INTRODUCTION

the Situationist International and for their applicability for social studies education. They argue that a Debordian vision of critical citizenship allows students to build and develop critical social understandings and is a way to live these transformative notions through practice. Throughout their chapter, they promote the social studies classroom as a space for constructing social meanings and encouraging social activism. In following chapter, Pofilio and Watz describe how a critical evaluation of world's fairs during the Victorian Era in the United States (and similar modern-day political and economic spectacles) have the potency to revitalize the social studies so that students (1) develop the critical literacy skills; (2) learn to interrogate hidden agendas; and (3) recognize the urgency to remake themselves, social institutions, and culture as part of an effort to build a society free from hate, hostility, and injustice.

Next, David Hursh further expands his work on neoliberalism and education. According to Hursh, neoliberalism, or the emphasis on "free markets", deregulation, privatization, competition and the entrepreneurial individual, has restructured education towards producing a society based upon greed, accumulation and competition and undermines our collective ability to make decisions that promote the common good and environmental sustainability. Through reimagining social studies education, these types of ideologies can be resisted and rethought.

Chapter 9 explores the convergences of human rights and social studies education. William T. Armaline argues that human rights must be fused with a social studies curriculum by deconstructing popular notions like community, justice, and humanity. This approach allows students and teachers to explore the notion and limits of human rights as a political project, specifically considering the rights of children. The potentialities of human rights as a legal discourse are also explored; the chapter closes with a description of how human rights education can resurrect and revise the notions of public and civic education in our contemporary era.

In Chapter 10, Wayne Au argues that social studies education has the potential to build critical consciousness with students that allows students to critically reflect on reality and its potential(s) for social actions. Through poignant examples of actual critical social studies education, Au illustrates how such critical consciousness can be developed.

In the final chapter, Stephen C. Fleury looks back across the arguments and questions presented throughout the book and offers a critical assessment of project of critical social studies education as represented in this volume and an in general.

Each of these chapters forces us to rethink social studies education in the current repressive and draconian climate that policies like *No Child Left Behind*, the U.S. Patriot Act and the wars in Iraq and Afghanistan have engendered. These larger societal issues are important for social studies educators to understand and to engage with. In this way, teachers can help deconstruct and name how oppressive ideologies and practices are enacted and deployed. This project has been an exhilarating and inspiring experience for us as editors—an opportunity to work with scholars who are brave enough to resist status quo thinking, but also providing the intellectual and creative space in which to rethink how oppression operates in today's society. We hope that you find the following chapters as engaging and provocative as we do and that they help generate much needed debate (and action) regarding the current direction of social studies education. Although currently mired in a reproductive framework, social studies has *potentialities* that can be realized through a dedicated cadre of committed, reflective, open and critical social studies teachers who open not only space to critique, but also offer us a space of infinite possibilities.

NOTES

[1] See for example: Anyon, 1980; Chant, 2009; Fickle, 2000; Jenne, 1997; Ross, Cornett, & McCutcheon, 1992; Slekar, 2009; Thornton, 2005.
[2] The mandated national accreditation of teacher education programs has, for the most part, functioned as reductive accountability system that promotes a division of labor in which teachers have lost control of their work as professionals as it is conceived, defined, monitored by the State.

REFERENCES

Andrzejewski, J., Baltdodano, M., & Symcox, L. (Eds.). (2009). *Social justice, peace and environmental education: Transformative standards.* New York: Routledge.
Anyon, J. (1980). Social class and the hidden curriculum of work. *Journal of Education, 162,* 67–92.
Au, W. (2008). *Unequal by design: High-stakes testing and the standardization of inequality.* New York: Routledge.
Bowles, S., & Gintis, H. (1976). *Schooling in capitalist America.* New York: Basic Books.
Brameld, T. (1956). *Toward a reconstructed philosophy of education.* New York: Holt, Rinehart, and Winston.
Chant, R. H. (2009). Developing involved and active citizens: The role of personal practical theories and action research in a standards-based social studies classroom. *Teacher Education Quarterly, 36*(1), 181–190.
Cherryholmes, C. H. (1999). *Reading pragmatism.* New York and London: Teachers College Press.
Counts, G. S. (1932). *Dare the school build a new social order?* New York: John Day.
Cuban, L. (1991). History of teaching in social studies. In J. P. Shaver (Ed.), *Handbook of research on social studies teaching and learning* (pp. 197–209). New York: Macmillan.
Darder, A., Baltodano, M., & Torres, R. (Eds.). (2009). *The critical pedagogy reader* (2nd ed.). New York: Routledge.
Dewey, J. (1916). *Democracy and education.* New York: Free Press.
Engle, S. H., & Ochoa, A. S. (1988). *Education for democratic citizenship: Decision making in the social studies.* New York: Teachers College Press.
Fickle, L. H. (2000). Democracy is messy: Exploring the personal theories of a high school social studies teacher. *Theory and Research in Social Education, 28,* 59–390.
Foner, E. (2010, April 5). Twisting history in Texas. *The Nation, 290*(13), 4-6. Retrieved from http://www.thenation.com/article/twisting-history-texas
Freire, P. (1970). *Pedagogy of the oppressed.* New York: Continuum.
Gabbard, D., & Ross, E. W. (Eds.). (2008). *Education under the security state.* New York: Teachers College Press.
Hinsdale, B. A. (1894). *How to study and teach history with particular reference to the history of the United States.* New York: D. Appleton and Company.
Hursh, D., & Ross, E. W. (Eds.). (2000). *Democratic social education: Social studies for social change.* New York: Falmer Press.
Jenne, J. T. (1997). Conserving the status quo in social studies teaching: The case of second career military teachers. *Theory and Research in Social Education, 25,* 446–469.
Leahey, C. R. (2010). *Whitewashing war: Historical myth, corporate textbooks, and possibilities for democratic education.* New York: Teachers College Press.
Mangan, J. A. (1993). Images for confident control: Stereotypes in imperial discourse. In J. A. Magnan (Ed.), *The imperial curriculum: Racial images and education in the British colonial experience* (pp. 6–22). London: Routledge.

Martorella, P. H. (1996). *Teaching social studies in middle and secondary schools* (2nd ed.). Englewood Cliffs, NJ: Merrill/Prentice Hall.
Mathison, S., & Ross, E. W. (Eds.). (2008). *The nature and limits of standards-based reform and assessment*. New York: Teachers College Press.
McGuire, M. E. (2007). What happened to social studies? The disappearing curriculum. *Phi Delta Kappan, 88*(8), 620–624.
McKinley, Jr., J. C. (2010, March 12). Texas conservatives win curriculum change. *The New York Times*. Retrived from http://www.nytimes.com/2010/03/13/education/13texas.html.
McLaren, P. (1998). *Life in schools* (3rd ed.). New York: Longman.
Nelson, J. L. (1985). New criticism and social education. *Social Education, 49*, 368–371.
Nelson, J. L., & Ochoa, A. S. (1987). Academic freedom, censorship, and the social studies. *Social Education, 51*, 424–427.
Nelson, J. L., & Pang, V. O. (2006). Racism, prejudice, and the social studies curriculum. In E. W. Ross (Ed.), *The social studies curriculum: Purposes, problems, and possibilities* (3rd ed., pp. 115–135). Albany, NY: State University of New York Press.
Ross, E. W. (2000). Redrawing the lines: The case against traditional social studies education. In D. W. Hursh & E. W. Ross (Eds.), *Democratic social studies: Social studies for social change*. New York: Falmer Press.
Ross, E. W. (Ed.). (2006a). *The social studies curriculum: Purposes, problems and possibilities* (3rd ed.). Albany, NY: The State University of New York Press.
Ross, E. W. (2006b). The struggle for the social studies curriculum. In E. W. Ross (Ed.), *The social studies curriculum: Purposes, problems and possibilities* (3rd ed., pp. 17–36). Albany, NY: The State University of New York Press.
Ross, E. W., Cornett, J. W., & McCutcheon, G. (1992). *Teacher personal theorizing: Connecting curriculum practice, theory, and research*. Albany, NY: State University of New York Press.
Ross, E. W., & Gibson, R. (2007). *Neoliberalism and education reform*. Cresskill, NJ: Hampton Press.
Saltman, K. J., & Gabbard, D. A. (Eds.). (2010). *Education as enforcement: The militarization and corporatization of schools* (2nd ed.). New York: Routledge.
Segall, A., Heilman, E., & Cherryholmes, C. (Eds.). (2006). *Social studies—The next generation: Researching in the postmodern*. New York: Peter Lang Publishing.
Shor, I., & Freire, P. (1987). *A pedagogy for liberation*. New York: Bergin & Garvey.
Slekar, T. D. (2009). Democracy denied: Learning to teach history in elementary school. *Teacher Education Quarterly, 36*(1), 95–110.
Stanley, W. B. (1985). Social reconstructionism for today's social education. *Social Education, 49*, 384–389.
Stanley, W. B. (1992). *Curriculum for utopia*. Albany, NY: State University of New York Press.
Thornton, S. J. (1996). NCSS: The early years. In O. L. Davis Jr. (Ed.), *NCSS in retrospect*. Washington, DC: National Council for Social Studies.
Thornton, S. J. (2005). *Teaching social studies that matters: Curriculum for active learning*. New York: Teachers College Press.
Vinson, K. D., & Ross, E. W. (2001). In search of the social studies curriculum: Standardization, diversity, and a conflict of appearances. In W. B. Stanley (Ed.), *Critical issues for social studies research in the 21st century: Research, problems, and prospects* (pp. 39–71). Greenwich, CT: Information Age Publishers.
Willis, P. E. (1977). *Learning to labor*. New York: Columbia University Press.

Abraham P. DeLeon
University of Texas, San Antonio

E. Wayne Ross
University of British Columbia

ABRAHAM P. DELEON

1. ANARCHISM, SABOTAGE, AND THE SPIRIT OF REVOLT

Injecting the Social Studies with Anarchist Potentialities

Anarchism is not, as some may suppose, a theory of the future to be realized through divine inspiration. It is a living force in the affairs of our life, constantly creating new conditions. The methods of Anarchism therefore do not comprise an ironclad program to be carried out under all circumstances. It does, however, stand for the spirit of revolt, in whatever form, against everything that hinders human growth.

Emma Goldman, *Anarchism and Other Essays*, p. 63

The opening quote by Emma Goldman is the spirit I want to bring to this chapter and the need for radical teachers and scholars to confront the current political climate. I hope by the end of this chapter that I will fruitfully convince you that we need to change our theoretical orientation to one that is adaptable, critical, radical, undomesticated, and necessary in the currently draconian State we find ourselves in today. In short, anarchists and radicals need to think about a *politics of infiltration*. There seems to be a popular perception among radical educators that, somehow, participating in institutional processes is akin to "selling" out. However, I want to challenge these critics to think about our practice in new ways that understands entering these coercive and hierarchical institutions as a form of infiltration, much like how the police and other State agents infiltrate radical political movements (Borum & Tilby, 2004). As educators, we have a special charge not only to prepare students for life after the classroom, but also to help them to be able to change the world around them. By inserting ourselves within these institutions and "being there," radical educational projects can begin (Fernandez, 2009). Education has a distinct social purpose and the current high-stakes model operating today demonstrates its role in reproducing the Market and the State and we have to resist these in unique and creative ways considering the current attacks on public education especially by powerful conservative political groups. Unfortunately in today's political climate in North America, the thought of including anarchism or other radical positions will engender a dismissive laugh or a downright puzzled look. What can anarchism add to social studies education?

As I will discuss throughout this chapter, anarchist theory provides ways in which to combine theory with praxis, situating our research and classroom practices as acts of resistance to the current statue quo. Heavily involved in activist practices, anarchist theory provides a theoretical framework in which to situate resistance both within and outside institutional realities. In social studies, this is especially relevant as history, sociology and civics allow for teachers to teach critically about society and history, injecting important questions about racism, sexism, classism, and other social ills. Critical pedagogy and its role in engendering critique and resistance has played a vital role in developing radical theory in education, but needs to be infused with anarchist notions of direct action and critiques of the State.

As a body of knowledge and as a discipline, social studies education is mired in a conservative and reproductive epistemological framework, liberal notions of multiculturalism and narrow definitions of civic engagement (Barton & Levstik, 2004; Evans, 2004; Hursh & Ross, 2000; Levstik & Barton, 2005; Segall et al., 2006). Important work has been done in social studies, with some scholars exploring critical or democratic approaches, and neo-Marxist critical pedagogy (Apple, 2004; Bigelow, 1999a, 1999b; Darder, 1991; Freire, 1970, 1985; Giroux, 1988; Hursh & Ross, 2000; Kanpol, 1999; Kincheloe, 2004; McLaren, 1994; Shor, 1992). Critical pedagogy has also been engaged by other voices in academia, pushing theory in new directions (Ellsworth, 1989; Gore, 1992, 1993; Lather, 2001; Weiler, 2001) and has countered the vicious attacks by right-wing organizations against academic freedom and progressive professors within the United States and elsewhere (Giroux, 2006).

Although there are several edited volumes that deal with radical theory in social studies, they omit anarchist praxis (Hursh & Ross, 2000; Ross, 2006; Segall et al., 2006) and critical pedagogy's neo-Marxist lineage has also been silent about anarchism (DeLeon, 2006, 2008). Anarchists employ a variety of means to achieve their goals, such as direct action, or, "communities of various sorts working together in a circulation of struggles that are simultaneously against capitalism and for the construction of alternatives to it" (Day, 2004, p. 735). For the context of this chapter, direct action *means* anti-capitalist action: whether that means feeding the homeless, freeing animals from cages, or other praxis that makes our communities more humane places to live. Social studies teachers interested in exploring direct action can also look to Graeber's (2009) ethnography about some of the features of anarchist communities he situated himself in.

Critical pedagogy has pushed us towards seeing the inherent political nature of school, but its foundations in neo-Marxist politics limit its ability to respond to the current neoliberal economic, social, academic and political climate. Anarchist theory appears to have a postmodern sensibility not found in neo-Marxist theory, since it focuses on economic terms (modes of production), but does not typically offer a fine grained enough approach to suggest action for non-economic/ State forms of power (the diverse practices of sexism, racism, etc.). Thus, anarchism recognizes all these oppressive expressions of power and promotes action and a more complex understanding against them. Or in simple terms, it pushes us to do things *now*, specifically resisting this "business as usual" paradigm that dominates most departments, schools, and colleges of education.

To address the domesticating nature of institutions, anarchists have employed various techniques of sabotage or "do it yourself" (DIY) techniques of social action (Holtzman et al., 2007). These techniques of disruption are often thought of within binary terms of "violent" or "non-violent". However, I urge us as social studies teachers to explore the grey area in-between that positions sabotage as creative and hopeful in remaking our world into something new. Social studies teachers should include sabotage as a viable classroom strategy and we should explore the literature on social movements and protest to give us new ideas as well (Crimethinc, 2001, 2005; Day, 2004; Della Porta & Diana, 2006; Goaman, 2005; Goodman & Jasper, 2003; Naples, 1997; Naples & Desai, 2003). Traditionally, "critical" methods in education have meant pedagogical practices specifically applicable to the classroom. Although critical pedagogy has included calls for teachers to resist in certain ways, sabotage as a "method" rings more clearly and urgently than similar positions in critical pedagogy, while also providing a more activist framework for engendering social change. *This approach also supports the notion that social change will have to occur both within and outside established institutional structures*, echoing Jean Anyon's call for economic change to accompany urban educational revitalization (Anyon, 2005). Sabotage is a way for anarchists to model direct action in their classrooms and using activist discourses allows students to become familiar with key concepts and strategies used by radical groups, a fact often overlooked or omitted in critical pedagogy (Martin, 2007).

Critical pedagogy forces us to conceptualize how we can teach against the status quo, but lacks simple urgency to counter current neoliberal onslaughts against public education (Hursh, 2008). Critical educators grounded in a neo-Marxist tradition have not engaged anarchist theory in most content areas including educational studies, which provides a framework for creative, direct resistance to neoliberal capitalism (DeLeon, 2006, 2008; Suissa, 2006). Marxists have added a strong and valuable contribution to radical theory in education (see specifically Peter McLaren's work), however, many people engaged in political struggles today have moved beyond Marxist politics and neo-Marxism as it has become an accepted and co-opted discourse in the academy (Martin, 2007; Shannon, 2009). Over-reliance on a mythical State that may or may not come into being is a tension that I believe neo-Marxists have not fruitfully addressed (DeLeon, 2009).

Anarchist theory and its conceptions of non-authoritative, autonomous, and direct action strategies bode well for activist teachers. Crispin Sartwell (2008) argues that anarchism, "yields a sharp set of critiques of existing institutions and efforts to reform them [and] provides the sort of vigilance that can help keep us free, even in a context where anarchism itself is not seriously contemplated" (p. 7). Sartwell forces us not only to view anarchism as a form of political organization (giving people the freedom to make their own decisions and destinies for example), but also as a mode of social, political, and cultural critique of coercive institutions and hierarchies that prohibit human beings from forming voluntary, free, and open associations. Social studies education needs to provide students the opportunity for a more positive political engagement and the space to think and dream of new possibilities.

Historically and globally, anarchists have participated in democratic schooling, as well as helping to organize and run alternative schools (Avrich, 2005; Gribble, 2004). As a result of an historical presence of anarchists in educational practice, anarchist theory can fundamentally inform the way we teach social studies and help us rethink our roles and functions as social studies teachers committed to social and ecological justice.

ANARCHIST THEORY AND PRAXIS: A BRIEF SUMMARY

Anarchism has a long history in radical social and political thought. From the Spanish Civil war, the Russian Revolution, Paris 1968, to the streets of Seattle in 1999, anarchists have been heavily involved in political struggles (Amster et al., 2009; Guerin, 2005). Whatever the scenario, anarchists have pushed for a more humane and just world. Anarchists combine radical political action with salient critiques of the State and the various oppressive conditions that arise out of coercive hierarchical systems. To anarchists, rigid State structures do not allow human beings the ability to coexist peacefully with their environment, are coercive and oppressively hierarchical which leads to an unhealthy and unnatural system of relationships (Berkman, 2003; Chomsky, 2005; Guerin, 1970). As Sartwell (2008) so eloquently claims, "the state has been able to render us dependent, and the extent to which it has educated, hectored, indoctrinated, beaten, nurtured, and executed us into taking it to be the only normal condition of human beings" (p. 5). Thus the State and its various coercive apparatuses of control have been brilliantly linked to human "instincts" to form complex institutions and reify hierarchies as "natural" ways to structure social organization.

Anarchism pushes us to recognize instead that this is tied to power relationships and the proliferation of global capitalism in our daily lives, instead of some innate human desire for hierarchical organization.

> Anarchist pedagogy breaks free from authoritarian modes of education and the regulatory mechanisms of the state. It actualizes its politics by functioning immanently in the here and now. This is the sense in which anarchist pedagogy is utopian. It is a gesture towards the future, akin to spraying a circle-A on a bank window before the bricks go in (Antliff, 2007, p. 248).

Anarchism and anarchist pedagogies affirm the wild spirit of revolt and resistance, pushing us to recognize the inherent contradictions within capitalism and its supporting ideological systems. It is a "pleasurable activity", recognizing the interrelated nature of social change and self-realization (Antliff, 2007). By doing this, anarchists are working towards resisting the status quo and disrupting the "business as usual" attitude of most hierarchical institutions, while simultaneously rethinking and envisioning a future free from capitalism. Adding to this however, is also a need to resist Western forms of thinking that result in reifying contemporary educational and economic structures. Because knowledge is bound to power relationships a la Foucault, we have to question what we know because of the power/knowledge relationship inherent in various coercive and oppressive paradigms (Foucault, 2000).

Outdated beliefs, rooted in the State and other hierarchies, support coercive institutions that require conformity and passivity, serving as domesticating institutions to global capitalism (Crimethinc, 2001, 2005; Sartwell, 2008). Hierarchies sustain traditional power structures and anarchists contend that human beings need to have the freedom to make decisions, participate in the political process and opportunities to build community through activism and political participation (Bowen, 2004; Bowen & Purkis, 2004; Guerin, 1970). Although these types of claims will make some liberals cringe, radical theory in education *should include* room for civil disobedience, sabotage, and direct action, such as what is covered by AK Press and Crimethinc (for example, Best & Nocella, 2006; Crimethinc, 2005). These particular works that I highlighted contain a milieu of examples of direct action techniques that have emerged and can serve as inspiration for us in education about how our praxis can be linked with anti-capitalist direct actions. Anarchists inspire me in ways that earlier radical theory in education was unable to do. Critical pedagogy needs to include ideas and debates for teachers who wish to conceptualize how anarchist direct action strategies can be folded into the work of radical educational scholarship: either through direct action, as a mode of critique, or as developing new and less coercive forms of pedagogy required under today's neoliberal educational regime.

TOWARDS AN ANARCHIST SOCIAL STUDIES

Social studies education combines several academic genres and is a great avenue for exploring social problems, forgotten or omitted histories, and civic participation (Loewen, 1995; Hursh & Ross, 2000; Ross, 2006). As I established earlier, some scholars have sought to ground social studies pedagogy in the critical tradition (Hursh & Ross, 2000; Segall et al., 2006). All too often the lived reality of social studies is one of innate boredom where students are drilled about dates, dead white men are worshiped and deified, history is offered as a totalizing narrative, and they are fed a decontextualized and sanitized curriculum. For anarchists, these types of educational experiences serve an important role in domesticating our bodies and minds to the will of capital and the State. To counter this idea, I want to provide some ideas for social studies teachers to ponder long after they read this chapter. What follows are not truths nor are they a prescribed method for teaching in the technocratic sense, but instead are *potential* ways in which anarchist theory can push us to think differently about social studies as a discipline and try to challenge and resist some of its coercive and domesticating functions. Hopefully this also serves as an example of how anarchist theory leads to a praxis that gives us new ideas and perspectives about resistance, sabotage, and direct action.

Social Studies has the Potential to be Subversive

This point appears fairly obvious to me personally and is a topic that has been explored within the literature about critical approaches in social studies education. However, it has not been addressed by anarchist theory in particular. Although the school will never likely possess revolutionary potential because its ties to the State and its role in reproducing labor for the whims of the capitalist marketplace, we have to act as subversive agents, infiltrating the capitalist training grounds that public schools represent. A common tactic utilized by agents of the State (such as the police) is infiltration in large protests in which to corner, frame, and provoke a violent response from protestors which leads to arrest, jail time and helps engender a popular representation of protestors as violent (Borum & Tilby, 2004; Graeber, 2009, p. 464).

Anarchists should provide a counter-narrative within these spaces, committing and performing *epistemological sabotage*. Deconstructing state exams, questioning the textbook, providing alternative histories and voices and openly discussing resistance are a beginning, but it also must move to actually showing students how to resist. This comes with great risk as the public school classroom is filled with students who represent varying levels of political ideologies and indoctrination. Thus, this must be done carefully if one is interested in keeping their employment. In my own teaching experiences, establishing trust and an open classroom in which all views are represented will often silence even the staunchest conservatives. In the university classroom, this type of action is a easier, but there is risk involved in speaking out against the status quo and each person must be comfortable with his or her own level of commitment and danger. I cannot, nor should anyone else, decide this for you. However, this models the idea that we need to have a plan and know the limits we are personally willing to push.

> You must always have a secret plan. Everything depends on this: it is the only question. So as not to be conquered by the conquered territory in which you lead your life, so as not to feel the horrible weight of inertia wrecking your will and bending you to the ground, so as not to spend a single night more wondering what there is to do or how to connect with your neighbors and countrymen [sic], you must make secret plans without respite. Plan for adventures, plan for pleasure, plan for pandemonium, as you wish; but plan, lay plans constantly (CrimethInc, 2005, para. 1, back cover).

Through this quote, CrimethInc captures the *wild* nature of anarchist theory and the importance of planning actions, adventures, and acts of resistance. By doing this, it keeps us diligent against the domesticating nature of capitalism, but also the importance of planning and following through with subversive acts of resistance. There is also a tension exists in this position as well. In fact, we have to be aware and cognizant of those around us and the actions we plan need to consider these variables. This also speaks to the need for constructing anarchist theory and actions within a context of community action combined with individual pursuits. We need to understand that our actions always occur within an interrelated context.

Social Studies can help Expose the Contradictions of the State

Let's face it, the State rests on hefty contradictions that can be easily deconstructed by teachers and embedded anarchists within hierarchical institutions. The State's reliance on overt and covert mechanisms of control, its role in the reproduction of social problems and in the reproduction of inequality make the State and its institutions a main focal point for anarchists and their direct action politics (Guérin, 2005, p. 151). Exploring State policies and functions for example, teachers can lead critical discussions about how States functions and for what purposes. For anarchists, the State has a powerful role in the reproduction of capital and in defending the interests of the owning class. Alexander Berkman (2003) reminds us, "... the government needs laws, police and soldiers, courts and prisons to protect capitalism" (p. 16). Berkman's point is that States function to protect the elite owning class and are structured to reproduce capitalist power relationships. As McKay, Elkin, Neal and Boraas (2008) argue further, "the main function of the state is to guarantee the existing social relationships and their sources within a given society through centralised [sic] power and a monopoly of violence" (p. 142). As anarchists have pointed out, the State needs to be dismantled and remade into something new and some anarchists have looked to other historical examples for alternative ways of organization (Arthur, 2008). By helping students to deconstruct the State and its legitimacy, this throws into question one of the most powerful ways that the ruling class has organized coercive social relationships.

Social Studies can Explore Social Movements and Other Acts of Resistance

Because of its ties to sociology and anthropology, social studies provide an avenue in which to examine social movements in their full historical and social context. This means that teachers can openly discuss acts of resistance and their ties to larger projects of economic and social justice. For example, an anarchist teacher can help debunk the myths surrounding important figures such as Rosa Parks, John Brown, Martin Luther King, Jr., Helen Keller and other radicals who have been sanitized to fit the needs of a liberal and status quo social studies curriculum. Linked to this, a curriculum can be centered upon historical justice movements. In much of mainstream social studies literature, some teacher educators advocate using "essential questions" as guiding frameworks for a curriculum (Lattimer, 2008). These can easily be adapted to fit the needs of activist teachers as these "essential questions" can arise from social justice movements, the literature on critical theory or critical pedagogy, and other transformative theoretical frameworks. By adopting more mainstream ideas, these can be easily sabotaged to reflect a radical political and teaching agenda.

Social Studies can be Utopian and Introduce Anarchist Communities and their Historical Legacies

Unfortunately, when one thinks of "utopian", it is immediately dismissed as "unrealistic." However, the utopian ideal that I seek to build in a social studies classroom is one in which students can see alternatives and the space in which to think of new possibilities. Thus, students can explore *potentially* new ways of organizing ourselves that rests outside of discourses of the State. Although Robert Nozick (1974) situates his ideas of utopia and anarchy within the individual and reeks of Western conceptions of individualism, his ideas can be a beginning point and pushed further.

> Utopia is not just a society in which the framework is realized. For who could believe that ten minutes after the framework was established, we would have utopia? Things would be no different than now. It is what grows spontaneously from the individual choices of many people over a long period

of time that will be worth speaking eloquently about. Many communities will achieve many different characters. (p. 332)

Although Nozick completely reifies the notion of the individual and some notion of a prescribed "framework", it provides an interesting starting point. A new society will not emerge after some mythical social revolution, but will take time and effort in remaking the world we inhabit into something new. This is utopian thinking. It is not the idea that we will all live in some "perfect" society once capitalism is overthrown, but there will be struggle, strife, disagreements, and contestation in building something new out of the ruins of the old. However, this is what makes community. We will all have to invest time into making our society into something different. Social studies can help begin the initial conversations by allowing students opportunities in designing their own social systems outside of a Market based society. Once a teacher helps students deconstruct the current neoliberal State, students should have the space in which to dream of new possibilities. Even if these may not be based in reality, it is important that students are given opportunities to think outside given parameters as this demonstrates the need for alternative vision and the importance of imagination and creativity in solving current social realities. This seems to capture the utopian element within anarchist theory without creating rigid frameworks and is an important way in which anarchists can begin dialogues of alternatives within their coercive and institutionalized classrooms.

Social Studies can Include Narrative Inquiry and Stress the Importance of Autoethnography in Telling Our Own Stories

A salient critique by scholars of color and other indigenous academics is the way in which Western epistemologies has constructed *the Other* through representations and ways of knowing that did not emerge from themselves, but through the gaze and watchful eyes of European colonizers (Tuhiwai Smith, 1999). However, narrative inquiry and autoethnography have emerged to counter this gaze. Academics who have been othered are beginning to tell stories through their own words, building theory from their lived experiences and using personal voice to construct knowledge.

> Autoethnography may teach us about self in that it challenges our assumptions of normalcy, forces us to be more self-reflexive, and instructs us about our professional and personal socialization ... (Hughes, 2008, p. 127)

Other scholars view autoethnographies as opportunities to, "interrogate and critique broader social issues", but also reify "narrative and storytelling as ways of knowing" (Morimoto, 2008, p. 30) that is, "embedded in theory and practice" (McIlveen, 2008, p. 15). Autoethnography is also positioned as being able to resist,

> Grand Theorizing and the façade of objective research that contextualizes subjects and searchers for singular truth ... situating the socio-politically inscribed body as a central site of meaning making" (Spry, 2001, p. 710)

In this way, many scholars view the autoethnographic project as a way to resist standardization, replication, and objectivity that is supposedly found and is often a privileged myth in academic and other scholarly discourses (Adams & Jones, 2008).

As anarchist teachers, this new development in research can be utilized for our advantage and if a teacher works with historically disenfranchised students, can serve as a point of departure from the standard curriculum to explore their own histories and pasts within the context of historical study and social studies in general. Autoethnography simply rejects feigns of objectivity found in Western forms of knowledge. Narratives include no such posture as theory begins from our lived experiences. If they are collected together, they can potentially form rhizomatic representations of contemporary life during late capitalism (Honan, 2007). Narratives simply subvert dominant mechanical academic paradigms. This subversive nature should not be underscored and can be conceptualized as a direct way in which to confront mainstreamed forms of knowledge.

Autoethnography can also potentially challenge privileged academic discourses. Our stories can connect us with each other. Because autoethnography does not assume a posture of objectivity or a rigidly normative stance, this already counters State policies and practices. The State is formulated around claims of hierarchical Truths that order our daily lives and are responsible for disciplining our bodies (Sheehan, 2003). By allowing space for these counter-narratives to exist, these stories can be organized and disseminated to help demonstrate other ways of knowing and understanding. In this way, this takes us out of State and Market discourses and adds a subversive element to how we come to understand the world around and our place within it.

RETHINKING THE SOCIAL STUDIES AS AGENT PROVOCATEURS AND INFILTRATORS: A POSTSCRIPT

Hopefully this chapter can begin new conversations in social studies education for those radicals, social activists and anarchists that wish to become teachers but are unsure of the implications of working in a rigid, coercive, and hierarchically based system. This should not deter us from becoming teachers, as students need stable, loving, nurturing, critical and caring teachers to guide them in their learning discovery. Most human beings are damaged, broken, and are often ill prepared for the reality after the school bell. It should be our charge, as radicals imbued with a sense of radical hope and love, to help alter and change these conditions. However, as anarchists, we also need to be embedded within oppressive systems and institutions to help sabotage the system that enslaves us all. With acts of micro resistance, this can be the beginning point of something new. Infiltration, as a strategy, is something that the State has employed against radicals for some time. I think it may be time to turn this tactic back upon them and start thinking about our pedagogy and praxis within this framework.

REFERENCES

Adams, T., & Holman Jones, S. (2008). Autoethnography is queer. In N. Denzin, Y. Lincoln, & L. Tuhiwai Smith (Eds.), *Handbook of critical and indigenous methodologies* (pp. 373–390). Thousand Oaks, CA: Sage.

Amster, R., DeLeon, A., Fernandez, L., Nocella II, A., & Shannon, D. (Eds.). (2009). *Contemporary anarchist studies: An introductory anthology of anarchy in the academy*. London: Routledge.

Antliff, A. (2007). Breaking free: Anarchist pedagogy. In M. Coté, R. Day, & G. de Peuter (Eds.), *Utopian pedagogy: Radical experiments against neoliberal globalization* (pp. 248–265). Toronto: University of Toronto Press.

Anyon, J. (2005). *Radical possibilities: Public policy, urban education, and a new social movement.* New York: Routledge.

Apple, M. (2000). *Official knowledge: Democratic education in a conservative age* (2nd ed.). New York: Routledge.

Arthur, S. (2008). *An anarchist study of the Iroquois.* anarkismo.net. Retrieved August 1, 2009, from http://www.anarkismo.net/article/4907.

Avrich, P. (2005). *The modern school movement: Anarchism and education in the United States.* San Francisco: AK Press.

Barton, K., & Levstik, L. (2004). *Teaching history for the common good.* Mahwah, NJ: Lawrence Earlbaum Associates.

Berkman, A. (2003). *What is anarchism?* Oakland, CA: AK Press.

Bigelow, W. (1999a). On the road to cultural bias: A critique of The Oregon Trail CD-ROM. In I. Shor, C. Pari (Eds.), *Education is politics: Critical teaching across differences K-12.* Portsmouth, NH: Heinemann Educational Books, Inc.

Bigelow, W. (1999b). Discovering Columbus: Rereading the past. In I. Shor & C. Pari (Eds.), *Education is politics: Critical teaching across differences K-12.* Portsmouth, NH: Heinemann Educational Books, Inc.

Borum, R., & Tilby, C. (2004). Anarchist direct actions: A challenge for law enforcement. *Studies in Conflict and Terrorism, 28,* 201–223.

Bowen, J. (2004). Moving targets: Rethinking anarchist strategies. In J. Purkis & J. Bowen (Eds.), *Changing anarchism: Anarchist theory and practice in a global age.* Manchester: Manchester University Press.

Bowen, J., & Purkis, J. (2004). Introduction: Why anarchism still matters. In J. Purkis & J. Bowen (Eds.), *Changing anarchism: Anarchist theory and practice in a global age.* Manchester: Manchester University Press.

Chomsky, N. (2004). *Hegemony or survival: America's quest for global dominance.* New York: Owl Books.

Chomsky, N. (2005). *Chomsky on anarchism.* Oakland, CA: AK Press.

CrimethInc. (2001). *Days of war, nights of love: Crimethink for beginners.* Salem, OR: CrimethInc.

Chomsky, N. (2005). *Recipes for disaster: An anarchist cookbook.* Salem, OR: CrimethInc.

Darder, A. (1991). *Culture and power in the classroom: A critical foundation for bicultural education.* New York: Bergin & Garvey.

Darder, A., Baltodono, M., & Torres, R. (2003). *The critical pedagogy reader.* New York: Routledge-Falmer.

Day, R. (2004). From hegemony to affinity: The political logic of the newest social movements. *Cultural Studies, 18,* 716–748.

DeLeon, A. (2006). The time for action is now! Anarchist theory, critical pedagogy, and radical possibilities. *The Journal for Critical Education Policy Studies, 4.* Retrieved January 5, 2007, from http://www.jceps.com/?pageID=article&articleID=67.

DeLeon, A. (2008). Oh no, not the "A" word! Towards an anarchism for education. *Educational Studies, 44*(2), 122–141.

DeLeon, A. (2009). Review of *Pedagogy and praxis in the age of empire: Towards a new humanism* by Peter McLaren and Nathalia Jaramillo (Rotterdam: Sense Publishers, 2007). *Workplace: A Journal for Academic Labor.* Retrieved from http://m1.cust.educ.ubc.ca/journal/index.php/workplace/article/viewFile/55/deleon

Della Porta, D., & Diani, M. (2006). *Social movements: An introduction.* New York: Blackwell.

Ellsworth, E. (1989). Why doesn't this feel empowering? *Harvard Educational Review, 59,* 297–324.

Evans, R. W. (2004). *The social studies wars: What should we teach the children?* New York: Teacher's College Press.

Fernandez, L. (2009). Being there: Thoughts on anarchism and participatory observation. In R. Amster, A. DeLeon, L. Fernandez, A. Nocella, & D. Shannon (Eds.), *Contemporary anarchist studies: An introductory anthology of anarchy in the academy* (pp. 93–102). New York: Routledge.

Foucualt, M. (2000). *Power. Essential works of Foucault, 1954–1984* (P. Rabinow, Ed.). New York: The New Press.
Freire, P. (1970). *Pedagogy of the oppressed*. New York: Herder and Herder.
Freire, P. (1985). *The politics of education: Culture, power, and liberation*. Westport, CT: Bergin and Garvey.
Giroux, H. A. (1988). *Teachers as intellectuals: Toward a critical pedagogy of learning*. Massachusetts, MA: Bergin and Garvey.
Giroux, H. A. (2006). Academic freedom under fire: The case for critical pedagogy. *College literature, 33*, 1–42.
Goaman, K. (2004). The anarchist traveling circus: Reflections on contemporary anarchism, anti-capitalism, and the international scene. In J. Purkis & J. Bowen (Eds.), *Changing anarchism: Anarchist theory and practice in a global age*. Manchester: Manchester University Press.
Goldman, E. (1969). *Anarchism and other essays*. New York: Dover Publications Inc.
Goodwin, J., & Jasper, J. (2003). *The social movements reader: Cases and concepts*. New York: Blackwell.
Gore, J. (1992). What can we do for you! What can "we" do for "you"? Struggling over empowerment in critical and feminist pedagogy. In C. Luke & J. M. Gore (Eds.), *Feminisms and critical pedagogy*. New York: Routledge.
Gore, J. (1993). *The struggle for pedagogies: Critical and feminist discourses as regimes of truth*. New York: Routledge.
Graeber, D. (2009). *Direct action: An ethnography*. San Francisco: AK Press.
Gribble, D. (2004). Good news for Francisco Ferrer – How anarchist ideals in education have survived around the world. In J. Purkis & J. Bowen (Eds.), *Changing anarchism: Anarchist theory and practice in a global age*. Manchester: Manchester University Press.
Guerin, D. (1970). *Anarchism*. New York: Monthly Review Press.
Guerin, D. (2005). *No gods, no masters: An anthology of anarchism*. San Francisco: AK Press.
Holtzman, B., Hughes, C., & Van Meter, K. (2007). Do it yourself … and the movement beyond capitalism. In S. Shukaitis & D. Graeber (Eds.), *Constituent imagination: Militant investigations/Collective theorization*. San Francisco: AK Press.
Honan, E. (2007). Writing a rhizome: An (im)plausible methodology. *International Journal of Qualitative Studies in Education, 20*(5), 531–546.
Horton, M., & Freire, P. (1990). *We make the road by walking: Conversations on education and social change*. Philadelphia: Temple University Press.
Hughes, S. (2008). Toward "good enough methods" for autoethnography in a graduate education course: Trying to resist the Matrix with another promising red pill. *Educational Studies, 43*(2), 125–143.
Hursh, D. (1997). Multicultural social studies: Schools as places for examining and challenging inequality. In E. W. Ross (Ed.), *The social studies curriculum: Purposes, problems, and possibilities*. Albany, NY: State University of New York Press.
Hursh, D. (2008). *High-stakes testing and the decline of teaching and learning: The real crisis in education*. Lanham, MD: Rowman & Littlefield, Inc.
Hursh, D., & Ross, E. W. (Eds.). (2000). *Democratic social education: Social studies for social change*. New York: Falmer Press.
Kanpol, B. (1999). *Critical pedagogy: An introduction* (2nd ed.). Westport, CT: Bergin & Garvey.
Kincheloe, J. (2004). *Critical pedagogy primer*. New York: Peter Lang.
Lather, P. (2001). Ten years later, yet again: Critical pedagogy and it complicities. In K. Weiler (Ed.), *Feminist engagements: Reading, resisting, and revisioning male theorists in education and cultural studies*. New York: Routledge.
Lattimer, H. (2008). Challenging history: Essential questions in the social studies classroom. *Social Education, 72*(6), 326–329.
Loewen, J. (1995). *Lies my teacher told me: Everything your American history textbook got wrong*. New York: Touchstone.
Martin, G. (2007). The poverty of critical pedagogy. In P. McLaren & J. Kincheloe (Eds.), *Critical pedagogy: Where are we now?* (pp. 337–353). New York: Peter Lang.

McIlveen, P. (2008). Autoethnography as a method for reflexive research and practice in vocational psychology. *Australian Journal of Career Development, 17*(2), 13–20.

McKay, I., Elkin, G., Neal, D., & Boraas, E. (Eds.). (2008). *An anarchist FAQ: AFAQ volume one*. San Francisco: AK Press.

McLaren, P. (1994). *Life in schools: An introduction to critical pedagogy in the foundations of education* (2nd ed.). New York: Longman.

Morimoto, L. (2008). Teaching as transgression: The autoethnography of a fat physical education instructor. *Proteus, 25*(2), 29–36.

Naples, N. (1997). *Community activism and feminist politics*. New York: Routledge.

Naples, N., & Desai, M. (Eds.). (2003). *Women's activism and globalization: Linking local struggles and transnational politics*. New York: Routledge.

Nozick, R. (1974). *Anarchy, state and utopia*. New York: Basic Books.

Parker, W. (1991). *Renewing the social studies curriculum*. Alexandria, VA: Association for Supervision and Curriculum Development.

Ross, E. W. (2000). Diverting democracy: The curriculum standards movement and social studies education. In D. Hursh & E. W. Ross (Eds.), *Democratic social education: Social studies for social change*. New York: Falmer.

Ross, E. W. (Ed.). (2006). *The social studies curriculum: Purposes, problems and possibilities* (3rd ed.). Albany, NY: State University of New York Press.

Sartwell, C. (2008). *Against the state: an introduction to anarchist political theory*. Albany, NY: State University of New York Press.

Segall, A., Heilman, E., & Cherryholmes, C. (2006). *Social studies –The next generation: Researching in the postmodern*. New York: Peter Lang.

Shannon, D. (2009). As beautiful as a brick through a bank window: Anarchism, the academy, and resisting domestication. In R. Amster, A. DeLeon, L. Fernandez, A. Nocella, & D. Shannon (Eds.), *Contemporary anarchist studies: An introductory anthology of anarchy in the academy* (pp. 183–188). New York: Routledge.

Shor, I. (1992). *Empowering education: Critical teaching for social change*. Chicago: The University of Chicago Press.

Spry, T. (2001). Performing autoethnography: An embodied methodological praxis. *Qualitative inquiry, 7*(6), 706–732.

Suissa, J. (2006). *Anarchism and education: A philosophical perspective*. London: Routledge.

Tuhiwai Smith, L. (1999). *Decolonizing methodologies: Research and indigenous peoples*. London: Zed Books Ltd.

Weiler, K. (2001). Rereading Paulo Freire. In K. Weiler (Ed.), *Feminist engagements: Reading, resisting, and revisioning male theorists in Education and Cultural Studies*. Routledge: New York.

Abraham P. DeLeon
University of Texas, San Antonio

NIRMALA EREVELLES

2. EMBATTLED PEDAGOGIES

Deconstructing Terror from a Transnational Feminist Disability Studies Perspective

INTRODUCTION

Over the past five years, I have found it very difficult as an educator to teach about issues of diversity and social justice without referencing the broader global social context into which we find ourselves relentlessly drawn by contemporary politics. I find it ironic that students and academic colleagues appear eager to discuss issues of diversity and social justice in the abstract - by which I mean that they assert a general openness to difference and social justice but are much more reticent and sometimes even hostile to the idea of exploring how their assertions of goodwill can be translated into transformative action in the concrete worlds (both local and global) where the politics of difference is materialized. By materiality I mean the actual social, political, and economic conditions within which difference is constituted, performed, and most importantly lived. By invoking the term global, I want to explore the complex ways in which the lived experiences of race, class, gender, and disability in the national context of the US exists in critical tension with similar lived experiences of race, class, gender, and disability in the international context, especially that of the Third World I will also engage the critical concept of invisibility as it plays out within the politics of difference.

To be invisible implies that for the Self, the other simply does not exist. To simply acknowledge that the other exists evokes a form of terror – a terror that demands a stifling silence; a desperate looking away; an urgency to bury the evidence of the other's existence. To engage this issue, in this chapter I will foreground two events in our recent history that continue to be spaces of terror: Hurricane Katrina and the Wars in Iraq and Afghanistan. I will foreground both the silences and the invisibilities and reflect on why our terror of the Other forces us to look the other way. Then drawing on a transnational feminist disability studies perspective, I will explore its implications for a transformative pedagogical praxis.

IN THE EYE OF THE HURRICANE

On August 30, 2005, the day after Hurricane Katrina made landfall as a Category 3 hurricane on the coasts of Louisiana and Mississippi, most of the nation who lived outside these affected areas watched in shocked outrage the scenes of despair, terror, and destitution that Katrina forced us to confront. We paid particular interest to the city of New Orleans. We watched in disbelief as television screens replayed in horrific monotony the walls of water that crashed through the city turning neighborhoods into a surging sea. We saw people stranded on rooftops, while others swam through brackish churning streets amidst bloated bodies, animals, and sewage. We waited breathlessly for the help that came too late while casting furtive glances at the crowded horror of the Superdome replete with rumor, fear, despair, and filth. And when the National Guard finally arrived on the streets fully armed with barbed wire and assault rifles to defend the wealth of the city from its impoverished residents (now refugees) and performed daring rescues, we watched spellbound unsure if our trembling was a result of our fear or our exhilaration.

The media chattered incessantly, making certain aspects of story lines hypervisible while rendering other aspects completely invisible. Take the example of the dapper figure of Anderson Cooper from CNN, live in New Orleans - gasping in horrified zeal while intoning, "Walking through the rubble, it feels like Sri Lanka, Sarajevo, somewhere else, not here, not home, not America" (Brinkley, 2006, p. 2004). I have been replaying those words in my mind for quite some time. Was he saying that this just could not be the United States of America? And why his horror at recognizing New Orleans as a "Third World country"? Did "Third World" symbolize for him pathological destitution as represented by the "dead disabled people" and "crazy, desperate people of color" he found in New Orleans? Was he shocked and outraged to confront these images in his own "backyard"? Actually, why was he even surprised? In examining the "news" from all angles (that's why his show is called 360, right???), had he never encountered news stories where poor disabled people as well as people of color with and without disabilities (all US citizens) have died/suffered because of poverty, lack of access to health care, environmental hazards, police brutality, and/or simply gross neglect – many of them in New Orleans and Mississippi in pre-Katrina times? Or was that even worthy of the news? Would exposing the failures of capitalism (otherwise touted as the best system there is) seem unpatriotic or heretical? Was this why it was easier to have a discussion of "third world poverty in the Ninth Ward" under the safe auspices of nature's fury? (Its natural! It could never be man-made!).

In what ways did Cooper and other journalists' preoccupation with "Third World Horrors" prevent them from raising other critical questions? Several journalists did acknowledge, in passing, that the bodies that kept surfacing in the brackish water, in abandoned houses, and on the streets were mostly poor, black, brown, elderly, critically ill, and or disabled. Why was it that this segment of the population did not figure in any official emergency evacuation plan? How did state and local officials envision that people (already marginalized because of inaccessible social structures) would magically propel themselves out of the city? Were there designated spaces that would be accessible to the varied needs of this population? Or did state officials simply assume that citizens who found themselves in these deplorable conditionswere also responsible for their own plight? These are the terrible costs of invisibility.

Disabled activist and author Anne Finger (2005) in a blog has written:

> Throughout this week, I've been struck by the presence of disability ... I read of a woman in the Superdome grabbing a reporter's arm, pleading for water for her daughter, a wheelchair user. "I'm afraid she's going to have a seizure," the mother cried. On NPR, I hear the voice of a man calling out, "Dilantin! I need Dilantin!" The President of Jefferson Parrish breaking down as he told of a man who'd been reassuring his mother, institutionalized in a nursing home, that help was on the way – only to learn that she had drowned – on Friday. And of course the image of the woman in the wheelchair dead outside the Convention Center. (para. 2)

Finger's quote reminds all of us of that lonely image of a dead woman in the wheelchair who haunted us all in her lonely tragic stillness. The only image of disability flashed so often on our television screens she served as the very embodiment of the metaphor for disaster, despair, and death – metaphors that have historically shaped the public's perception of disability and disabled people (Lubet & Johnstone, 2005). The ultimate symbol of pity, revulsion, and uselessness; it was an image that caused us to either turn away from our television sets and/or startled many of us into a guilty charity. But as Anne Finger (2005) again notes:

> ... though the impulse to reach out and offer help is a good one ... charity keeps in place the notion that the "problem" is located in the bodies of disabled people; in the individuals who [died] or who were displaced rather than in social structures and in economic policies that often ignore and usually render the objects of charity as invisible. (para. 6)

FEMINIST POLITICS AND THE PATHOLOGIZING OF DIFFERENCE

In many ways our own responses to disability mirror the imagery put forth by the media. And it is this very critique that the Disability Rights Movement and scholars in the associated field of inquiry disability studies make. From a disability studies perspective, disability appears on the landscape of difference as a hypervisible identity, commonly associated with denigrating terms like 'cripple', 'moron', 'gimp', and 'freak'. On the few occasions when disability is celebrated, the focus has generally been on narratives depicting individuals single-handedly overcoming the stigma of disability in order to pass almost as normal, thereby attaining the dubious distinction of 'super-crip' (Clare, 1999). At other times, disability appears as the ultimate symbol of tragedy, despair and misery – a symbol actively propagated by the telethons that raise millions by marketing this particular image. In contrast, conscious of their experiences of social, economic, and political subjugation, disabled scholars and activists have struggled to claim space, voice, and power to disrupt the normative ideals of the social world that has historically ignored them. To achieve this end, they have sought to define a disability culture that is based on the recognition of their differences – not in spite of their disabilities but because of them. As disabled feminist Susan Wendell (1996) explains:

> We are dis-abled. We live with particular social and physical struggles that are partly consequences of the conditions of our bodies and partly consequences

of the structures and expectations of our societies, but they are struggles which only people with bodies like ours experience. (p. 24)

These critiques have also implicated feminist scholarship. In an essay that makes the case for the inclusion of feminist disability studies in mainstream feminist discourse, Judy Rohrer (2005) asks that feminists formulate a "disability theory of feminism" (p. 40) – one that "upsets old frameworks and allows new questions to be asked" (p. 41). Rosemary Garland-Thomson explains this further:

> Seldom is disability presented as an integral part of one's embodiment, character, life, and way of relating to the world. Even less often do we see disability as part of the spectrum of human variation, the particularization of individual bodies, or the materialization of an individual body's history. Instead we learn to understand disability as something that is wrong with someone, as an exceptional and escapable calamity rather than as what is perhaps the most universal of human conditions ... A feminist disability studies teaches us that we are better off learning to accommodate disabilities, appreciate disabled lives and create a more equitable environment rather than trying to eliminate disability. (2005, p. 1568)

While it is true that feminist disability studies poses a fundamental challenge to feminist concepts of the (ab)normal body, there is an implicit assumption in her argument that the acquisition of a disabled identity always occurs outside of historical, social, and economic contexts. This position becomes especially problematic when issues of race, class, gender, sexuality, ethnicity and nation intersect with disabled identity. For example, how can acquiring a disability be celebrated as "the most universal of human conditions" if it is acquired under the oppressive conditions of poverty, economic exploitation, police brutality, neo-colonial violence, and lack of access to adequate health care and education? What happens when human variation (e.g. race) is itself deployed in the construction of disabled identities for purely oppressive purposes (e.g. slavery, colonialism, immigration law etc.)? How can cyborg subjectivities be celebrated when the manufacture of prostheses and assistive technology is dependant on an exploitative international division of labor? How does one "value interdependence" (Rohrer, 2005, p. 47) within imperialist/ neo-colonial contexts that locate consumers and producers of goods and services within a network of fundamentally unequal social relationships? (Erevelles, 1996). And finally, how do we build solidarity across difference even while we negotiate the dis-stances that simultaneously separate and divide us within the contemporary context of transnational capitalism?

Like feminist disability studies, third world feminism also offers a critique of the normative tendencies in (western) mainstream feminism. Here, "western" is used to describe a certain normative construction of "woman" (read: educated, modern, having control of one's body, and the freedom to make their own decisions) against whom the "average third world woman" is compared and who is found to be lacking. Thus, "the average third world woman" is generally represented as leading an "essentially truncated life on account of her gender (read: sexually constrained) and her being 'third world' (read: ignorant, poor, uneducated, tradition-bound, domestic, family oriented, victimized, etc.)" (Mohanty, 1997, p. 80). Constituted as the very embodiment of lack, such representations of third world women mirror ableist representations of disabled women (Fine & Asch, 1988; Morris, 1991; Garland-Thomson, 1997; Thomas, 1999; Ghai, 2003). And yet, notwithstanding this obvious connection, third world feminists have consistently ignored issues of disability.

This occlusion of disability issues in third world feminism is costly. For example, significant in third world feminist analyses are theorizations of the experiences of women under the postcolonial nation-state (Mohanty, 1991; Rai, 1996; Kaplan, Alarcon & Moallem, 1999). Rai (1996) points out that in Third World contexts, the state "looms large in women's lives only when women transgress the boundaries set by the state in various areas of public and private life over which it has jurisdiction" (p. 36). Thus, an ableist state would also closely patrol the boundaries of female bodily difference as is evident in state practices that seek to control (disabled) women's reproduction - sterilization (Ghai, 2004; Molina 2006); (disabled) women's immigration and citizenship rights (Molina, 2006); and (disabled) women's economic (in)dependence (Chang, 2000; Livngston, 2006; Erevelles, 2006).

Additionally, notwithstanding "different histories with respect to the particular inheritance of post-fifteenth-century Euro-American hegemony: the inheritance of slavery, enforced migration, plantation and indentured labor, colonialism, imperial conquest, and genocide" (Mohanty, 1991, p. 10), third world feminists should have common cause around at least one issue – that of disability – an inevitable repercussion of the violence of such oppressive practices/structures. So then, in which spaces do disabled third women claim sisterhood? How do they relate to their disabled sisters who derive certain privileges from residing in the very imperialist states that facilitated their becoming disabled in the first place? More urgently, how do they challenge their invisibility among their third world sisters who, while critiquing the imperialist state refuse to foreground its ableist assumptions that ultimately work against all third world women?

THE INVISIBLE TERROR OF GENDER, RACE AND DISABILITY IN WAR TIME

I now turn to the very real and immediate context of war. Almost daily, on the news, there are reports of roadside bombs detonating, the launching of military offensives, the consistent regularity of power failures and shortages of food, drinking water, and fuel in the "post-war" contexts of a devastated Afghanistan and an occupied Iraq. In the United States, we keep a diligent count of the number of U.S. soldiers killed in the wars in both Iraq and Afghanistan. Even more infrequently, and almost always as a passing note, we hear a rare report of US disabled war veterans returning from combat (iCasualities.org, 2009). In Afghanistan, the first country targeted in the "War on Terror", the number of civilian deaths reported in 2002 was around 3,800 (Herold, 2002). The escalation of combat in 2009 has now brought that total to 6534 (The Guardian, 2009). On the Iraqi side, the numbers of civilian and military deaths reported is contested, with reports varying from 40,000 (iCasualities.org, 2006) to around 103,000 (iraqbodycount.org, 2009). I was unable to find any statistics on

Afghan and Iraqi civilians and members of the military (and now the insurgency) who have become disabled as a result of the war and the post-war conflict.

I find these omissions extremely troubling. In moving from a national to a transnational context, why has there been little outrage and protest not just by Anderson Cooper but also by his U.S. audience, when for the last 5 years similar devastating accounts of death, destruction, and disability from Afghanistan and Iraq have briefly appeared on television before disappearing forever with little debate and or discussion? This is extremely problematic in light of the fact that this devastation was on a much larger scale and was a direct result of US imperialist policies. Even more troubling has been the unemotional response from both people of color and disabled communities in the US. After all, this war has created more disability in people of color communities with very little or no social and economic support.

Third world feminists Jacqui Alexander and Chandra Talapade Mohanty (1997) argue that "militarized [hyper]masculinity" (p. xxv) has a strategic function in the reproduction of (neo)colonialism and the (re)organization of gendered hierarchies in the nation state. As a result, in war time, the nationalist popular media creates a seemingly facile relationship between violent male behavior and hyper-masculinity by glorifying tough, aggressive, and robustly masculine soldiers (Myrttinen, 2004), while ignoring women unless they appear in "recognizable and traditional roles such as the mourning widow or the all-feeling mother" (Lindinski, 2005, p. 142). Moreover, in an effort to maintain its robustly masculine image, the military exists in persistent terror of being emasculated (Pin-Fat & Stern, 2005). Thus, even though both women and gay men serve in the U.S. military, gay men, in particular, who represent a "feminized masculinity" in the popular imagination are required to maintain a "silent" presence, in order to sustain the mythical image of the hyper-masculine imperialist army.

However, even tough and aggressive U.S. soldiers are humbled while living through the actual materiality of war. War injuries produce disability - another threat to the hyper-masculine imagery. Many of the soldiers who are diagnosed with depression, post-traumatic stress, and mental illness are afraid to admit their vulnerability and dependence on others – traits that appear so contradictory to their fictional ideal of masculinity because of their association with disability (Glaser, 2005). In Operation Iraqi Freedom, soldiers are reported to have access to the best emergency medical attention and advances in medical technology during the time period immediately after acquiring their injuries[1], especially in relation to prosthetics. Proud of its technology in this area, the military has announced new efforts to keep certain disabled personnel on active duty if they can regain their fitness after being fitted with a prosthetic (Hull, 2004). One such example is David Rozelle, who having being fitted with a prosthetic leg was slated to be deployed to Iraq as commander of the Third Armored Cavalry Regiment. One of the few disabled soldiers celebrated in the mass media, Rozelle is seen as the very embodiment of the saying – "once a soldier, always a soldier" – because he is also seen as the very embodiment of the fabled toughness and manliness of the U.S. military.

In fact, disabled soldiers like Rozelle could be seen to represent a new identity in contemporary military discourses – "the cyborg soldier ... the juncture of ideals, metals, chemicals, and people who make weapons of computers and computers of weapons and soldiers" (Masters, 2005, p. 113). The cyborg soldier is the new posthuman subject who is intimately interconnected with modern technologies of war (e.g. the Patriot missile; smart bombs, etc.) that are infused with the ability to reason and think without being interrupted by emotions, guilt, or bodily limitations. In fact, the cyborg soldier, in almost every way, is in constant battle against the normal human male body using "technological prostheses that replicate biological senses while circumventing human biological limitations: poor eyesight, hearing and discernment" (Masters, 2005, p. 122). Masters describes this cyborg soldier as "a much more resilient subject, a hegemonic technological subject animated by masculine subjectivity, effectively mitigating against the imperfections of the human body while simultaneously [forging] a close identification with white, heterosexual, masculine subjectivity" (p. 121).

From a feminist disability studies perspective, the cyborg soldier is a cause for celebration. The cyborg soldier as posthuman[2] subject troubles the boundaries of normal/abnormal humanity – creating a transgressive image of disabled subjectivity that modernist discourses have historically denied. Whereas disabled subjectivity has historically been categorized as effeminate, disability as embodied via the hyper-masculine cyborg soldier challenges oppressive images of weak, pitiable, broken, and wounded human flesh and offers more empowering and transgressive imagery of possibility and potential. Additionally, one of the benefits of militarism is that advanced technologies developed in the battlefield often trickle down to domestic markets (cell phones, video games, and now high-tech prostheses) to enhance the quality of (disabled) civilian life. Thus, some feminist disability studies theorists could argue that the cyborg soldier can offer transgressive possibilities for the category of disability.

But what if, we actually looked at the "other' face of disability – one that resists codification as cyborg because of actual social, political, and economic deprivation? As mentioned earlier, war produces disabilities that include loss of limbs, paralysis, emotional trauma - disabilities that challenge families, communities, and government agencies (Safran, 2005). For example, in Afghanistan, vast numbers of people have physical disabilities arising from polio; blast injuries, visual disabilities from untreated eye diseases and blasts; mental disabilities associated with malnutrition, iodine deficiency disorders, and trauma; and epilepsy associated with trauma or with untreated malaria (Miles, 2002). Moreover, Afghan refugees wounded and/or disabled as a result of "friendly fire" have had to depend on the meager resources of their families for survival. Miles (2002) has reported that access to disability services for women is very limited and during Taliban rule these services ceased functioning. In addition, access to even, community rehabilitation is restricted for women and children. In an interesting observation, the restriction of mobility of Afghan women has actually resulted in fewer women being killed or disabled by fighting, landmines, and unexploded bombs. Women, also participate disproportionately in the informal home care and assistance – a major source of disability services in the country. Given these material realities, neither feminist disability studies nor third world feminism can dismiss disability in third world contexts as either a troublesome trope or an irritating detail.

In Iraq, the situation is even more sobering. Like Afghanistan, Iraq has also suffered 15 years of war, economic sanctions, and now the US invasion and ongoing occupation of Iraq. A new study by the United Nations Development Program (UNDP) contains the following indices of what they term the "social misery" in Iraq:
- Nearly a quarter of Iraq's children suffer from chronic malnutrition
- The probability of dying before 40 of Iraqi children born between 2000 and 2004 is approximately three times the level in neighboring countries
- 40 percent of families in urban areas live in neighborhoods with sewage on the streets
- More than 200,000 Iraqis have "chronic" disabilities caused by war (Walsh, 2005)

In addition, lessons learned from other war-torn countries like Bosnia, Sierra Leone, and Kosovo demonstrate that there is also a proliferation of other invisible disabilities among civilian populations living through a war. For example, McKay (2004) reports that in Sierra Leone, children participating in war return to rural communities with memories of terror and day to day suffering. Additionally, children exposed to war experience post-traumatic stress, anxiety and depressive symptoms, psycho-physiological disturbances, behavioral problems and personality changes, in addition to physical traumas resulting from injury, physical deformities and diseases such as tuberculosis, malaria, and parasites (Kuterovac-Jagodic, 2003; McKay, 2004; Al-Ali, 2005).

Ghoborah, Huth, & Russett (2004) describe some major influences wars have on public health infrastructures. First, wars increase the exposure of the civilian population to conditions that increase the risk of disease, injury, and death as a result of displacement. Bad food, water, sanitation, and housing turn refugee camps into vectors for infectious disease. With the destruction of the health care infrastructure, prevention and treatment programs are weakened and often in these circumstances new strains that are drug resistant (e.g. tuberculosis, HIV/AIDS) evolve. Secondly, wars reduce the pool of available resources for expenditures on health care for the general population as well as constrain the level of resources allocated to the public health care system in their aftermath. Thirdly, war time destruction of the transportation infrastructure weakens the distribution of clean water, food, medicine and relief supplies to both refugees and those who remain behind in these war torn areas.

In citing these statistics, I am attempting to show how the proliferation of disability in war, actively affects positive and negative meanings that are attributed to the category of disability. In third world contexts, international organizations like the World Bank and the International Monetary Fund are often instrumental in defining and administering disability with devastating consequences for disabled people themselves as exemplified by the use of the concept of the DALY – disability adjusted life years. Using the DALY, the World Bank prioritizes health interventions by calculating their relative cost effectiveness. (SLIDE 31) Hence, children and the elderly have lower value than young adults, and presumably disabled persons who are unable to work are awarded zero value and therefore have little or no entitlement to health services at public expense (Erevelles, in press). Thus, the DALY, constitutes disabled people as a liability to the state rather than as a valued investment.

Additionally, state-initiated policies that have been celebrated for their cost-effectiveness are actually geared to "[mobilize] ... people's resources for government programs" (Kalyanpur, 1996, p. 125), where the additional costs of these services continue to be absorbed by both the lowly paid and unpaid labor of poor third world women. In a context where war is responsible for the proliferation of disability, it is critical that third world feminists examine the impact of disability on (both non-disabled and disabled) third world women's lives as they struggle against the oppressive policies and practices of the imperialist, neocolonial state.

IMPERIALISM/NEOCOLONIALISM AS THE NEW EUGENICS

In this final section of my chapter, I make the case for a *transnational feminist disability studies perspective* – a perspective that engages gender and disability and their intersection with race, class, and sexuality within the material context of the post/neocolonial state. Such a perspective is neither ahistorical, nor limited by national/ethnic boundaries. It is neither burdened by narrow class interests nor restricted by normative modes of being. Rather, this perspective maps both the continuities and discontinuities across different historical periods that have both separated and connected women along the axes of race, class, disability, sexuality, ethnicity, and nationality by foregrounding not just discursive representations but also the material (read actual) conditions of their lives.

As an example, I will very briefly map out the historical continuities and discontinuities between racism, sexism, and ableism embodied in the eugenics practices of the early 20th century and the contemporary context of neo-colonialist wars and their impact on disability, race, and gender in the third world. The term "eugenics" was coined in 1883 in Britain by Francis Galton to describe a program of selective breeding. Within the imperialistic context of colonialism, eugenics thrived on the fear of racialized Others fueled by racist associations of genetic degeneration and disease. By hinting at the imminent possibility of social decay if certain degenerate "bodies" were not brought under control, the segregation and/or *the destruction of the colonized races was regarded as necessary for the public good* because maintaining biological distance was critical to preventing degeneracy. Fearing that such characteristics could be passed down from generation to generation and further pose a threat to the dominant white race, "protective" practices such as forced sterilizations, rigid miscegenation laws, residential segregation in ghettoes, barrios, reservations and other state institutions and even genocide were brought to bear on non-white populations by bringing into play the oppressive practices of eugenics. In this way, according to feminist scholar Leslie Roman (2003) the project of colonialism and nation-building was intimately intertwined with eugenics policies that contributed to the social and material construction of people of color and people with disabilities as 'unfit bodies' or 'unworthy citizens.'

Similarly, by foregrounding disability as an imperialist ideology that equates certain racialized, gendered, sexual, and class differences as "defect," it is possible to also foreground the eugenic impulses articulated via the "War on Terror" and that have oppressive implications for both poor non-disabled and disabled women of color living in both the first and third worlds. The sheer scope of this violence should be difficult to ignore and yet it is ignored; its invisibility justified by the imperialist/neocolonial state through its claims of regulating and controlling differences that are seen as disruptive to the "natural" order of global civil society. This is where the echoes of eugenics policies of the late nineteenth and early twentieth centuries resonate in contemporary times. For example, Iraqis and Afghans who are killed or disabled in their "Occupied" countries are not thought of as "civilians" resisting an imperialist force but as "terrorists/insurgents" – a term that negates any rights to enfranchised citizenship. If civilian deaths and/or disabilities caused by the war are acknowledged, they are dismissed as collateral damage. When an odd discussion comes up regarding the meager pensions and lack of disability benefits made available to widows/mothers/caregivers whose family members have been affected by the War on Terror, it is explained away as a luxury they did not even enjoy prior to the Occupation. And in spaces where concepts like the DALY are deployed to determine who has access to health services at public expense, there will be oppressive outcomes for the thousands of civilians disabled on account of war and their care-givers, most of whom will be poor women of color.

Persistent invisibility and occasional hypervisibility exact a heavy price from its victims. On February 1st, 2008, for a brief moment race, disability, and gender claimed center stage in the news regarding the war in Iraq. The FOX News Headline read, "Mentally Disabled Female Homicide Bombers Blow Up Pet Markets in Baghdad, Killing Dozens." The AOL news headline put it even more tersely and coarsely, "Mentally Retarded Pair Used in Bombing." Moral outrage is the only appropriate response to these headlines. But what exactly has caused our outrage? Was it the fact that the two women who literally exploded in the market place were "mentally retarded"? Were we outraged because we presumed they were unwilling pawns used by unscrupulous individuals for whom barbarism has no boundaries? Does our outrage reinforce our belief in the righteousness of our stance against the "terrorists'? Or do we give pause amidst this moral outrage to reflect on several issues I have raised in this presentation that demonstrate that we have always used poor disabled third world women as pawns in our mythical struggles over good and evil – allowing them a "deadly" recognition – only when it suits our purposes.

A transnational feminist disability studies perspective will force us to see that the embattled bodies of (disabled) (third world) women wear scars that speak of centuries of violence – representational, physiological, and material – and still live to tell their stories in the breathless whisper of exploding bodies and shattered bones. As witnesses to this violence, our only recourse is to forge a transnational theory and praxis that would work across the boundaries of race, class, gender, disability, and sexuality to end this violence now.

AND SO ... WHAT IS TO BE DONE?

So what does all this mean pedagogically? Should not discussions like this cause us all to be outraged? Where is there place in our curriculum for us to address issues like this? Why is it that even progressive pedagogues in Feminist Studies,

Disability Studies, Anti-Racist, and Social Education have done little to reflect on the implications of contemporary history on issues of race, gender, and disability? Is it because we perceive these populations as "backward, irrational, undeveloped"– whose claims to personhood are questionable? Are we conscious of both racist and ableist metaphors that we deploy to justify and therefore silence the critical dialogue as well as action that may be required of all us to stop the violence? How do we go about business as usual...making blithe assertions of our respect for our common humanity in a context rife with the real material violence of social and economic inequality?

To educate for social justice it is imperative that we ask the hard questions. To be an ethical educator would require that we have the moral courage to seek the answers to those questions. And to claim our own humanity necessitates that we care about the Other as much as we would our own.

NOTES

[1] Here I am referring only to the emergency care soldiers receive at the military bases and at hospitals like Walter Reed in Bethesda, Maryland. Follow up medical care and access to medical benefits that occurs in VA hospitals in the months following emergency care are reported by several news media sources to be far from satisfactory.

[2] Judith Halberstam and Ira Livingston (1995) define posthuman bodies as "the causes and effects of postmodern relations of power and pleasure, virtuality and reality, sex and its consequences. The posthuman body is a technology, a screen, a projected image; it is a body under the sign of AIDS, a contaminated body, a techno-body, ... a queer body." (p. 3)

REFERENCES

Al-Ali, N. (2005). Reconstructing gender: Iraqi women between dictatorship, war, sanctions, and occupation. *Third World Quarterly, 26*(4–5), 739–758.
Brinkley, D. (2006). *The great deluge: Hurricane Katrina, New Orleans, and the Mississippi Gulf Coast.* New York: Harper Collins.
Chang, G. (2000). *Disposable domestics: Immigrant women workers in the global economy.* Boston: South End Press.
Clare, E. (1999). *Exile and pride.* Boston: South End Press.
Erevelles, N. (2006). Disability in the new world order: The political economy of world bank intervention in (post/neo) colonial context. In INCITE, *The Color of Violence.* Boston: South End Press.
Fine, M., & Asch, A. (Eds.). (1988). *Women with disabilities: Essays in psychology, culture, and politics.* Philadelphia: Temple University Press.
Finger, A. (2005, September 12). *Anne Finger reflects on Hurricane Katrina.* Retrieved from http://www.rollingrains.com/archives/000644.html
Garland-Thomson, R. (2005). Feminist disability studies. *Signs: Journal of Women and Culture, 30*(2), 1557–1587.
Garland-Thomson, R. (1997). *Extraordinary bodies: Figuring physical disability in American culture and literature.* New York: Columbia University Press.
Ghai, A. (2003). *(Dis)embodied form: Issues of disabled women.* New Delhi: Har-Anand Publications.
Ghobarah, H. A., Huth, P., & Russett, B. (2004). The post-war health effects of civil conflict. *Social Science and Medicine, 59,* 869–884.
Glasser, R. J. (2005, July). A war of disabilities. *Harper's Magazine, 311*(1862), 59–62.
Herold, M. W. (2002, March). A dossier on civilian victims of United States aerial bombing of Afghanistan: A comprehensive accounting (revised). Retrieved from http://www.cursor.org/stories/civilian_deaths.htm

Hull, A. (2004, December 1). Wounded or disabled but still on active duty. *The Washington Post.* Retrieved from http://www.washingtonpost.com/ac2/wp-dyn/

iCasualities.org. (2009, December). Iraq coalition casualty count. Retrieved from http://www.icasualties.org/

Iraqbodycount.org. (2009, December). Iraq body count. Retrieved from http://www.iraqbodycount.net

Kalyanpur, M., Kaplan, C., Alarcon, N., & Moallem, M. (Eds.). (1999). *Between women and nation: Nationalisms, transnational feminism, and the state.* Durham, NC: Duke University Press.

Kuterovac-Jagodic, G. (2003). Posttraumatic stress symptoms in Croatian children exposed to war: A prospective study. *Journal of Clinical Psychology, 59*(1), 9–25.

Lidinsky, A. (2005). The gender of war: What "Fahrenheit 9/11's" women don't say. *International Feminist Journal of Politics, 7*(1), 142–146.

Livingston, J. (2006). Insights from an African history of disability. *Radical Review of History, 94,* 11–126.

Masters, C. (2005). Bodies of technology: Cyborg soldiers and militarized masculinities. *International Feminist Journal of Politics, 7*(1), 112–132.

McKay, S. (2004). Reconstructing fragile lives: Girls' social reintegration in northern Uganda and Sierra Leone. *Gender and Development, 12*(3), 19–30.

Miles, M. (2003). Formal and informal disability resources for Afghan reconstruction. *Third World Quarterly, 23*(5), 945–959.

Mohanty, C. T. (1997). Under Western eyes: Feminist scholarship and colonial discourse. In N. Vishwanathan, L. Duggan, L. Nissonoff, & N. Wiegersma (Eds.), *The women, gender, and development reader,* (pp. 79–93). Atlantic Highlands, N.J.: Zed Books.

Mohanty, C. T. (1991). Introduction. In C. T. Mohanty, A. Russo, & L. Torres (Eds.), *Third world women and the politics of feminism,* (pp. 1–50). Bloomington, IN: Indiana University Press.

Molina, N. (2006). Immigration, race, and disability in early 20th century America. *Radical History Review, 94,* 11–126.

Morris, J. (1991). *Pride against prejudice.* London: Women's Press.

Myrttinen, H. (2004). 'Pack your heat and work the streets'—Weapons and the active construction of violent masculinities. *Women and Language, 27*(2), 29–34.

Pin-Fat, V., & Stern, M. (2005). The scripting of Private Jessica Lynch: Biopolitics, gender, and the "feminization" of the U. S. Military. *Alternatives, 30,* 25–53.

Rai, S. (1996). Women and the state in the third world. In H. Afshar (Ed.), *Women and politics in the third world* (pp. 25–39). New York: Routledge.

Rohrer, J. (2005). Towards a full-inclusion feminism: A feminist deployment of disability analysis. *Feminist Studies, 31*(1), 34–61.

Roman, L. (2003). Education and the contested meanings of 'Global Citizenship.' *Journal of Educational Change, 4*(3), 269–293.

Thomas, C. (1999). *Female forms: Experiencing and understanding disability.* London: Open University Press.

Safran, S. P. (2001). Movie images of disability and war: Framing history and political ideology. *Remedial and Special Education, 22*(4), 223–232.

Walsh, D. (2005, May 18). U.S. war in Iraq yields a social tragedy. *World Socialist Web Site.* Retrieved from http://www.wsws.org/articles/2005/may2005/iraq-m18.shtml

Wendell, S. (1996). *The rejected body: Feminist philosophical reflections on disability.* New York: Routledge.

Nirmala Erevelles
The University of Alabama

REBECCA A. MARTUSEWICZ AND GARY R. SCHNAKENBERG

3. ECOJUSTICE, COMMUNITY-BASED LEARNING, AND SOCIAL STUDIES EDUCATION

INTRODUCTION

Global climate change is suddenly on our radar screens as the primary challenge facing us in the 21st century. The use of fossil fuel-based energy and the economic system it supports has had enormous effects on the all aspects of the life systems that we depend upon for survival—from soil to water, to air, to plant and animal species. And, despite promises that this system provides a better quality of life for all, there is growing evidence that human communities across the planet are actually experiencing widening economic inequalities and insecurities as material wealth becomes consolidated in the hands of fewer and fewer people. While "bigger and better," faster and faster, and the mantra of "more, more, more" continues to saturate our lives, actual incomes and buying power for the bottom 90% of people in the United States has actually declined steadily. Meanwhile, "the world's Social majorities" (Esteva and Prakash, 1998) who have historically lived largely outside of this industrialized economic system, are steadily being forced off their land and into exploited labor where they are told that real economic success comes in the form of two dollars or less a day. Food and water security become increasingly rare as traditional cultures around the world are brought under the mantra of "development." Communities are suffering, and while the fate of polar bears may be our current "canaries in the mine shaft," the crises that we face are much closer and more complex than those distant polar ice caps may indicate at first glance.

Social Studies education has historically been argued for by radical educators as the discipline most suited to taking on issues related to equity, social justice, and the promotion of democratic ways of living/being. For the most part issues related to ecological sustainability have been relegated to the sciences or to environmental education, separated off from the treatment of concerns about poverty, racism, sexism or other forms of social violence. In this chapter, we argue for an approach to social studies education that takes seriously the interdependence of human communities (and thus social justice) within a larger ecological system. Further we argue for turning traditional social studies disciplines—history, economics, and civics, for example—toward an understanding of the ecological crisis as a *cultural crisis*, the same cultural crisis causing impoverishment and oppression among humans.

INTRODUCTION TO THE ECOJUSTICE FRAMEWORK

EcoJustice is an approach to education that has two major goals. First, to engage an analysis of the linguistically rooted patterns of belief and behavior in Western industrial cultures that have led to a logic of domination leading to social violence and ecological degradation, and secondly to identify and revitalize the existing cultural and ecological "commons" that offer ways of living more sustainably in our own culture, as well as in diverse cultures across the world. Within these two broad goals, six specific tasks are delineated: (1) to identify, disrupt, and shift the socio-linguistic foundations that lead to interrelated forms of ecological and social violence; (2) to identify and eliminate the ways marginalized groups across the world disproportionately suffer from the ravages of pollution, species extinction, topsoil loss, fisheries loss and other forms of ecological degradation; (3) to end the cultural, economic and environmental exploitation by modern industrialized nations of the "North" of non- or less-industrialized cultures of the "South" (Third World cultures); (4) to recognize and support efforts to revitalize the world's diverse cultural and environmental commons in order to achieve a healthier balance between market and non-market aspects of community life, (5) to protect the renewing capacity of natural systems in order to ensure the prospects of future generations; (6) to support local decision making that takes account of the rights and integrity of the more than human world, and healthy human communities as they are nested in living systems, or in the words of Vandana Shiva (2005), to support processes that lead to earth democracies.

Emphasizing "ecology" to mean the complex network of living relationships creating the community within which we live, EcoJustice perspectives understand issues pertaining to social justice to be inseparable from and even imbedded in questions regarding ecological well-being. For K-12 teachers, the first goal of this framework offers an analytic path for learning to identify and disentangle the ways language and a complex socio-linguistic system has been established historically to frame the assumptions, relationships, identities, institutions, policies, and general worldview that Western industrialized cultures depend upon and take for granted as universal. Foundations of education scholars are probably most familiar with the body of work put forward by C. A. Bowers over the last twenty or so years offering an analysis of "double-bind thinking" resulting from the deeply held cultural assumptions that get created and carried forward within the very structure of our day-to-day language as well as within the policies and discursive practices organizing K-12 and higher education. As he wrote in a recent online publication (2009):

> What the vast majority of Americans, as well as citizens in other western countries, fail to recognize is that words have a history. If the history of words is ignored, the analogs chosen in response to a different set of social circumstances will continue to frame how we understand today's problems. This history also influences the silences that are clearly present when people claim that they are concerned about changes in the environment, but have few ideas beyond embracing the technological solutions being promoted by experts who share similar silences about the deep cultural changes that must be undertaken. (p. 11)

Bowers uses the concept "root metaphors" to get at the ways that language operates analogically to create foundational discourses such as ethnocentrism, individualism, mechanism, scientism, and anthropocentrism (Bowers, 1997; 1999). The idea of "root" here is important because the metaphors at the heart of these discourses are old and deeply entrenched; they shape our beliefs and behaviors, making possible both the institutional structures and individual relationships and identities implicated in both social and ecological violence. For example, an instrumental view of knowledge as made up of discrete disciplines can be linked to mechanism, a fundamental way of seeing the world that is exemplified by the Newtonian idea of "universe as clockwork" or a natural system as a machine able to be taken apart, manipulated, and thus controlled by science (See Merchant, 1980). While all cultural systems use metaphor and are socio-symbolic systems, many non-western peoples use more organic or even familial/kinship metaphors to describe their relationship to the cosmos. These different worldviews create very different relationships to the living world.

The important analysis put forward by this part of the EcoJustice framework is that the ecological crisis is really a *cultural* crisis. To understand the processes leading to the devastation of the world's diverse living systems or the impoverishment of communities, we must look at historically codified patterns of belief and behavior. These powerful discursive practices result in social policies, economic decisions, and educational institutions that continue to reproduce unsustainable overconsumption of the resources we need to survive. Further, they produce subjective formations and collective psychological patterns that make certain relationships seem normal, natural, or universal. The words we use on a day- to-day basis help to maintain and recreate "master narratives" structure complex hierarchized systems of identity, value, and material realities. In an analytic vein similar to what post-structuralist philosophers have offered us, EcoJustice analyses expose the power-knowledge dynamic within discourses used to rationalize the hyper-separation of human communities from the natural world, and the reification of living creatures and eco-systems as resources designed for human use and exploitation.

Related work by ecofeminists Val Plumwood (1997, 2002), Karen Warren (2003), Carolyn Merchant (1980) and others offer further insights to support this sociolinguistic analysis. Plumwood's detailed analysis of what she calls "centrist" modes of thinking exposes the intertwined nature of age-old patterns of hierarchized belief leading to both social and ecological oppression. "A hegemonic centrism," she writes, "is a primary-secondary pattern of attribution that sets up one term (the One) as primary or as centre and defines marginal others as secondary … as deficient in relation to the centre. Dominant western culture is androcentric, eurocentric and ethnocentric, as well as anthropocentric" (2002, p. 101). For example, the historical deprivation and exploitation of enslaved African communities, or the genocidal actions taken against Native Americans was rationalized historically via analogic comparisons of non-white peoples to "savages," "beasts," or "farm animals." Slave narratives reveal, for example, the discursive and thus psychological struggle to be considered human rather than mere animals: "Us ain't hogs, us is human beings!" (see Haymes, 2001). Similarly, examination of the history of the scientific revolution in Enlightenment thought reveals "Woman" defined as having a different nature, and thus is inferior to man based on her lack of reason and her closeness to "nature" which is "defined as constituting a lower order of life and radically excluded from humans" (Plumwood, 2002, p. 102). Thus, she is the social and political analogue to radically excluded nature.

It would be impossible to degrade humans on the basis of their likeness to animals or to broad conceptions of "nature" if we did not first believe in the inferiority of non-human species, and our right to exploit them. While on the surface we may find the above beliefs and practices difficult to swallow today, they are a powerful part of our discursive, subjective, and material history, and remain part of the deeply internalized rationalizations for both social inequality and ecological degradation. Today we use other descriptors to marginalize and degrade. Using the language of market liberalism, we talk about "undeveloped" nations and "undeveloped" land.

Corporate outsourcing of work to areas of the world where "labor is cheap," using female and child labor in sweat shops, buying up forests to be turned into paper commodities, turning once rich farmland into desert via unsustainable industrialized agricultural practices, polluting or privatizing the world's potable water sources, and stripping the ocean's fisheries are all processes rationalized by a mindset that backgrounds and instrumentalizes the living systems being harmed, and values individual profit over life. The powerful assumption that humans are unavoidably self-interested, that the "individual" is the most basic unit of the human species (which is superior to all other species), and that the most successful societies will be those organized to effectively capture that individualist drive and make it productive dominates our social, political, and economic organizations. Our culture is so steeped in metaphors that valorize competition, "progress," and unlimited "growth" as the way to satisfy individual profit motive as a core human trait, that we accept as inevitable the attending exploitation of human and non-human life to get what we are told we "need." "Hey, that's Progress!" The drive to consume our forests and fisheries, and impoverish our rural and urban communities in the process is "just the way it is." These deep cultural meanings are internalized and passed down over many generations through specific metaphors that are so internalized as to seem natural. While they may be shifted as they are exchanged and applied over time, in general they frame and normalize they ways we think and they show up in our everyday words and texts, as well as in our relationships, and this includes those exchanged and reproduced in schools.

An EcoJustice framework also emphasizes the ways that various communities and cultures around the world actively resist these globalizing neoliberal forces, protecting and revitalizing their cultural and environmental Commons (the social practices, traditions, and languages, as well as relationships with the land necessary to the sustainability of their communities). The recognition that diverse cultures across the world live within very different cosmologies that have very different effects on the natural world is an important aspect of this work. This includes listening carefully to the voices of North American indigenous peoples, for example, as they teach us about their ancient belief systems and practices as models of more sustainable ways of living. It means that we introduce our students to a way of thinking about economics beyond the usual liberal ideologies and systems that dominate modernist cultural ways of knowing. Students learn to analyze the ecological consequences of different economic approaches, identifying ancient and existing economic ideologies and relationships that are operationalized by the specific needs of communities first, as opposed to those market liberal systems where specific demands of "the economy" frames social life. An EcoJustice approach emphasizes the more than 5000 languages that are still spoken worldwide, and the important relationship between linguistic, cultural and bio-diversity (Nettle and Romain, 2000). Where linguistic diversity is lost, there is a clear connection to ecological degradation, as cultural practices and knowledge related to sustainability are also lost.

Further, and perhaps most important of all, EcoJustice insists on reconnecting students and teachers to their own local communities: to their shared relationships within neighborhoods, landscapes, and with the more than human creatures that often go unnoticed as primary sources of knowledge and life-sustaining support. In this sense, we find it useful to reconsider place-based education within a distinctly EcoJustice theoretical framework. Place-based education offers students the opportunity to connect their studies with relevant and authentic experiences within places that are already imbued with meaning for them (Sobel, 2005; Gruenewald and Smith, 2008). They learn to identify both problems and assets in their own neighborhoods, collaborating with local stakeholders, family members, and elders, as they engage in critical problem solving around issues that matter to them. The idea here is that learning is more powerful when made relevant to personal understandings and relationships, and that learning to protect the places we love is most likely when those places are studied in all their living complexity, rather than dispassionately or as abstractions. When the issues plaguing our communities are analyzed using the wider EcoJustice framework, students learn to recognize the ways deep cultural constructs and assumptions lead to social structures and decisions that affect their specific situations. Thus, the local is made sense of in terms of its imbeddedness in global, cultural, economic and political systems.

Further, when students are encouraged to identify the aspects of their cultural and environmental commons that lead to mutual well-being and a smaller ecological footprint, they are offered the opportunity to understand these practices and relations as important assets needed to address current social and ecological injustices that are the consequence of a "hyper-consumer culture." Thus, EcoJustice education is about more than recognizing and analyzing problems. It is also crucial that students and teachers can recognize, celebrate, and help to revitalize a community's existing strengths—the often overlooked skills, traditions, and practices that have been passed down over many generations that don't require money to access, but that are aimed at helping or nurturing each other. This is what we mean by the cultural commons. We emphasize these age-old ways of knowing as critical to more sustainable societies.

This chapter argues that the purposes of public education and more specifically the responsibility of Social Studies education ought to be to develop citizens who can understand, identify, and make collective decisions to remediate problems in their communities as a matter of basic survival as well as happiness and overall well being. In the sections that follow, we discuss the relevance of an EcoJustice framework to social studies education and examine several current examples where K-12 teachers use these ideas to guide their approach to social studies, developing civic awareness, activism and "earth democracy" in their students. Given the crises we face, we can no longer afford to choose to ignore EcoJustice as a framework for the social studies curriculum.

THE PURPOSES OF SOCIAL STUDIES EDUCATION

With this EcoJustice approach we are calling for a rethinking of what citizenship means, what it means to be educated for citizenship, and what the purposes of social studies education ought to be. Today, and over the past several decades, those of us involved with U.S. public schooling have witnessed and experienced federal and state policies that define the purposes of schooling in terms of the preparation for work and the need for the US to be economically dominant on a world-wide scale. Ironically, this demand that schools prepare people for work is made concurrent with an increasingly deregulated and globalized economic system that normalizes outsourcing, leaving hundreds of thousands of people out of work and without hope of employment as they watch their jobs leave the country.

Rather than being educated to reproduce a culture and economic system whose short term profit motive and ideology of unlimited growth dangerously overshoots the carrying capacity of the bio-systems depended upon for life, we argue that the purpose of public education must be to develop citizens who can actively work toward a democratic and sustainable society, one that values cultural diversity for what it offers to community problem solving and for the essential role that bio-diversity plays in the very possibility of living systems. Such a citizenry requires a developed eco-ethical consciousness, people who recognize the importance of protecting their local communities' health and welfare, while understanding the ways larger social, political, and economic systems function historically to degrade the social and ecological relationships necessary for life. And, it requires teachers who can take on responsible pedagogy necessary for confronting the deadly consequences of these current systems. Many teachers have learned that schools often reproduce the inequalities of race, class, gender, homophobia and other oppressions, but they have little understanding of how these inequalities intertwine with the suffering of non-human creatures, the loss of habitat, the degradation of soil, water, forests, or air.

ON THE ISSUE OF STANDARDS

Not surprisingly, when we talk to prospective or practicing teachers about shifting their pedagogical frame to EcoJustice many react with certainty that we are asking them to do more, that it feels like a burden too large to carry in light of all their other responsibilities, or that it means subverting state mandates. They are right that it takes more work in the sense that it means the same old-same old approaches or activities won't suffice. They will indeed have to rethink what they are doing and that takes some work, but it is our experience that good teachers do this periodically as a matter of professional practice and in fact welcome ways to make learning more authentic for students. Mostly, adopting this framework means that the sort of questions they raise with students and the activities, projects, readings and other materials will begin to shift as their own personal understandings and commitments shift; it also means moving the learning beyond the classroom walls, getting students out into and involved in their communities to address critical ecological and social problems. But the idea that this approach must necessarily go against state standards is not accurate. In fact, as we'll show in the specific examples below, benchmarks in science, language arts, and social studies as well as the arts can all be used to support this approach.

As defined by most states in their educational benchmarks or standards, social studies normally consists of instruction in four main disciplinary focus areas or content strands: history, economics, geography, and civics/government. In addition, some states include several other social science fields such as sociology, anthropology, philosophy, and psychology to some degree in their frameworks or standards. Each of the four primary categories and several of the secondary ones can be addressed effectively through the utilization of an EcoJustice framework at different grade levels. For example, New Hampshire's History strand includes "investigate the evolution of the United States economy from farms and small stores to [industry and services]" for students in grades 3–4, its Economics strand indicates that students in grades 9–12 will "examine how various national economic policies have led to changes in the international economy, and the Geography strand for grades 5–6 reports that students will "understand the consequences of human modification of the physical environment" (Department of Education, State of New Hampshire, 2006).

In the state of Michigan, the History strand requires that later elementary students "select decisions made to solve past problems and evaluate those decisions in terms of ethical considerations, the interests of those affected by the decisions, and the short- and long-term consequences [of] those decisions," while middle school students will "compare various methods for the production and distribution of goods and services." At the high school level, students will "explain the causes and importance of global issues involving cultural stability and change, economic development and international trade, resource use, environmental impact, conflict and cooperation, and explain how they may affect the future." (State of Michigan Department of Education, 1996). Thus, rather than being restricted by state frameworks and standards, we argue that these typical examples of social studies standards directly support teachers' utilization of an EcoJustice framework in fulfilling the responsibilities of social studies education. Our examples below help make this clear.

FOOD FOR THOUGHT, SUSTAINABILITY AND FOOD SYSTEMS: SOUHEGAN HIGH SCHOOL, AMHERST, NH

In the fall of 2005, three teachers from Souhegan High School in Amherst NH, representing Social Studies, English/Language Arts, and Science, launched an interdisciplinary seminar for 12th graders focused on food systems and sustainability.

Gary Schnakenberg, Ken Boisselle, and Melissa Chapman, joined by Rebecca while on sabbatical, planned and implemented this course, and were supported by a faculty Committee on Sustainability that served in an advisory capacity. At Souhegan, students in their senior year receive English credit either through an Advanced Placement course (a minority take this route), or a two-credit interdisciplinary Senior Seminar where one credit is dedicated to English and one credit to another discipline, creating a specific elective course dedicated to a particular topic. There are several such seminars from which students choose including an Arts Seminar, Nature Seminar, Ethics Seminar, Conservation Biology Seminar, and the Sustainability and Food Systems Seminar. These seminars are organized in a modified block scheduling structure, utilizing two back-to-back course periods every day, and as close to a two-course enrollment as possible. Each section enrolls between 30 and 45 students.

The structure and context of this school made this interdisciplinary approach not only possible but a *normal* part of the school's curricular commitments. Founded according to principles set out by the Coalition of Essential Schools, Souhegan embraces interdisciplinary instruction, teams, advisory groups and assessment by "Exhibition." Teachers are accustomed to high degrees of collaboration throughout grade levels, and work in an atmosphere of trust and democratic decision-making. Thus, the context in which this course was developed is probably uncommon—but not entirely unique—for a public school.

Nonetheless, all seminars including this course are required to meet state mandates and benchmarks in all three disciplines, and serve a very heterogeneous group of students in terms of ability. While many of the Amherst students come from white professional affluent families, about one third of the students in this seminar the year it was launched came from lower socioeconomic segments of the community and upon graduation planned to move into the workforce rather than pursue higher education. This variety made for a very rich set of discussions, activities, and relationships that ultimately evolved into a strong community over the course of the year. The description for the Sustainability and Food Systems course reads as follows:

> This interdisciplinary course examines the various aspects of the U.S. and global food production, allocation, and distribution. It draws on environmental, botanic, cultural, geographic, economic, civic, and ethical lenses of focus, utilizing fiction, poetry, and nonfiction literature to provide perspectives on place, nature, food, and agriculture.

The course, now in its fourth year, intentionally utilizes the six key aspects of EcoJustice education, offering students an analytic frame for understanding the processes and politics of food on both global and local scales. Students begin the year reading *Ishmael*, a novel by Daniel Quinn (1992), as an introduction to the idea that there are diverse cultural worldviews leading to very different ways of organizing societies and relating to the surrounding natural systems. Students are introduced to key concepts—individualism, ethnocentrism, anthropocentrism, "progress," and mechanism as tools for examining the workings of socio-linguistic systems on their own thinking and on western industrial/consumer cultures more generally.

Exploring Quinn's example of a "Taker" worldview under the banner, "The World Belongs to Us," Rebecca (on sabbatical and supporting the initiative) led a discussion one day on anthropocentrism. She asked the students to imagine and list out examples of the sorts of things they might see in a culture organized by anthropocentric ways of thinking. We defined the concept carefully and they thought a while, soon offering examples like "roadkill," mountaintop mining, deforestation, animal abuse, zoos, and so on. After several examples were on the board, a young woman raised her hand. "I might be way off here," she started, "but I think in a culture where humans are defined as superior to animals, it would be a short leap to believing that some people are superior to others." There was quiet, and then we were swept up in a flurry of other examples of how value hierarchy works to structure our thinking. "There would be poverty!" "Men would think they're better than women!" "Yeah! It's why we had slavery! We thought they were 'like animals!'" Our journey was underway.

Later, using concepts from human geography, the students explored cultural points of view akin to Quinn's notion that "We belong to the world." They were introduced to Ladakh, a culture perched on the edge of the Himalaya in northwestern India who continue to use traditional and highly sustainable food production practices even while they experience the intrusions of a globalized economic system (Norberg-Hodge, 1991). Human geography concepts were introduced that enabled students to analyze in a non-deterministic way the manner in which the Ladakhis developed a "culture complex" that helped them to thrive in this physically harsh environment. For example, water is a precious resource (the region receives an average of only 4 inches of rain per year), and the Ladakhis use a carefully managed system of distribution and community maintenance of irrigation channels in order to not overtax the glacial meltwater "reservoir" on which their agriculture depends (allowing, incidentally, bumper harvests of wheat and barley, with apricot and apple orchards at lower elevations!). A lesson to take from this is not that we should or could "become Ladakhis," but rather to understand that there are different ways that cultures see themselves in relation to the world, and that "technology" encompasses a wide range of possibilities—some more sustainable and community-building than others. Students were also exposed to Hopi, Quechua, and the local Abenaki First Nations peoples as a means of exploring diverse cultural patterns and belief systems, especially related to their relationships with the land and food production. Focusing closer to home, students study the history of these different worldviews in their own bio-region, reading William Cronon's *Changes in the Land: Indians, Colonists and the Ecology of New England* (1983). Cronon's work is a classic environmental history comparing land conservation practices and attitudes of native peoples versus commodification-based views of colonizing New Englanders and the effects of these differences. They also read Wendell Berry's novel, *Jayber Crow* (2000), a tale of the ways a Kentucky farming community was changed in tragic ways after World War II as the country shifted to an industrialized food production system.

Alongside these explorations of diverse cultural perspectives and practices, students studied their own food commons. They learned to grow, preserve, and cook food themselves, building six raised-bed gardens where a wide range of vegetables and herbs were grown. The class harvested lettuces and other greens to supply the school salad bar for two weeks in the fall. With the science teacher they examined soil science and soil analysis, nutrients and nutrient cycling, soil conservation practices, and the ecological impact of synthetic fertilizers. A major research project and exhibition was organized around the science of composting, including the construction and implementation of a school composting system. They read most of Michael Pollan's *The Omnivore's Dilemma* (2006) and portions of Barbara Kingsolver's *Animal, Vegetable, Miracle* (2007). Mixed in were also lectures on physical geography: world soil-type distributions and classification systems, world climate, glaciers and glaciation, soil forming processes, and "agricultural revolutions." In a major project, teams of students studied the history of the town's food commons, interviewing descendents of some of Amherst's long-established farming families. This project was designed to connect the students to their community's not-too-distant past, examining the specific knowledge and memories of food production from elders who still live among them. They used the community library and town hall to access records and historical archives about the agricultural history of their now largely suburban community.

While space does not permit to examine all the aspects of this course, it is important to emphasize that, as the course continues to be developed, these three disciplines are woven together to help students examine the multidimensionality of sustainability. All three teachers are often present in full class discussions of these topics, or outside with students working in the gardens. There is substantial effort by all three teachers to weave into their assignments the key aspects of the EcoJustice framework and to continually pose questions about the ecological effects of specific practices or policies. Students work back and forth between projects that ask them to inquire into the policies of modernization and the effects the industrialized food system on their own bioregional and community history and land-use patterns. An oral history project requires students to research agricultural history of their town of Amherst, while a "commons" project gets them involved in one-on-one mentoring relationships to learn about the value of particular non-monetized skills and traditional practices. All through these activities and assignments they were constantly reminded to use the EcoJustice analytic tools to think about the way that language operates to keep the market-based/consumerist systems functioning, as well as the existence of practices in their own and other cultures that leave a smaller ecological footprint.

Our experiences in this seminar paved the way for the development of a major project currently underway in Michigan. Teams of teachers in partnership with non-profit community organizations are learning to use EcoJustice education to frame community-based learning projects with their students.

THE SOUTHEAST MICHIGAN STEWARDSHIP COALITION

The Southeast Michigan Stewardship Coalition (SEMIS) at Eastern Michigan University is one of four "hubs" established in 2007 by the Great Lakes Stewardship Initiative. The primary goal of the SEMIS Coalition is to develop students as citizen stewards able to understand and promote healthy ecological and social systems affecting the Great Lakes basin and their communities. In SE Michigan, a steady decline in manufacturing jobs and sprawling suburban development has led to a declining tax base in the city and inner ring of suburbs, as well as loss of farmland, inadequate infrastructure, and negative environmental and public health impacts throughout the region. The statistics are grim: 390,000 additional acres of farmland lost by 2030; 240,000 manufacturing jobs lost since 2000; 21% of Detroit's population lost since 1980; $52 billion needed for regional infrastructure renovations; regional asthma rates nearly twice the national average; the sixth highest adult-obesity rate in the nation; and 52 school closings in Detroit alone. Water pollution caused largely by storm-water run off is a major result of these land use problems. As more open land and tree cover are lost to roads, parking lots, and buildings, storm water carrying chemical fertilizers, pesticides, oil, and other pollutants enters the surface water, degrading area water quality at higher rates.

According to the U.S. Census Bureau, 2006–2008 American Community Survey, Detroit is approximately 90% African American and Latino; 28% of households live below the poverty level, three times the national average. Using data from the U.S. Department of Health and Human Services, the National Center for Children in Poverty reports that "a higher percentage of [Detroit] children are poor than in any other major city in the nation except Atlanta. Detroit's child poverty rate is 39 percent, and a startling 72 percent of Detroit's children live in families that are low income, defined as twice the official poverty level" (Dinan et al,. 2006). Literacy rates are low and violent crime in the city is high. Given this context, it is very important that teachers begin to introduce their students to the tools that they need to respond. Supported by the resources offered through SEMIS, students, teachers and community members learn to work together effectively to address the intersecting social, economic, and ecological problems in their communities, and their underlying root causes.

Working in schools and communities across southeastern Michigan, the Coalition's objectives are to: (1) offer sustained professional development for teachers using a model of community-based education within an EcoJustice framework; (2) develop partnerships between schools and community organizations working on social and ecological problems; (3) promote collaboration among community organizations in the service of schools; (4) help these school and community partners to develop community-based learning projects that engage students in addressing critical ecological and social problems in their own neighborhoods. Working with seven schools and 16 non-profit grassroots community organizations in the region, the SEMIS Coalition is the only one of these four hubs that emphasizes the intersection and inseparability between social and ecological justice and uses a cultural ecological analytic approach for solving these problems. Meeting about once a month with teams from all the other schools for full-day professional development workshops that introduce the primary ecojustice concepts, teachers are learning to focus on the specific social and ecological problems in the communities where our schools are located, while studying the larger economic, political, and sociolinguistic context in which these problems occur.

In all the schools where we work, administrators are highly supportive of the teachers' participation. Indeed, this is a requirement to become a member school in SEMIS. Administrators must agree to release their teachers for both full-day professional development workshops and field trips when they take their students out into the community. Even if a school's scheduling and programming does not explicitly create opportunities for school-wide reform, collaborative associations among teams of teachers with community organizations, and with teachers from nearby schools can inspire the sorts of curriculum reform needed for student engagement.

Hope of Detroit Academy

At a K-8 charter school in Southwest Detroit, 4th through 8th grade students are learning to think about how they can contribute to making their community a safer, healthier, more sustainable place by studying the history of land use, wildlife habitat, and brownfield remediation. This school serves a largely Latino community in a section of Detroit highly impacted by the ravages of industrialization, outsourcing, and immigration policies.

Since February 2008, 6 teachers from Hope of Detroit Academy have participated in professional development workshops introducing them to a cultural ecological analysis and supporting them as they translate that framework into curricula for 250 elementary and middle schools students. In the spring of 2008, a handful of 6th graders took a walk around their SW Detroit neighborhood with several of their teachers and interested community members. The group walked about a square mile through a neighborhood of small clapboard houses and neat yards, but also plagued by abandoned lots and high levels of illegal dumping, toxic soil, and "tagging" by gangs. As they walked, the students pointed out where they lived, where they rode their bikes and played, which yards had gardens with fresh vegetables, and who nurtured those gardens. One ten year-old boy, George[1], was particularly passionate about pointing out the piles of old tires and other debris in abandoned factory lots surrounding the school. He was upset and perplexed about these lots, asking questions about why those tires and piles of construction material got dumped in his neighborhood. Listening to stories told by the other children about the time the factory behind the school burned while the children were in school, the teachers and other adults began to talk with the students about ways to clean up those lots and recycle the tires. George spoke up again, quick to point out places where tires had been placed in the openings of storm drains. "Yes! We need to do something, and soon! But, don't take those tires away! I put those there so my sister wouldn't fall in with her bike!" Many of the grates and manhole covers have been stolen, and sold as scrap metal.

This community walk was the beginning of our community-based learning project and stewardship initiative with this school, and the use of community mapping as a standard practice among the other schools as well. A decision was made to help the Hope of Detroit students figure out how to work in this neighborhood in an effort to clean up the schoolyard and adjacent lots. Using curriculum planning strategies developed by the Coalition of Essential Schools and other national school reform programs, the teachers chose an "essential question" and several sub-essential questions to organize their project: What is Community? How do communities change over time? How are decisions made and what effects have decisions had on social and ecological aspects of community? What kind of community do we want to live in?

Using these questions as a general guide, the middle school social studies and science teacher planned an interdisciplinary project with the 6–8th graders to study the history and science of land-use in SW Detroit, especially focusing on the shift from agriculture to industrialization, the development of the auto industry, and the problem of brownfields in the community. Students are conducting surveys and oral histories engaging parents, business owners, community leaders and elders in discussions about the neighborhood, their memories of work, politics, and land use. They are learning to test soil and water, studying the remediating properties of some plants, and communicating with local officials about their interest in and potential plans for rehabilitating their schoolyard neighborhood. In May 2009, supported by the Southwest Detroit Environmental Vision, a local non-profit, about thirty, eighth graders participated in a neighborhood Tire Sweep, first mapping the location and then collecting a truckload of illegally dumped tires that were taken to a local Detroit social services agency where homeless men are employed to turn the tires into mud mats. As one student told a local news station, "anything can make a difference."

At the same time, 4th and 5th graders studied the need for wildlife habitats even in urban settings, planning and planting a small habitat in a side yard of the school. Becca Nielson, regional representative of the National Wildlife Federation worked closely with the teachers to support this elementary initiative. The Matrix Theatre Company, a Detroit-based ecology-oriented performance troupe, collaborates to help the students communicate the importance of this work to the public. A major part of our work is dedicated to coalition building among these organizations, helping them to build capacity for collaboration that reflects regional thinking and cooperation in order to best serve schools and communities. These organizations participate with the schools in all parts of the professional development workshops, as well as developing relationships with specific schools and helping to mentor individual teachers.

Divine Child Catholic High School, Dearborn, MI

A second school in the Southeast Michigan Stewardship Coalition project is Divine Child High School located in a suburb of Detroit, Dearborn, MI. While Dearborn is home to the largest Arab population outside the Middle East, this school enrolls students from primarily white middle class families from across the region. Approximately 8 teachers from DCHS began working with the Coalition in November 2008. Several students from the school's Green Team, a student led ecological organization, have also been involved in workshops that help participants unpack the cultural foundations of the ecological crisis. Having attended several foundational workshops introducing them to the socio-symbolic foundations of social and ecological problems, this team of teachers and students are working on a variety of stewardship projects with the essential question, "How do we work together to create a sustainable community for the 21st Century?" Friends of the Rouge (a local non-profit organization that works on issues related to the River Rouge Watershed), and University of Michigan Dearborn's Student Environmental Association are two key community partners, but the school is beginning to draw on other resources in their community on their own as well. 150 ninth graders were taken on a day long retreat where stewardship oriented community service was the primary theme. With some of this groundwork underway, the first phase of this school's implementation was planned for a two-week Summer Institute for students in June 2009.

Six interdisciplinary courses involving social studies, science, religion, media, technology and language arts were planned with a water stewardship theme and interrelated community-based learning projects. Teachers were coached by SEMIS staff to develop these courses with clear EcoJustice criteria as the primary framework, and required to get students directly involved in authentic problem solving in their community. For students more accustomed to going to the mall or sporting events, or partying with their friends, paying attention to what's going on in the river nearby is a totally new experience.

A course on "Urban Ecology" was developed between Social Studies, Science, and Religion teachers. This course brings together study about the civil rights movement in Detroit, its relation to white flight and suburbanization, and the ecological impacts of that movement, especially on the Rouge watershed. In addition to working closely with Friends of the Rouge to plan this course, Divine Child teachers also invited other community groups (Spinscape and Detroit Options for Growth) into the school to talk with students about documenting and mapping solutions to urban sprawl, water and sewage treatment, industrial waste and brownfield remediation, as well as light rail and economic stimulus. A focus on community service as eco-ethical responsibility runs through the work of the teachers at Divine Child; school administration is so supportive of this unfolding approach to the schools' service requirement that they have begun to hire young teachers specifically for their interest in pursuing professional learning communities that result in relevant, interdisciplinary community-based learning projects tied to their curriculum and state standards.

Nsoroma Institute

Another school involved in the Southeast Michigan Stewardship Coalition is the Nsoroma Institute, a K-8 African-centered charter school. At Nsoroma, the school-wide focus on food security is a response to the "food desert"[2] in Detroit especially among the African American population. Malik Yakini, the principal, is also the founder and chairman of the Detroit Black Community Food Security Network:

> We have an organic farm that we maintain in a city-owned park that we hope is creating a template for other groups who might want to utilize some of the under-utilized land owned by the city of Detroit ... All members of a community should have access to affordable, nutritious, culturally appropriate food ... As of 2007, the last major grocer left the city of Detroit which was Farmer Jack. Now, I grew up in Detroit—I'm 53 years old—and when I was a child there were many national chains in Detroit ... but now there are no

major grocers in the city ... we have a serious problem both in terms of access to fresh produce in the city of Detroit and we also have a problem in terms of the quality of food, because often the quality of food is markedly different in the city of Detroit than the quality of food that is available in the suburban rings that surround the city. (Malik Yakini, Ecology Center, 2009)

Under Mr. Yakini's leadership and with the support of the SEMIS Coalition, the three lead teachers from Nsoroma are working to design interdisciplinary curriculum materials around food security that can be adopted by their colleagues throughout the school.

Other schools in the SEMIS Coalition are using community-mapping strategies with their students to begin to identify assets and problems that will become the focus of community-based learning projects. In all of these schools, social studies teachers collaborate with teachers from other content areas, developing EcoJustice-oriented activities and practices that encourage their students to think differently about their responsibilities to their communities. We see this interdisciplinary approach using EcoJustice theory as a great model for school reform.

CONCLUSION

At the conclusion of the Souhegan seminar's inaugural year, students were asked to write a critical reflection on their experiences in the course, and present pieces of their reflections to the class. For us as teachers, the presentations were an emotional and powerful experience. One after another, the students gave deeply personal testimony about the ways that the course had changed their lives; they were awakened to cultural and ecological issues they had never thought about or acted upon before. They saw possibilities that they had never considered. An ecojustice framework is aimed at undoing the primary cultural discourses that form the powerful rationalization for a whole array of violent attitudes, relationships, and behaviors woven throughout Western industrial societies. Similar to sociolinguistic frameworks that examine the ways racism, sexism and other forms of social injustice are constructed via our discursive practices, EcoJustice scholars argue that to really understand culture one must understand the ways language works to shape thought. However, what distinguishes our work is the refusal to separate ecological degradation from social violence resulting from discourses that depend upon value-hierarchized metaphors. Students who study history, geography, and economics framed by EcoJustice learn to examine the specific social and ecological consequences of anthropocentric as well as ethnocentric, Eurocentric, and androcentric discourses on their own lives and communities.

In this sense, citizenship education within an EcoJustice model is a radical challenge to the reproduction of neoliberal faith in "growth" or "development" that requires the perpetual exploitation of people, land, and nonhuman creatures worldwide to fulfill our addiction to consumption. To be a "citizen," therefore, requires that teachers and their students actively engage in critical and ethical analysis of how their own identities are formed within this cultural matrix. There is no way to stop the violence without also understanding our own active complicity in the problem.

All too often "citizenship education" within social studies means socializing the next generation to accept and take their place in the exploitive relations that characterize the Western productionist-consumerist system. Making visible the ways these discourses work in day-to-day interactions creates the ability to shift these relationships, attitudes, and actions.

Further, educators who internalize an EcoJustice framework create pedagogical opportunities for their students to value commons-based ways of knowing still circulating in their communities. Students learn to identify and practice sustainable ways of being as a necessary component of citizenship as they create relationships with elders and actively collaborate with other community stakeholders in authentic problem solving. Community-based learning, therefore, provides a necessary context for the application of EcoJustice concepts and principles, an essential pairing evidenced in the practices and relationships among the teachers and students described here. We have no illusions that these teachers are going to "bring down the system," nor are we confident that their students are suddenly going to eschew consumerist habits. However, they are also not simply reproducing the age-old violent hierarchies. Instead, their work together creates the ability to see and embrace pathways towards healthy communities and living systems.

NOTES

[1] Not his real name. We use a pseudonym to protect his identity and anonymity.
[2] The term "food desert" was first coined by S. Cummins in 2002 in an article published by the British Medical Journal (Vol. 325, p. 436). Food deserts are generally defined as "Large and isolated geographic areas where mainstream grocery stores are absent or distant." Retrieved from the Food Desert website on Sept. 22, 2009: http://fooddesert.net/

REFERENCES

Apffel-Marglin, F., & PRATEC. (1998). *The spirit of regeneration: Andean culture confronting Western notions of development*. New York: Zed Books.

Berry, W. (2000). *Jayber Crow*. Washington, DC: Counterpoint.

Bowers, C. A. (1997). *The culture of denial: Why the environmental movement needs a strategy for reforming universities and public schools*. Albany, NY: State University of New York Press.

Bowers, C. A. (1999). Changing the dominant cultural perspective in education. In G. Smith & D. Willams (Eds.), *Ecological education in action: On weaving education, culture, and the environment*. Albany, NY: State University of New York Press.

Bowers, C. A. (2006). *Revitalizing the commons: Cultural and educational sites of resistance and affirmation*. Mahwah, NJ: Lawrence Erlbaum Associates.

Bowers, C. A., & Martusewicz, R. (2008). Eco-Justice pedagogy and the revitalization of the commons. In E. Provenzo Jr. (Ed.), *Encyclopedia of the social and cultural foundations of education*. New York: Sage Publishers.

Bowers, C. A. (2009). *Educating for ecological intelligence: Practices and challenges*. Retrieved September 28, 2009, from http://www.cabowers.net/CAPress.php

Cronon, W. (1983). *Changes in the land: Indians, colonists, and the ecology of New England*. New York: Hill and Wang.

Department of Education, State of New Hampshire. (2006). *K-12 New Hampshire Social Studies CurriculumFramework*. Retrieved February 5, 2010, from http://www.ed.state.nh.us/education/doe/organization/curriculum/SocialStudies/documents/K-12SocialStudiesFramework.pdf

Dinan, K. A., Fass, S., Chau, M., & Douglas-Hall, A. (2006, November). *Struggling despite hard work: Michigan and Detroit*. National Center for Children and Poverty. Retrieved February 8, 2010, from http://www. nccp.org/publications/pub_694.html#3

Ecologist, The. (1993). *Whose common future?* Gabriola Island, BC: New Society.

Esteva, G., & Prakash, M. S. (1998). *Grassroots postmodernism*. New York: Zed Books.

Gruenewald, D. A., & Smith, G. A. (2008). *Place-Based education in the global age: Local diversity*. New York: Lawrence Erlbaum Associates.

Haymes, S. N. (2001). "Us ain't hogs, us is human flesh:" Slave pedagogy and the problem of ontology in African American slave culture. *Educational Studies, 32*(2), 129–157.

Kingsolver, B. (2007). *Animal, vegetable, miracle: a year of food life*. New York: HarperCollins.

Martusewicz, R. (2009). Educating for 'collaborative intelligence:' Revitalizing the cultural and ecological commons in Detroit. In M. McKenzie, H. Bai, P. Hart, & B. Jickling (Eds.), *Fields of green: Re-storying education* (pp. 253–270). Cresskill, NJ: Hampton Press.

Martusewicz R., & Edmundson, J. (2005). Social foundations as pedagogies of responsibiity and eco-ethical commitment. In D. W. Butin (Ed.), *Teaching social foundations of education: Contexts, theories, and issues* (pp. 71–92). Mahwah, NJ: L. Erlbaum Associates.

Merchant, C. (1980). *The death of nature*. San Francisco: Harper Collins.

Nettle, D., & Romaine, S. (2000). *Vanishing voices*. New York: Oxford University Press.

Norberg-Hodge, H. (1991). *Ancient futures: Learning from Ladakh*. San Francisco: Sierra Club Books.

Plumwood, V. (2002). *Environmental culture: The ecological crisis of reason*. London: Routlege.

Plumwood, V. (1997). Androcentrism and anthropocentrism: Parallels and politics. In K. Warren (Ed.), *EcoFeminism: Women, culture, and nature* (pp. 27–35). Bloomington, IN: Indiana University Press.

Pollan, M. (2006). *The omnivore's dilemma: A natural history of four meals*. New York: Penguin Press.

Quinn, D. (1992). *Ishmael*. New York: Bantam/Turner Books.

Shiva, V. (2005). *Earth democracy: Justice, sustainability, and peace*. Cambridge, MA: South End Press.

Shiva, V. (1993). *Monocultures of the mind. Perspectives on biodiversity and biotechnology*. London: Zed Books.

Sobel, D. (2005). *Place-based education*. Great Barrington, MA: Orion Society.

United States Census Bureau. Retrieved February 8, 2010, from http://factfinder.census.gov/servlet/ACSSAFFFacts?_event=Search&geo_id=04000US26&_geoContext=01000US|04000US26&_street=&_county=Detroit&_cityTown=Detroit&_state=04000US26&_zip=&_lang=en&_sse=on&ActiveGeoDiv=geoSelect&_useEV=&pctxt=fph&pgsl=040&_submenuId=factsheet_1&ds_name=ACS_2008_3YR_SAFF&_ci_nbr=null&qr_name=null&reg=null%3Anull&_keyword=&_industry=

United States Department of Education. (1984). *A nation at risk*. Washington, DC: U.S. Dept. of Education, Office of Educational Research and Improvement.

Warren, K. (2003). The power and promise of ecological feminism. In D. VanDeVeer & C. Pierce (Eds.), *The environmental ethics and policy book: Philosophy, ecology, economics*. Belmont, CA: Thomson/Wadsworth.

Yakini, M. (2009, August 8). *Ecology center: Malik Yakini, Chairman, Detroit Black Community Food Security Network* [video]. Retrieved September 22, 2009, from http://www.channels.com/episodes/show/6349233/Malik-Yakini-Chairman-Detroit-Black-Community-Food-Security-Network#/ajax/feeds/show/16954/Ecology-Center.

Rebecca A. Martusewicz
Eastern Michigan University

Gary R. Schnakenberg
Michigan State University

RICH GIBSON

4. WHY HAVE SCHOOL?

An Inquiry through Dialectical Materialism

Criticism is no passion of the head, it is the head of passion. It is no anatomical knife, it is a weapon. Its object is its enemy, which it will not refute but destroy.

Karl Marx, *A Criticism of the Hegelian Philosophy of Right 1843*

Having a good school within this capitalist society is like having a reading room in a prison. Not acceptable.

Statement of students seizing the administration building at the University of California Santa Cruz, November 2009

The core issue of our time is the reality of the promise of endless war and booming inequality met by the potential of mass, activist, class conscious resistance.

We witness an international war of the rich on the poor in which the children of the poor, everywhere, fight and die on behalf of the rich in their homelands.

The core of dialectical materialist analysis insists that things change. But how and toward what end? More: Why?[1]

In this context, schools are the centripetal organizing point of de-industrialized North American life, and much of life elsewhere. Evidence: School workers, not industrialized workers, are by far the most unionized people in the USA, more than 3.5 million union members. School unions are growing, if slowly, while industrial unions collapse, evaporate, because, in part, industry evaporates, and because industrial union leaders abandoned the heart of unionism—the contradictory interests of workers and employers.[2]

In fall 2008, about 74.1 million people were enrolled in American schools and colleges. About 4.6 million people were employed as elementary and secondary school teachers or as college faculty, in full-time equivalents. Other professional, administrative, and support staff at educational institutions totalled 5.2 million. (National Center for Education Statistics, 2009)

Nearly one-half of the youth in high school today will be draft-eligible in the next seven years.

It is in school where, theoretically, mind meets matter. Schools claim to gain and test knowledge in a reasonably free atmosphere. Capitalism, rooted in exploitation, a reality that works best when hidden, overpowers freedom.

Matter intervenes. Capitalism meets democracy. Capital dominates. The relationship of schools to society where schools are, for the most part, capitalist schools is a reality ignored by liberal and even radical educators, particularly in the field of social studies education.

The education agenda is a class war agenda, and an imperialist war agenda. One begets the other (Gibson & Ross, 2009).

Let us tick off the emerging realities of our times as highlighted by the last election; the results of the many crises of capital contradicted by the promises of democracy. The recent election should not only be studied as how voters chose who would most charmingly oppress the majority of the people from the executive committee of the rich, the government. It should be studied, more importantly, as how an element of capitalist democracy, the spectacle of the election, has speeded the emergence of fascism as a mass popular force; that is:

- the corporate state, the rule of the rich, near complete merger of corporations and government;
- the continuation of the suspension of civil liberties (as with renditions);
- the attacks on whatever free press there is;
- the rise of racism and segregation (in every way, but especially the immigration policies);
- the promotion of the fear of sexuality as a question of pleasure (key to creating the inner slave), and the sharpened commodification of women (Sarah Palin to pole dancers);
- the governmental/corporate attacks on working peoples' wages and benefits (bailouts to merit pay to wage and benefit concessions);
- intensification of imperialist war (sharpening the war in Afghanistan sharpens war on Pakistan which provokes war on Russia, etc, and the US is NOT going to leave Iraq's oil);
- the promotion of nationalism (all class unity) by, among others, the union bosses,
- teaching people the lie that someone else should interpret reality and act for us, when no one is going to save us but us;
- trivializing what is supposed to be the popular will to vile gossip, thus building cynicism—especially the idea that we cannot grasp and change the world, but also debasing whatever may have been left of a national moral sense;
- increased mysticism (is it better to vote for a real religious fanatic or people who fake being religious fanatics?); and
- incessant attacks on radicals (Bill Ayers is not a radical; he is a foundation-seeking liberal now, once he was a liberal with a bomb, but people see him as the epitome of a radical and he is connected to Obama) (Gibson & Ross, 2009; Moore, 1957; Singer, 2002).

Capitalist schooling exists within these social rising circumstances. It's a litany of the emergence of fascism (Gibson, 2000).

Following the election, the demagogue Obama who was wildly backed by post-analytical hysterics like Tom Hayden, Barbara Ehrenrich, and liberal academics as well as dreamy students and sincere but deluded anti-racists, finalized what can only be called the corporate state, not merely the domination of capital over democracy, but the merger of the two at every level, desperately chasing capital itself. The corporate state deals with its own contradictions—a key one being social control versus profiteering and their interrelationship. Sometimes they merge neatly, other times one must dominate the other, all under beneath the veil of exploitation.

The demagogue, Obama, turned $12.9 trillion over to the banks, no strings, on the grounds they are too big to fail. Then he bailed out the auto industry to the tune of more than $400 billion, but Obama effectively killed Chrysler and became the de-facto president of General Motors ($12.9 trillion for economic recovery. Where is it?, 2009).

Those who seek evidence about what specifically I suggest to do about the rise of corporate state fascism would expect me to ignore the Patriot Act. I write, instead, of a more hopeful future, if a slimmer possibility rooted in the fact that things do indeed change, that we can comprehend and change our world. A revolution, a full overturning, is possible. Not likely soon, but possible. Dialectical materialism is not a crystal ball, but a navigation tool to the past, present, and future.

Now, back to school.

CAPITALIST SCHOOLING IS PART OF THE CAPITALIST STATE

Al Szymanski (1978) outlined the basic functions of the capitalist state's democracy three decades ago. This is a reminder:
– To guarantee the accumulation of capital and profit maximization and make it legitimate.
– Preserve, form, and temper, capitalist class rule.
– Raise money to fund the state.
– Guarantee and regulate the labor force.
– Facilitate commerce.
– Ensure buying power in the economy.
– Directly and indirectly subsidize private corporations.
– State sanction of self-regulation of corporations.
– Advance the overseas interests of corporations.

Democracy does not dominate capital. Democracy submits, atomizes voters to individuals huddled in ballot booths asking capital's favorite question: What about Me?

We have evidence from the past when the rise of fascism begins to overwhelm the relationship of capitalism and democracy in schools.

> The Nazis education project which was riddled with contradictions of mysticism and science, for example, nevertheless followed the broader Nazi effort, to protect capital itself and to extend the empire via preparing citizens for endless war. The educators were "converted into priests (and nuns) of the new creed, which made them responsible ... for undertaking to create a militarized society that accepted war as a normal condition of life." (Blackburn, 1984, p. 182)

The demagogue, Obama, then turned to the schools with his Race to the Top (RaTT) project personified by Chicago's education huckster Arne Duncan. The RaTT speeds what was already happening in capital's schools and adds a few factors for spice.

The RaTT's predecessor, a bi-partisan project touted by Democrats and Republicans alike called the No Child Left Behind Act had at least these key factors: (1) The development of a regimented national curriculum to promote nationalism; (2) High stakes standardized tests to promote segregation and ignorance through with a pretense of scientific backing; and (3) the militarization of schools in poor and working class areas. RaTT makes the logical extensions:
– Sharpened demands for a national curriculum,
– merit pay based on student test scores,
– attacks on all forms of tenure (made palatable to the public because they know through experience that there is no shortage of incompetents in schools),
– Layoffs, hits on pay and benefits, increases in class size,
– Tuition hikes driving youth out of college with razor-like precision, typically rooted in inherited wealth.
– Some privatization, but hardly only privatization (the corporate state reflects both the unity and contradictions internal to the ruling classes who have different short term views of profitability).
– Calls for national service setting up a syphon for middle class opposition to a draft.
– Intensified moves into cities and schools in crisis, like Detroit, demonstrating the contradictory goals of social control and profiteering.
– Ruthless competition between school districts and states for limited RaTT reward dollars.
– A harsh rule of fear and intimidation sweeping across all of capitalist schooling (Gibson, 2010).

Fear seems to be the core emotional value in schools today. After a long trip visiting schools in about one-half of California's counties, my colleague and friend Susan Harman (a former principal) and I concluded that fear overwhelms much of educational work. It travels down, from superintendents through principals through education workers to kids and parents. It has many secondary sources (secondary to profiteering and social control) like high stakes exams and constant surveillance. Fear also travels horizontally. It is produced by school workers who believe they have more to fear than they actually do. They give in with no struggle, even before demands are made. As they do, fear accelerates as all conclude that no one can win.

This, then, begins to describe the conflicting material bases of capitalist schooling. Social control meets profits. That, however, is but a small part of the story.

While the central issues of human life—labor (communists–oh my!); reproduction (sex and creativity–pleasure oh no!); the struggle for the truth (nationalism, racism, sexism, tolerance for mysticism, etc.); and freedom (not in *our* school); are commonly illegal to teach in school, they remain an opposing force because schools are not Ford plants. Schools hold out a promise of freedom, inquiry, and creativity that many people take to heart, and it is almost impossible to successfully impose Ford plant discipline in school. Even so, it is important not to confuse resistance with rule. Schools are not contested terrain unless they are fully disrupted by forms of civil strife, which does happen, as we shall see.[3]

WHY HAVE SCHOOL?

A Radical Question: Why have School?

Schools are huge multi-billion dollar markets where profit and loss influences almost everything. Consider the buses, the architects, textbook sales, consultants, the developers for the buildings, the upkeep, the grounds, the sports teams, salaries, etc. Cost is always an issue in school. This is, after all, capitalism (a maneuver drawn from dialectical materialism, abstracting, looking to history–the Church–and locating school in its historical place: capitalist schooling).

> The average salary for public school teachers in 2006–07 was $50,816, about 3 percent higher than in 1996–97, after adjustment for inflation (table 78). The salaries of public school teachers have generally maintained pace with inflation since 1990–91. (National Center for Educational Statistics, 2009)

Multiply $50,816 by the total number of school workers, above. That's a tidy sum.

These relatively good salaries, in comparison to the crash of industrial wages and jobs, served as a bribe to educators, winning them to conducting the child abuse that is high-stakes exams and regimented curricula, for example. But, as economic break-downs caused by overproduction and war evaporated at least some of the ability to make the pay-off—and as school workers became more and more alienated from each other, their communities and students, through those same processes—the bribes and jobs began to vanish–as we witness today.

The capitalist market necessarily creates pyramid-like inequality, not only in the pocket, but in the mind. Is there a single public school system in the US (or wherever)? Actually, there is not. There are five or six carefully segregated school systems, based mostly on class and race.

> The actual image of education in the minds of philanthropic economists is this: "Every worker should learn as many branches of labor as possible so that if ... he is thrown out of one branch, he can easily be accommodated in another." (Marx, 1975, p. 25)

There is a pre-prison school system in Detroit, Michigan or Compton, California; a pre-Walmart system in National City, California; a pre-craft worker system in City Heights, California; a pre-teacher or social worker system in Del Cero, California; a pre-med or pre-law system in Lajolla, California and Birmingham, Michigan; and a completely private school system where rich people send their kids, like George W. Bush or Mitt Romney.[4]

Rich schools teach different realities using different methods from poor schools. In rich schools the outlook is: "This globe is ours; let us see how we can make it act." In the poorest schools, the outlook is, "Tell me what to do and I will do it."

"Public schools" are, in fact, funded by an unjust tax system that forces the working classes to pay for their own mis-education. These are not just schools but, again, capitalist schools. There is little democratic about them.

It is usually easy to track the role of the market in schools by checking the campaign contributors to school board members. The sources of their power are the Men, and Women Behind the Screen, who have very special interests in determining how schools function.

There is, in schools unlike most factories, a tension between elites' desire for social control and profitability. This can be seen in the contradictions within elite groups about the privatization of schools. Old guards like the Rockefeller Foundation oppose privatization, perhaps because they rightly see they can exert a great deal of control over tax funded schools, while new entrepreneurs like Bill Gates and Eli Broad pour millions into privatization schemes. Who will win? I bet on the old guard.

Battles over the market in schools, as in wage strikes, test boycotts, etc., have been rare in the last thirty years as the consumer economy diverted people, on one hand, and the obvious corruption of union leaders (as we shall see) on the other hand, held people back. Such fights were disappointingly uncommon in schools where, for at least two decades, the work force has overwhelmingly been guided by at least four things: Opportunism. Racism. Sheer ignorance. Cowardice. However, things change.

More answers to why have school:

Skill and ideological training. Under skill training we might list, of course, "the three r's," along with music, art, athletics, theater, science, etc. That list comes fast and easy.

But ideological training is another thing. Ideological grooming would include nationalism (the daily salute to the flag, school spirit, etc.) as well as the training in viewpoints established by teaching distinct curricular substance in the segregated schools, using different methods. Beyond nationalism, one clear purpose of most schooling is to make the system of capital natural, almost invisible, and to present it as the highest, last, stage of human development. Further, students must become so stupefied that they see no real contradiction between nationalism and the other central tenet of capitalist thought: individualism. Me!

The upshot of capitalist schooling is that many students, surrounded by the unsystematic, incoherent, mystical worldviews of both the curricula and most teachers, come away learning not to like to learn. Curiosity, a birthright of all children, gets crushed. Parallel to that dubious success, children in exploited areas learn they cannot understand or alter the world. So, people in pacified areas become instruments of their own oppression.

Baby-sitting and warehousing kids. Babysitting is a key role played by capitalist schools. One way to find out, "Why have school," is to experiment; close them. In our case, teacher strikes serve as a good test subject. In school strikes (no sane union shuts down a football program), the first people to begin to complain are usually merchants around middle schools–who get looted. The second group is the parents of elementary students, quickly followed by their employers. (These realities can help demonstrate to elementary educators their potential power— along with setting up kids' entire world views).

The baby-sitting role is, again, funded by an unjust tax system and serves as a giant boon to companies that refuse to provide day care for their employees–but are able to duck taxes as well.

Schools fashion hope: real and false. On one hand it is clear that societies where hope is foreclosed foster the potential of mass uprisings: France in the summer of 1968 is a good example of what can happen; uprisings starting in school and quickly involving the working classes nearly overthrew the government (Singer, 2002).

Real hope might be found in showing kids we can comprehend and change the world, collectively, and teaching them how. Ask, "Why are things as they are?" every day. Or, in demonstrating that we are responsible for our own histories, but not our birthrights. Must we be lambs among wolves? Does what we do matter? False hope might be the typical school hype: Anyone can make it, all you must do is work hard. Trumpery. Inheritance is, more than ever, the key to understanding social mobility, or immobility.

To the contrarians: there is nothing unusual about elites picking off children of the poor, educating them, and turning them back on their birth-communities as a form of more gentle rule. Obama would be one example of such a success. Skanderberg, the Albanian rebel trained by the Turks, would be a failure.

Schools create the next generation of workers, warriors, or war supporters. Automatons or rebels, or something in between, a process with some witting direction. Those workers need to be taught to accept hierarchy, to submit, to misread realities like class war and endorse nationalism (school spirit) or racism (segregated schooling products). They need to accept their lot, to be unable to notice why things are as they are; why some live in abundance while others have no work—when there is plenty of work to do—why drudgery is so much part of most jobs. The core project here: obliterate the possibility of class consciousness.[5]

And what of the school unions that claim to protect educators' rights from academic freedom to job security and to defend "public" education as well?

Another Tick-List, this Time about the School Unions

No leader of any major union in the US believes that working people and employers have, in the main, contradictory interests, thus wiping out the main reason most people believe they join unions. The bosses (for that is what they are) of the two education unions (the National Education Association and the American Federation of Teachers (AFL-CIO) by far now the largest unions in the USA) openly believe in what former NEA president Bob Chase called "New Unionism," the unity of labor bosses, government, and corporations, "in the national interest." There is nothing new about company unionism, however, nor the corporate state.

Both unions are utterly corrupt. There has been a steady stream of AFT and NEA leaders to prison on charges ranging from child molestation to the more common embezzlement. Top NEA and AFT leaders will make nearly $500,000 a year in 2009 and can live on their expense accounts. While nothing like the difference between finance capitalists and industrial workers, the union bosses enjoy extraordinary privileges while claiming to represent many people who have to live in trailers. The corruption runs deeper, though, as shown below.

The AFT is completely undemocratic and impossible to change without violence. The NEA, not a part of the AFL-CIO, has a somewhat more democratic structure but no one with a grasp of the "rule of the people," would confuse NEA with democracy.

The school unions draw on a member base that is about 90% white and reflect the racism that such a base inherently creates. Rather than fight to integrate the teaching force, the unions urge more and more "education" classes, adding on expenses for students, meaning those with the least get shaved out with razor sharp precision–by class and race.

The unions, like all US unions, do not unite people, but divide them along lines of job, race, years of tenure, staff and leaders from rank and file, that is, down to the narrowest interest–capital's favorite question: What about me? Unions typically recreate and mimic the hierarchies of the industry they represent, in our case, school worker versus school worker for petty positions of power that offer high pay and distance from the work place.

Unions mirror their industries. Thus, school unions create hierarchies (that reformers tend to mimic), which resemble the management structures of schools. These structures promote the quasi-religious view that someone else will solve key problems that must, in fact, be resolved by the solidarity and direct action of the rank and file–a group that would include parents and students but, since these are capital's unions, those people do not pay dues and are excluded. The unions promote a vending machine ideology ("I paid my dues now do for me") rather than solidarity and direct action, thus making the members reliant on people whose interests are not their own.

Union bosses recognize their opposing interests to the rank and file. They learn a variety of strategies to manipulate people and, "protect the contract." These maneuvers, like grievance procedures, move workers away from the locus of their power, the work place, to geographically distant spaces where "neutral" arbitrators decide on vital issues. But the unions rarely file cases to arbitration and, nevertheless, lose about 2/3 of the cases they file. Union bosses also divert member action to the ballot box–any place away from the job site—where, in the words of one top NEA organizer, "if voting mattered, they wouldn't let us do it." But electoral work keeps member volunteers busy and it reinforces the false notions school workers have about professionalism (professionals set their own hours and wages, they determine the processes of work–teachers typically are called professionals by people asking the workers to buy textbooks for their kids), allowing educators to win hollow "respect," the chance to dress up and rub elbows with Important People, away from school.

Since the mid-1970's, union bosses have supported every measure that elites used to regain control of schools which were, in many cases out of control. The NEA and

AFT bosses today support curricular regimentation, high stakes racist exams, the militarization of schooling, merit pay, and charter schools (a key new source of dues income).

The AFT organized the decay and ruin of urban education in the US, while the mostly suburban NEA let urban schooling be devastated, failing to recognize the truth of the old union saw, "an injury to one only goes before an injury to all." That both unions steeped themselves in volumes of forms of racism (racist exams, racist expulsions, racist segregation, etc.) should not go unnoticed or excused. Indeed, the teacher work force is an apartheid force, about 90% white.

These are the empire's unions. Top leaders are fully aware that a significant portion of their sky-high pay is made possible by the empires adventures. NEA and AFT bosses work with a variety of international organizations on behalf of US imperialism. These adventures are frequently deadly as with the AFT's unwavering support for Israeli Zionism, support for the recent oil wars, and, precisely to the point, work throughout the world with the National Endowment for Democracy, a Central Intelligence Agency front, in wrecking indigenous leftist worker movements. While the AFT has been the spearhead of US imperialism inside the wholly corrupt "labor movement," NEA has also been deeply involved. There is a long history to this, back to World War I and the AFL's support for that horrific war. The theory behind it: US workers will do better if foreign workers do worse.

The education unions serve to peddle the wage labor of education workers as a commodity to employers and to guarantee labor peace, as Los Angeles teacher Neil Chertcoff has repeatedly demonstrated. In this context, there is a direct trade off: no strikes or job actions in exchange for guaranteed dues income, the check-off. That is precisely the historical origin of the agency shop. It is also a big reason why union bosses obey court injunctions against job actions; threats to the union's bank account, that is, the union staff salaries.

School unions attack the working class as a whole. The most recent example (May 2009) of this was the support the California Teachers Association and the NEA gave to a series of ballot propositions that would have dramatically raised the taxes of poor and working people while leaving corporations and the rich off the hook, again. NEA and CTA combined spent more than $12.2 million dollars on the campaigns, and lost overwhelmingly. CTA-NEA demonstrated to poor and working families that organized teachers are enemies—yet those same people are educators' most important allies (Gibson, 2002).

Unlike the private sector where less than 10% of the people belong to unions, school workers are the most unionized people in the country. It follows that it is important for change agents to be where the people are. But one must keep one toe in and nine toes out of the unions. It is as important to build outside organizations, like the Rouge Forum, which actually unite people, urge job actions and freedom schooling, which seek to unite people rather than structurally divide them, and which can take a strategic and tactical plan into the unions to fight for justice.

Still, it is not hard to see why there is so much fear in schools. Although most education workers don't have the analysis of why there is no protection on the job, why the union is always telling people to vote but never organizes anything to prepare for job actions, they still recognize their own vulnerability. They know the union is an opposing force, not their friend.[6]

Jean Anyon (1997) famously says,

> Doing school reform without doing social and economic reform in communities is like washing the air on one side of a screen door; it just won't work. (p. 182)

Surely this statement nicely sums up a clear relationship of school and society that is routinely denied, both by the disingenuous powerful as well as too-kind people who work in schools. Anyon, however, explodes her own analysis and suggests that the only hope for poor kids' schools is for the rich to give them money.

The role of de-industrialization means that school workers are centripetally positioned in a powerful spot: the place where most people organize their daily lives. Schools do not just teach, but in many cases offer food, medical care, meeting places, etc. Schools produce, presumably, ideas. Perhaps they could be ideas about new and better ways to live. In any case, school workers have incredible potential power. What we do counts more than ever. Since good teaching and organizing are very much alike, school worker potential power is redoubled.

How do educators get the power to teach toward the truth, rather than toward capital's cruel desires? Clearly, one answer is dedication to the kids, parents and community; teaching well every day. The unions must be overcome, in part by transcending the boundaries of unionism and, beyond that, by violating the norms that keep the union bosses in power. Storm the podiums and seize the union offices. Another is in solidarity across lines of class, race, gender, nation; building close personal ties—tight friendships. And another is direct action on the job, the real battle for control of the work place linked to corresponding freedom schools in the midst of strikes or civil strife.

And this then leads to yet another demonstration of how capitalist democracy, which is a perversion of what people think of as democracy and not democracy, works. In the schools of capitalist democracy, as with any other form of capitalist government, lies the *violence* that is the iron fist inside the velvet glove of the system. That violence can be portrayed as the kind of drill and skill pedagogy that succeeds in making kids learn to not like to learn, or more graphically, it can be see in truancy laws. If you do not come to school, you or your parents face arrest and fines: cops.

CAPITAL IS THE ALL-DOMINATING POWER OF BOURGEOIS SOCIETY[7]

Let us abstract now, step back and consider the rise of capitalist, or bourgeoisie, democracy, it's current reality, and peer into what might be.[8]

Slave-holding Greeks are credited with the invention of democracy, but it's slave-holding American revolutionaries who took the notion to new heights in their battles with British tyranny, a turning point in what most people see as democratic rule.

Howard Zinn, a liberal pacifist who borrowed from Marx but wrote out the concept of revolution, suggested in his popular *People's History of the United States* (2005) that what was truly up was not so much democracy, rule of the people, but the enriching of hegemony, and elites, who used the myth of democracy, first under the Articles of Confederation, then on a lower plane, with the US Constitution, not to empower the people, but to establish the rule of property law, class domination in a somewhat new form, replacing a King with a local not-so chosen few. It was 55 rich men who wrote the Constitution in secret, after all, shifting the Declaration of Independence "Life, liberty and happiness," to "Life, Liberty and Property."[9]

But the abstract idea of democracy still holds a powerful grip on people, left to right and in-between. Let us quickly toss away the idealist abstract pretense of democracy standing by itself.

Here are three telling quotes about Democracy:

Democracy is the name we give the people whenever we need them. (Marquis de Flers Robert and Arman de Caillavet)

The whole dream of democracy is to raise the proletarian to the level of stupidity attained by the bourgeois. (Gustave Flaubert, 1821 – 1880)

Under democracy one party always devotes its chief energies to trying to prove that the other party is unfit to rule—and both commonly succeed, and are right. (H. L. Mencken, 1880 – 1956) [10]

We can see how US democracy deals with popular Hamas, crushes democratically elected regimes it does not like as in Guatemala, Nicaragua, Haiti, and Chile, seeks to murder popular leaders like Castro, creates bogus democratic movements in accompaniment with the CIA as in Kosovo or Poland, promotes democracy in the USSR and calls the KGB leadership "democracy advocates," restores drug gang warlords in Afghanistan and calls that democracy, invades and Balkanizes Iraq, for oil and regional control while waving the flag, and props up tyrants like the Saudis all over the world. The US uses the National Endowment for Democracy as a front for the CIA all over the world, and inside the US as well, to destroy indigenous movements that fight for equality.

Internally, US democracy, often with liberals in the lead, fashions the theft of the public treasury in maneuvers like Enron which involved every sector of government, demolishes the environment and gets the citizens to pay for the superfund sites, cheats at the ballot box, as in 2000, how the rich use the sheer power of their money to deceive and exclude people in national elections.

Democracy relies on a tax system that forgives the rich their riches and punishes workers for having to work. Greek democracy and US democracy were stacked on slavery. US democracy is a untrustworthy privilege won through the plunders of vicious imperial violence, part of the buy- off of the population of the empire's citizens, just as the nationalist loyalty of top union leaders is purchased by the CIA and imperialist war. US abstract democracy sits on the false idea that we are all in this nation together, when we writhe in the midst of class warfare, our side losing for now.

The one place we might expect to see some kind of abstract democracy operating, in the unions, we witness the most grotesque perversions of abstract democracy, as in the American Federation of Teachers or the United Auto Workers unions, both functioning with a caucus system that locks out any dissent whatsoever, a system upheld by the democratic Supreme Court. Union democracy is a myth. The unions, decidedly a part of the system of capital, are reduced to capital's motive: chase the dues money.

Every big city in the US is polluted with political corruption, from Mayor Kilpatrick's disgrace in Detroit to Mayor Murphy's disgrace in San Diego, just as the cities were utterly corrupt 100 years ago, as Lincoln Steffens demonstrated in *Shame of the Cities*, but Steffens (2009) was never able to connect incidents of corruption and the necessary tie of a system of exploitation and buy-offs, so he treated each city's rot as a fluke, just as Jonathon Kozol continues to do with education reform today, calling for "democracy" (Gibson, 2007). When US anti-war activists in the Vietnam era wanted to organize a vote against the war, they arrogantly forgot about the Vietnamese vote taking place on the battlefield.

Plunkett of Tammany Hall begat Randy "Duke" Cunningham. The current election spectacle is going to cost more than one billion dollars, for TV ads alone. The offer is, now, two demagogues declaring they can out-superstition the other and one war criminal. Such is abstract democracy in the US.

In philosophy, abstract democracy is religion, dialectics without materialism, the dead end of critique, a source of class rule. You suspend your critical thought, agree to one Imaginary Friend or another, enter an arena run by self appointed translators for the IF, pay them, accept the hierarchies they created before you arrived, take direction and adopt the rules of the translators for the IF, and since your IF has to expand or collapse, and since there is no way to resolve religious disputes, no way to offer proofs, others become enemies: Rivers of blood!

I do not want to hear about abstract rule of the people. Rather than vote in this system, the best move might be to turn the tables and, instead of buying a politician, get some pals and collectively sell your votes. I dismiss the abstraction of democracy.

CAPITALIST DEMOCRACY

I do want to address capitalist democracy, which Marx described as the best fit for the social system when under expansion. To grasp the relation of capital and democracy we must understand that they are not piled, one on the other, but fully imbued with each other. They developed together in history. It is like a mathematical fraction in which the numerator exists as a full partner with the denominator. But it, capitalism and democracy, is a zipped up relationship that is ignored or denied in civics classes, and which can ebb and flow depending on power relations between classes. We know US democracy can vanish, fast, as in Detroit in 1967 when all laws were suspended and the military invaded the city. Same is true of Canada, with the War Measures Act enforced in 1970.

What, then, is capitalism? It is, first, a system of exploitation, a giant sucking pump of surplus labor, a relentless quest for profits in which those who do not expand, die, as with the US auto industry. Capitalism is born in inequality and violence. Those who own, stole, and the rest, who must work to live, work under an unjust condition that claims to give us a fair day's pay, when in fact that days pay begins with the violence of being dispossessed and ends with our being paid but a portion of what our labor creates–the source of profit. Over time, production becomes increasingly social, yet the value of that production is looted by those few who hold power and capital. Still, at least in theory, the revolutionary system of capital, which demolished feudalism (then gave it new life in the Taliban) creates a world in which all people could live fairly well, if they shared.

So, capitalism is a system of exploitation in which those who must work to live must vie with each other for jobs, while nation based owners vie with each other for cheap labor, raw materials, and markets, often using militaries made up of workers who are sent off to fight the enemies of their real enemies: the rich at home.

Capitalism is a system rooted in alienation and exploitation: People who must sell their labor to live; that is, the vast majority of people, are drawn together in systems of production which, over time, are more and more socialized (bigger plants, more interconnected forms of exchange, technology, and communication, etc).

However, the people who must work, who form a social class, are set apart from each other in competition for jobs and do not control the process or the product of their work. We see that as school layoffs prompt educators to point at one another, suggesting someone else should go first, while the curriculum and teaching methods are imposed from the top down. Kids really need more educators, not less, and corporate profits and CEO pay still boom.

While educators have more control over our time than most workers, school workers do not determine how the work will be done, nor do we choose what will be done with the product and don't own the profits gained (whether it is a Pinto of child or a chocolate). The more they engage in this form of exploited work, the difference between them and their employers increases. At the same time, the more workers labor, the more they enrich their rulers, and wreck themselves. Alienation is a loss of self, indifference to others, and a surrender to passivity. Each group forms, in essence, a competing social class, hence Marx says, "history is the history of class struggle." Alienated individuals, though, become increasingly isolated while, simultaneously, they are driven together in ever more distinct, separated, classes.

Alienation and exploitation lead to commodity fetishism: Capitalism is propelled, in part, by the sale of commodities, for a profit (as in surplus value). Over time, both workers and the employer class relate more to things than they do to other people, indeed people begin to measure their worth by commodities, especially the chief commodity, money, which in many instances becomes an item of worship. Businesses no longer focus on making, say, steel for use, but on making money, for profits.

Finance capital begins to dominate industrial investment, or such is the path in the US. People who must sell their labor become commodities themselves, and often view themselves and their own children that way. How much you make determines who you are, who you meet, who you marry, where you travel. You are not what you are, but what you have.

People then begin to see what are really relations between people, as relations between things (every human relationship mainly an economic one), which leads to the connection of commodity fetishism and reification. In discussing the stock market, most economists treat it as if it had a wisdom and life of its own (remember the religion metaphor). In schools, children have been routinely commodified, sold to companies like McGraw-Hill (textbooks) and Coca Cola—and most teachers would agree that this process has accelerated in the last decade. Commodification means that people become things, less human, less connected so Marx argued, "the more you have, the less you are."

Test scores are a good example. No Child Left Behind sets up an appearance of equality, just like the myth of a fair day's pay for a fair day's work. The myth is that children enter the testing room as equals, the harder they prepped, the better they will do. The reality is that the more their parents earn, the higher the scores. The more you are concerned about test scores, the less you are learning anything important. The more you are learning, for example, subservience. In school the battle for profits meets the battle for social control.

As with capital, the more you concentrate on test scores, the more stupefied you become. But, the politicians ask, "how else can we measure learning?" while masses of people forget we could just ask the kid.

War, on one hand, and unconcern, on the other, are results of commodity fetishism. Greed, domination and fear are the underlying ethic.

Combined these three processes—exploitation, alienation, and commodity fetishism—forge reification: "All reification is a form of forgetting" (Horkhiemer & Adorno, 2002, p. 230).

The relations of people, disguised as the relations between things, become so habitual that it seems natural. Things people produce govern peoples' lives. Commodity production and exchange are equated with forces of nature. "Natural laws," really inventions of people, replace real analytical abilities (as in seeing supply and demand, or scarcity and choice, as the center pieces of economics, rather than seeing economics as the story of the social relations people create over time in their struggle with nature to produce and reproduce knowledge, freedom, and life—or in political science, discussing democracy as if it had nothing to do with social inequality).

Reified history is abolished, capitalism assumed to be the highest attainable stage of human development. Nothing changes. Normalcy in some capitalist countries is really store-bought assent to exploitation—masked as freedom. Test scores are good examples of reification in school. Measuring little but parental income and race, test scores are worshiped uncritically, influencing peoples' live far beyond their real value. Real estate salespeople love test scores, churn the market.

Reification hides the system of compulsion and disenfranchisement, a push-pull from the powerful, that mystifies a social system of exploitation so thoroughly that it is able to seriously call itself a centripetal point of freedom, producing a mass neurosis so powerful that it encourages it subjects to steep in two decades of consumerist euphoria while their social superstructure, like schools, their social safety net, like welfare or health services, evaporated underneath them.

Their industrial base vanished as well—a hangover from euphoria, the Golden Calf becoming the Trojan Horse—not wise for a nation promising to wage meat-grinder perpetual wars on the world to have the steel industry owned by outsiders from India, Germany and Japan. One has to worry about what happens when the US population cannot use its PlayStations or get to the mall. They may be the most dangerous people in the history of the world—or real rebels.

These processes of capital give those who own an enormous machine for lying and deceiving.

This background sets up our look at capitalist democracy as the best system for capital as it expands. The capitalist state is an executive committee of the rich, not an autonomous neutral, but their debate forum where they iron out their differences, then allow the vast majority of people to choose which of them will oppress best. The capitalist democracy is also an armed weapon in service to property rights. As the ruled far outnumber the rulers, and since coercion and force alone cannot sustain capitalist production, to pacify areas people must be turned into instruments of their own oppression.

We can see now how the one-person-one vote mythology would appeal both to rulers who seek to divide and conquer, and to individuals isolated by the system of alienation, fooled by the atomizing deception apparatus that promotes individualism–voting promotes the lowest forms of opportunism, boils down to "what about me?"—and the false notion that a vote can bring fundamental social change.

People hide from one another in voting booths wrongly thinking they are making real public decisions when they really have no control over the processes and products of the system–and most cynically know politicians always lie–yet they vote thinking they are exercising their only public or social power, when in fact they are just setting themselves off from others and the reality is that their real power lies in unity with other workers—at work, their ability to build solidarity to fight to control the value they create. The crux of capitalist democracy is revealed in the fact that nearly no one expects to have a vote on anything significant at work, unless they own the workplace.

Fundamentally powerless student councils are practice areas for future political leaders, councils where all concerned pretend they have influence, when they are mere performers reading blank scripts–sandboxes where the children at play are quickly put back in place should they wander out of bounds.

Others, excluded, (by Jim Crow laws or chicanery) might be disgruntled, while those who don't vote can be attacked for being responsible for the bad choices voters make.

The masses of people are told this is the law, which is alienated law, the will of the ruling class exalted into statutes, a sandbox of property laws overseen by millionaire judges that only incidentally considers people. The mythological rule of law is sheer class rule that shifts as class struggle and largess or bankruptcy meet one another.[11]

Within this law, as in religion, people deepen their alienation, choose, and pay, others to think and act for them, others who operate behind the habits of hierarchy and the force of arms. When serious differences, collisions of interests, appear between the capitalists of a given nation, they conduct civil war. The base for capitalist law is the same as the capitalist ethic: Profits are good, losses are bad, keep a careful count. Capitalist law is the law of property, ownership, not humanity.

The religion metaphor works well with schooling in the industrialized world. In the abstract, as with abstract democracy, public schools are there for the common good. But they are capitalist schools, above all, while, granted, opposition exists in some ways like it does in a factory. Educators in capitalist schools are somewhat like missionaries for capitalism. Look at the hierarchies: men run the administration (Bishops), and women (Nuns) do the front line work. School workers, who have more freedom than other workers, have a clear choice, be a missionary for the system of capital—or not.

No one ever voted themselves out of what is, at base, a Master/Slave relationship. The Masters will never adopt the ethics of the slaves. The singular path of reason alone will not overcome the system of capital, though reason must be our light and beacon. Our choice today is between community or barbarism.

Marx was correct in seeing that capitalism is a giant worldwide company store, an international war of the rich on the poor, and most importantly that the dispossessed of the world, probably all of us, have a real interest in overcoming that system and, not replacing it with another form of dictatorship, but with an ethic and reality of reasonable equality.

The logic of the analysis of capitalist democracy leads directly to revolution. There is no other way out. While we should abhor violence, we should not reify it, treat it as if abstract violence stands on a plane similar to abstract democracy, beyond history, social conditions, or the legitimate arts of resistance.

This is true especially now when finance capital in the US, though continuing to expand, is challenged by capital in other nations, like China which has a well motivated, not exhausted, military and needs that oil just as much as the US. Oil moves the military, which in turn is absolutely key to any empire's ability to expand, which is why saving gas will do little or nothing about the perpetual oil wars. US finance capital is hit by the crises we are familiar with: the inflation resulting from the lost war, $108 a barrel oil, the mortgage, personal debt, and national debt crises the ghastly rise in food and transportation costs, and so on. Yesterday's run on Bear Stearns, a big Wall Street bank bailed out by the government, the capitalist government in service to the rich, may be a harbinger of harsh times coming fast.

It follows that capitalist democracy in the US is rapidly contracting, and fascism emerges. As class antagonism grows, state power becomes an ever more national power over labor. There are no more labor laws of any worth, no civil rights laws, habeas corpus, rights of privacy, free speech (remember, "watch what you say") are gone, through bi-partisan legislative action as well as the courts.

The fight-back to transform the system of capital needs to look carefully at the rise of fascism (merger of the corporate and political elites, suspension of common laws, racism, nationalism, a culture writhing in violence in search of a strong leader– all moving at hyper speed within the national election now). Saying "emergence of fascism," does not mean fascism is arrived, but it does mean that fascism exists for some people in the US now, say a young black man in Detroit or Compton, while it is appearing before the eyes of others–volunteers drafted by the economy in Iraq.

But the left of the US anti-war movement, and the education reform movement, abandoned the critique of capitalist democracy (as in the current March 4, 2010 slogan, "Defend Public Education"), meaning they have no basis for analysis, no ability to develop strategies and tactics across a nation or even in unique communities—because they do not grasp how power works or why it is that the power of people who work lies, not in the voting booth—where odds are the voting machines are owned by their enemies–but at work where they can collectively win control of the processes and products of their work, in communities, or in the military where the working classes are already organized and armed.

At the same time, the left has made a fetish of Abstract Democracy, following the postmodernist coalitions where the notion of class struggle or the word, capitalism, is banished and people are urged to go off in narrow race/nation/sex/language, "autonomous," grouplets taking up their constricted issues, as did the 10,000 people meeting in Atlanta last year, thinking this will somehow lead to real resistance to a ruthless enemy with a long history of rule and a centralized command. To quote America's last remaining moral compass, Judge Judy, "it doesn't make sense and it is just not true." It won't work. Judge Judy is a perfect example of the appearance of judiciousness, when it is really the application of the values of the bourgeoisie, and the sale of judiciousness, as the filler between commercials.

Inside the trap of Abstract Democracy, the left has shown it is unable to get its ideas to leap ahead of daily social practice, and absolute necessity if we are to envision a better world and set about creating it.

In order to make a fight, people must trust one another. That means they must meet with each other in integrated groups that recognize that class remains the key issue at hand, of course mediated by questions of race, language, sex, gender, nation.

That, coupled with its ceaseless enchantment with nationalism, is the main reason the US left has had no impact whatsoever on the last seven or more years of imperialist war, even though a million and more people hit the streets in the first week of the Iraq invasion. They evaporated into their semi-autonomous worlds and have not exercised their potential power since. A somewhat similar thing happened to the school reform movement which, other than parts of the Rouge Forum, simply refuses to address the connections of the system of capital, imperialism, the regimentation of school life and the curriculum, oversight through high stakes exams, militarization, and privatization as well (Gibson, Queen, Ross, & Vinson, 2009).

It is fair to say, I think, that the dominant elements of public life in the US are opportunism, racism, nationalism, ignorance, and fear (surely that is true of the professoriate) though we have to recognize that the sheer perseverance of continuing to work, in our case on behalf of kids, has considerable courage built into it—and things do change, as we shall see.

Anyone interested in confronting our conditions today must follow Hegel's dictum: "The truth is in the whole." The whole is capitalism. Some live in capitalist democracies, and most do not, but it is the whole that must always be addressed, like keeping the front sight aligned with the rear sight. Even reforms will not be won without both sights on the target. The failure to create a mass base of class conscious people, which is our life and death high stakes test, remains the Achilles heel of nearly every revolutionary social movement. It follows we need to openly talk about what capitalism is, why class struggle takes place, what can be done, and what a better future might be. We need to answer the pedagogical question: *What do we want people to know, and how do we want them to come to know it?*–inside every action we take.

CONNECTING REASON TO PASSION TO POWER, ORGANIZATION, AND ACTION

> An educated man is...one who hears the entire concert being performed around him, all the sounds are within his range, they all blend together in a single harmony which we call culture. And at the same time he himself is playing one instrument in it, he plays well and makes his contribution to the common wealth, and this common wealth is all as a whole reflected in his consciousness, in his heart. (Lunacharsky, 1981, p. 49)

How is it that those who are aware of the enormous sacrifices that must be made to forge and sustain real social change, a full transformation beyond capital, offer a chance to be whole, creative, caring, either inside this ensnaring social system, or in the process of changing it? Such is the conundrum in schools and out.

We need to connect reason to passion to power, organization, and action.

We need to find ways to allow people to be as fully human, celebratory, as possible, connected, each demonstrating their creativity and connectedness with unfreedom as a commonly understood problem to be solved, because we are lambs among wolves.

It is this condition that can allow us to connect passion to the willingness to sacrifice that fundamental change, or any important social change now, will require to create and sustain. This is not going to be easy. This path beyond reason demands that people sacrifice treasure, sleep, sometimes jobs, certainly time and promotions, maybe jail or life, for the common good. Without that sacrifice, which can be achieved with collective joy, nothing.

We must not promise ourselves a future of material abundance. That will not happen. The ruling classes will destroy their own factories, hospitals, and even the water supply. What can transport us to a world where people can share is the idea that we might have to share misery for a while because, per Marx, ideas can be a material force—and have been.

The Rouge Forum

The ethic-as-material-force that guides work in the Rouge Forum, for example, is equality, not as an abstraction, but a guide (Gibson, Queen, Ross, & Vinson, 2009). Taken from the other direction: it is wrong to exploit.

This brings us to organization, power and action. Surely we can see that justice demands organization. The Rouge Forum has changed the discourse in the education reform movement. Our insistence on the role of capital, on class struggle is best illustrated by Wayne Ross' immortal comment—interrupting a particularly boring opening plenary of the College and University Faculty Association of the National Council for the Social Studies in Anaheim, CA—"Hey, this is a lot of nonsense, We Need To Read Marx and Make Class War."

We have had a dramatic impact on academic historians, whole language specialists, the critical pedagogy crowd, and the K-12 world as well. The conversation always has to, at worst, worry about us saying, "hey, wait a minute." We ruptured the habits of daily academic life that only reproduces the system of capital, diminishing all it touches.

The Rouge Forum has brought together people throughout the US, Canada, Mexico, South Africa, Great Britain, and India within an organization that has grasped, for eleven years, that it is possible to have an organization, be friends, and be both critical and self-critical. We united parents, kids, school workers, and community organizers.

We predicted both these wars and what became the NCLB as early as 1997 and published much of the initial research on the real impact of NCLB in academic and popular journals. We were among the first to plan ways to fight it. We traveled the US and other nations pointing out the centripetal power of educators in de-industrialized nations, among the last workers who have health benefits or predictable wages.

We have organized and led direct actions in workplaces and communities like the high-stakes test boycotts in Michigan, Florida, New York, and California. We did not just breach discourse and habits, we disrupted the unjust social relations in schools, shutting them down and, in very limited ways, offered youth freedom schooling. We marched on May Day before the massive immigrant May Day marches, and happily joined those huge outpourings of the working class when they took place. Now, with activist groups such as Calcare and others, we participate in a mass testing opt-out campaign, hoping to lead test boycotts to cut the school to war pipelines. We are building a base of thinking activists inside and outside the unions to reject the coming demands for school worker concessions, teaching people how to strike in solidarity—and to supply the Freedom Schools that can show how the future might be.

Today, the ground of the resistance appears to have shifted from test resistance and a focus on curricula or militarism, to battles about layoffs, wage and benefit cuts, tuition hikes, booming class size, etc. At this point, people resist in segments: teachers fight for teacher jobs, students against tuition boosts, support personnel for support jobs—even private sector workers versus public sector workers around the question of taxation. The only proper response is the one we developed here, addressing the whole, the key question being overcoming the system of capital as a whole. Fighting back within its fragmented framework, following the natural lines of the war of all on all economy, simply means we organize our own loss; divided and ruled again.

The Rouge Forum played a pivotal role in the March 4th 2010 Strike and Job Actions to Defend Education From the Ruling Classes, to Transform Education.[12] This movement, initiated by students in the Northern California University of California system, taking the direct action tact of building occupations, teach-ins, demonstrations, etc., drew opportunists and sectarians of all kinds, vampires to blood. We assisted in the building occupations and took on the combined reactionaries, union bosses and a variety of Bolshevite imitators, in meetings, online, and in direct action struggles–urging an analysis of the whole.

From an online debate:
People can be told that this is capitalism,
– that there is a connection between capitalism and imperialism,
– that the key reasons for the attacks on working people and schools are rooted in those two,
– the education agenda is a class war agenda and an imperialist war agenda,
– that the government is an executive committee and armed weapon of the ruling class and there they work out their differences, allowing us to choose which one of them will oppress us best,
– that the overwhelming majority of union bosses have chosen the other side in what is surely a class struggle and the union hacks gain from the wars and capital by supporting those wars, winning high pay and benefits, and betraying workers, they're a quisling force,
– that we can build a social movement that rejects the barriers US unionism creates, from job category to industry to race and sex and beyond.
– The core issue of our time is the reality of endless war and rising inequality met by the potential of mass, active class conscious resistance.

We can fight to rescue education from the ruling classes.[13]

The Rouge Forum has operated loosely. That worked for about eleven years, now with about 4700 people steady on our email lists, our yearly conferences, our publications, our joint work with *Substance News*, Calcare, the Whole Language Umbrella, TASH, and Susan Ohanian.[14] We have developed an organizational structure, a Steering Committee, the *Rouge Forum News*, Rouge Forum updates, that not only won the respect of educators, but community people and students. More, people can see where they may fit in, play a leading role, using their own creative abilities in the cause of social equality.

What we do counts now more than ever. We must plan the resistance with care, hopeful that things change, recognizing they do not always change the way we wish.

We are lambs among wolves. Kindness, reason, organization, must prepare to meet those willing to spill—rivers of blood.

Everything negative is in place for a revolutionary transformation of society (distrust of leaders, collapse of moral suasion from the top down, financial crises, lost wars, massive unemployment, booming inequality, imprisonment of only the poor, growing reliance on force to rule, eradication of civil liberties, corruption and gridlock of government at every level, etc.) What is missing is the passion, generalization, organization, and guiding ethic to make that change.[15]

In this chapter, I have sought to show that we have the positive aspects of change in embryo, that change can be initiated, if not completed, in social studies classrooms, in schools, that students are likely to take the lead as they have while I write, and—Yes. We can win.

NOTES

1. Rather than interrupt readers with long renditions about the nature of dialectical materialism, I seek to offer an analysis that relies on the outlook *vis a vis* capitalist schooling–and revolution. For a brief outline of dialectical materialism see Gibson, R. (2004) http://richgibson.com/diamatoutline.html And here http://richgibson.com/scedialectical4.htm. There is an excellent bibliography at the conclusion of Bertell Ollman's *Dance of the Dialectic* (2003). If pressed for one book, I recommend Ira Gollobin, (1983) *Dialectical Materialism, Its Laws, Categories, and Practice*. It is very hard to find. To see Lenin's advancing view, check *Materialism and Empiro-Criticism*, compared to his *Philosophical Notebooks* on Hegel (Vol. 39 Collected Works).
2. For a close examination of the wreckage of what was once the leading industrial union in the USA, see "The Torment and Demise of the United Auto Workers Union," (2006) at http://clogic.eserver.org/2006/gibson.html
3. Liberal post-modernists like Henry A. Giroux repeatedly insist schools represent "contested terrain." Postmodernism, religion with an angry cloak per historian Ernest Breisach in *On the Future of History: The Postmodern Challenge and its Aftermath* (2003), plays with dialects lifted up and away from the material world where the contest may be on, but somebody is on top. See for example, H. Giroux, *Slacking Off Youth* online at http://www.gseis.ucla.edu/courses/ed253a/Giroux/giroux5.html
4. On February 12, 2010, Walmart announced a partnership with four Detroit schools, training youth for jobs in their stores. This is a link to the Detroit Free Press announcement. http://www.freep.com/article/20100211/NEWS01/100211049/Walmart-offers-job-training-via-DPS Cranbrook Schools, an elite private both Mitt Romney and I attended, has a web site linked here http://www.cranbrook.edu/
5. I credit my many conversations online with Wayne Ross, David Hill, and Glenn Rikowski for fleshing out my thought on this. A good introduction to the latter comes from a joint interview linked here: http://clogic.eserver.org/4-1/mclaren&rikowski.html An introduction to Hill is here: http://clogic.eserver.org/2004/hill.html
6. For lengthy examinations of the role of the school unions in specificity, see the Unions section linked to my web page here http://www.richgibson.com/gibson.htm
7. Marx, K. (1858). *Grundisse*, linked online at http://www.marxists.org/archive/marx/works/1857/grundrisse/ch01.htm#3
8. Bertell Ollman in *Dance of the Dialectic*, now online (http://www.nyu.edu/projects/ollman/docs/dd_ch05a.php), argues that Abstraction is the key issue with dialectics while Raya Dunayevskaya argues it is revolution (http://www.newsandletters.org/Raya_Dunayevskaya.htm). I'll side with Dunayevskaya, but appropriate Ollman's thought here.
9. See: Zinn (2005), pp.77-102.
10. Quotes sourced at http://www.quotationspage.com/quote/856.html
11. For a detailed examination of the rule of property law, see essays in, Ollman (1990).
12. See: http://defendcapubliceducation.wordpress.com/
13. Gibson, R. (February 26, 2010). "The UCSD Occupation: What to Think and Do" for the Rouge Forum. The notion of rescuing education from the ruling classes comes from the Communist Manifesto, Part II linked online here: http://www.marxists.org/archive/marx/works/1848/communist-manifesto/ch02.htm. This view opposes the liberal call, Defend Public Education, which would in fact only strengthen the capitalist state.
14. See: Substance News (http://www.substancenews.net/); Whole Language Umbrella (http://www.ncte.org/wlu), TASH (http://www.tash.org/), and Susan Ohanian (http://www.SusanOhanian.org).

[15] Note the convergence of analysis about passion, the key role of morals, ideas, and organization in two apparently very different authors. Georg Lukacs in *Defense of History and Class Consciousness, Tailism and the Dialectic* (2000) Verso Press, p. 67; and Chalmers Johnson in *Revolutionary Change* (1982), Stanford University Press, p. 99.

REFERENCES

$12.9 trillion for economic recovery. *Where is it?* (2009, June 19). Retrieved March 1, 2010, from http://www.bloggingstocks.com/2009/06/19/12-9-trillion-for-economic-recovery-where-is-it/

Anyon, J. (1997). *Ghetto schooling.* New York: Teachers College Press.

Blackburn, G. (1984). *Education in the third Reich.* Albany, NY: State University of New York Press.

Breisach, E. (2003). *On the future of history: The postmodern challenge and its aftermath.* Chicago: University of Chicago Press.

Gibson, R. (2000). Teaching about the Holocaust in the context of comprehending and overcoming fascism. *Cultural Logic, 4*(1). Retrieved March 1, 2010, from http://clogic.eserver.org/4-1/gibson.html

Gibson, R. (2002). NES-AFT-AFL-CIO "Not just no. But HELL NO!". *Cultural Logic, 2*(1). Retrieved March 1, 2010, from http://clogic.eserver.org/2-1/gibson.html

Gibson, R. (2006). The torment and demise of the United Auto Workers Union. *Cultural Logic, 9.* Retrieved March 1, 2010, from http://clogic.eserver.org/2006/gibson.html

Gibson, R. (2007). *Going beyond Jonathan Kozol's manifesto: How can we overcome the weapons of mass indoctrination?* Retrieved March 1, 2010, from http://richgibson.com/beyondkozol.htm

Gibson, R. (2010, January 8) The Detroit Federation of Teachers contract; The worst ever? *Substance News.* Retrieved March 1, 2010, from http://www.substancenews.net/articles.php?page=1063&section=Article

Gibson, R., Queen, G., Ross, E. W., & Vinson, K. D. (2009). The rouge forum. In D. Hill (Ed.), *Contesting neoliberal education: Public resistance and collective advance* (pp. 110–136). New York: Routledge.

Gibson, R., & Ross, E. W. (2009). The education agenda is a war agenda: Connecting reason to power and power to resistance. *Workplace: A Journal for Academic Labor, 16,* 31–52.

Gollobin, I. (1983). *Dialectical materialism, Its laws, categories, and practice.* New York: Petras Press.

Horkheimer, M., & Adorno, T. W. (2002). *Dialectic of enlightenment* (G. S. Noerr, Ed., & E. Jephcott, Trans.). Stanford, CA: Stanford University Press. (Original work published 1947)

Lunacharsky, A. (1981) *On education.* Moscow: Progress Publishers.

Marx, K. (1975). *The Karl Marx library: On education, women, and children* (Vol. 6). New York: McGraw-Hill.

Moore, S. W. (1957). *Critique of capitalist democracy.* New York: Paine-Whiteman.

National Center for Education Statistics. (2009, March). *Digest of education statistics 2008.* Retrieved March 1, 2010, from http://nces.ed.gov/programs/digest/d08/#top

Ollman, B. (1990). *The United States Constitution: Two hundred years of anti-federalist, abolitionist, feminist, muckraking, progressive, and especially socialist criticism.* New York: NYU Press.

Ollman, B. (2003). *Dance of the dialectic.* Urbana, IL: University of Illinois Press.

Scipes, K. (2005, May). Labor imperialism redux. *Monthly Review, 57*(1). Retrieved March 1, 2010, from http://www.monthlyreview.org/0505scipes.htm

Singer, D. (2002). *Prelude to revolution.* Cambridge, MA: South End Press.

Steffens, L. (2009). *Shame of the cities.* London: General Books.

Szymanski, A. (1978). *The capitalist state and the politics of class.* Cambridge, MA: Winthrop.

Zinn, H. (2005). *A people's history of the United States.* New York: Harper.

Rich Gibson
San Diego State University

ANTHONY BROWN AND LUIS URRIETA, JR.

5. GUMBO AND MENUDO AND THE SCRAPS OF CITIZENSHIP

Interest Convergence and Citizen-making for African Americans and Mexican Americans in U.S. Education

CITIZENSHIP AND CRITICAL RACE THEORY—INTEREST CONVERGENCE

The conceptual and political meaning of "citizen" has remained foundational to the discourse and pursuits of equity and social justice in the U.S. The origins of this discussion start in early U.S. history, which promoted an ideological belief that only a select group of men would serve as the citizens of this nation. The social engineers, framers, creators and purveyors of democracy were then only white, land-owning, presumably heterosexual, men. Those who did not fit this category of citizen and potential citizen were not seen as having the proper temperament, class privilege, gender, sexuality, ancestry and race. Subsequently, for at least the first two and half centuries of U.S. history, the material and discursive category of the "American citizen" remained entrapped within the conceptual and legal framework of "white, landowner, heterosexual male." As political theorist Rogers Smith (1993) explains: "For over 80% of U.S. history, its laws declared most of the world's population as ineligible for full citizenship solely because of their race, original nationality, or gender ...." (p. 549)

In keeping with critical scholars of race and citizenship (Smith, 1988; Bell, 1980, Mills, 1997), we contend that the historical antecedents and contemporary discussions about citizenship have remained explicitly and subtlety defined by constructed meanings of "race." Numerous scholars (Smith, 1993; Mills, 1997; Horseman, 1981) have argued that the most effective way to justify for why non-whites could not be citizens was through the production and circulation of erroneous scientific and theological theories about the mental, spiritual, and social deviance of non-white populations. The tool thus for defining the U.S. citizen was through the persistent and on-going construction of legitimizing discourses employed to quantitatively and qualitatively measure and describe why particular groups did not have the mental capacity, character and temperament to engage in democratic affairs as full citizens.

These discourses certainly were the ideological apparatuses used for centuries to explain why black Americans could not be U.S. citizens, and why Mexican Americans would only be citizens in name, but not in practice. By this we mean that Mexican Americans were citizens, according to the Treaty of Guadalupe Hidalgo (1848), but did not enjoy the full rights and privileges of citizenship, as we will discuss later. For this chapter, however, we contend that despite such ironclad, and yet ambiguous, definitions of U.S. citizenship, at different moments in history both

African Americans and Mexican Americans were offered either a promise or even the expanded legal definition of citizenship, but only in the event that they fulfilled white power interests. In this chapter, we show how the expanded and inclusive discourses of education and citizenship for all people, generally served as proxy to promote larger white interests. We also show that the convergence of interest between white elites and the interests of African Americans and Mexican Americans' desire to change their material and educational realities often resulted in outcomes that disproportionately privileged white's political and economic interests over the immediate and long-term needs of African American and Mexican American communities.

This work is significant to the field of social studies education because it provides an historical context to the racialized dimensions of race and citizenship in the U.S. This work seeks to address this theoretical and historical gap in the literature in social studies education, which countless scholars have expressed in recent years (Epstein, 2009; Ladson-Billings, 2003; Howard, 2003; Tyson, 2003). Our intent is to provide historical illustrations of the manner in which the notion of the citizen (a core issue to the field of social studies) is historically entrenched in both explicit and implicit racialized discourses.

THEORY, RACE, AND THE SOCIAL STUDIES

This paper purposefully draws from the theoretical lenses of *racial contract theory* and *interest convergence*. Charles Mills' (1997) *racial contract theory* posits that civil democratic societies, are political spaces where whites regulate, control and define the moral and juridical standards of society. In such societies, like the U.S., there is a "differential privileging of whites as a group (p. 11)." Non-white subordination, in such societies, includes the "exploitation of their bodies, land, and resources, and the denial of equal socioeconomic opportunities." (Mills, 1997, p. 11) These conditions constitute what Mills calls a *racial contract*.

In societies functioning under a racial contract, non-citizens or the racialized Other are left out of the body politic because of a tacit contractual agreement that only certain populations of men can provide the governorship, legislation and leadership to maintain a free market liberal democracy. We maintain however, that historically in the U.S. when white interests converged with black Americans or Mexican Americans' interests, the terms of the racial contract would change, but only to the extent to which white interests and gains could outweigh the benefits gained by non-white groups. Legal scholar Derrick Bell (1980) defines this kind of political relationship as *interest convergence*. Bell argues that historically the advancement of racial inequality causes for blacks only became a priority in the U.S. if they converged with the ideological interests and economic gains of white Americans.

Drawing from these theories, we contend that the history of citizenship for African Americans and Mexican Americans (and Puerto Ricans) in the U.S. remained constructed by an explicit and implicit *racial contract*. In this racial contract Anglo American men and later white men, in general, were/are the model or standard of the full "American" citizen (Urrieta, 2004). The terms of the racial contract, however, expanded during specific historical moments to benefit black or brown interests, so long as they *converged* with Anglo and later white interests.

RACE, EDUCATION, AND THE CONSTRUCTION OF THE BLACK CITIZEN

The odyssey of African American education has historically helped and hindered African Americans' efforts to gain full citizenship in the U.S. For close to two centuries the topic of African American education has centered on the question of whether African Americans had the moral, social, psychological and intellectual capacity for full citizenship. Within different historical periods, white manumission societies, industrial philanthropists, educators, government officials and researchers both implicitly and explicitly developed curriculum and schools with the intent of creating a particular kind of African American citizen.

This section of the paper focuses on three historical periods when African American education was discussed in relation to their "capacity" to be citizens. Each period highlights how the exchange for education often came because of the overt and sometimes subtle interests of white elites. In addition, each period illustrates how education was created based on an imaginary of African American morality and psychology. The first period is the early 1800s when free and freed African Americans were educated by manumission societies. The second period examines the context of black education and citizenship after Reconstruction. The final section discusses the implicit ideological interests that helped to advance the legal victory of *Brown v. Board of Education*. In addition, we discuss how the findings from the Clark Doll studies that were used to sway the opinion of the courts, helped to set in place a construction of African Americans as psychologically damaged (Scott, 1997), which had lasting implications to the research on African American students.

Manumitted Negroes: The Taming of Moral Debauchery

As historian John Rury (1985) explains, directly after the American Revolution a wave of liberal sentiment emerged in the U.S., particularly in the North. A focal point of this emergent liberalism was the abolishment of slavery throughout the U.S. From this surfaced anti-slavery societies that fought for the abolishment of slavery as well as serving as the "moral and political guardians" of the local free African American populations. One of the more prominent anti-slavery societies to surface was the New York Manumission Society. While the initial goals of the Society were to protect the human rights of free African Americans from local acts of racism, it gradually shifted its focus onto ways of controlling the behavior of free African Americans. Rury (1985) illustrates this point:

> At its third meeting, in May, 1785, the Manumission Society ordered its standing committee to "Keep a watchful eye over the conduct of such Negroes as have been or may be liberated; and ... to prevent them from running into immorality or sinking into idleness." (p. 233)

The discourse of "sobriety," "idleness" and "immorality" were employed to make sense of and address the social needs of African Americans in New York, led to the development of a standing committee charged to develop a method to control the behavior of African Americans. The committee cautioned against free African

Americans to allow slaves or servants into their homes or to engage in any kinds of behavior such as "fiddling, dancing or any other noisy behavior" (Rury, 1985, p. 234). In short, the effort of the Society was to come up with a way to insure that African Americans' moral conduct was congruent with the elite New York communities. Thus, what emerged was a discourse that constructed African Americans as immoral, idle, lacking character and prong to criminal behavior. The effort then was to identify a suitable method to insure the control of African American behavior. From this, the Society opened schools that would educate a select few of African American leaders served to meet the objective of controlling the so-called "immorality" of African Americans. Here Rury (1985) explains the purpose of the African Free School:

> Moral education remained the essential purpose of the African Free School throughout its initial twenty-five years. Rules concerning matters of appearance, conduct to and from school, behavior in class, as well as respect for property and "our Great Maker's awful name were rigidly enforced." If they learned nothing else, the students at this school would have a clear understanding of the moral expectations they faced upon graduation. (p. 236)

In this context, the notion "citizen" was constructed in relation to an erroneous imagery of African Americans as prong to moral debauchery.

The African Free Schools created a tacit agreement between the Society and a select population of African Americans who received an education so long as they became leaders who could socially control the growing population of African Americans in New York. The African Free Schools certainly met some of its goal of fostering African American leadership by educating some of the most respected African American leaders of the 19th century—including luminaries such as Dr. James McCune Smith, the first African American to earn a medical degree, Ira Aldridge, the most famous black actor of this time and prominent abolitionists such as and Henry Highland Garnet and Alexander Crummel. In fact, the development of a highly educated population of African Americans eventually led to African Americans opening their own schools that directly challenged the curricular efforts of the Society. Yet, despite the persistent agency of African American communities, the approach of the African Free School would set a precedent of black education reform, where African Americans were provided an education and some civic "privileges" as community leaders so long as it fulfilled white ideological interests. In addition, the efforts to open African Free Schools helped to set in place a discourse about African American education that would endure for the next two centuries. In particular, the belief that African Americans possessed a common set of cultural or social dispositions that was oppositional to a mainstream white civil society.

The Hampton Idea: Education in Exchange for Political Disenfranchisement

The years after Reconstruction led to another significant period for how African American education and citizenship was conceptualized. Similar to the efforts of the New York Manumission Society, white philanthropists and governmental officials sought ways to educate the recently freed African Americans. The Hampton

Institute and the efforts of General Samuel Chapman Armstrong provide a powerful illustration of how the concerns of African American education and citizenship converged.

As historians note, directly after the Civil War marked a period of rapid social, political and economic change (Berlin, 1974; Foner, 2005). This was a period of reform and nation building. Central to these concerns was the question of how to "transition" the "roaming masses" of African Americans from their status as "enslaved non-citizen" to their new political and social status as outlined in the 13th, 14th and 15th amendments. Similar to the Manumission Societies of the early 1800s, federal agencies and philanthropists were charged to come up with viable solutions to "reform" African Americans. Samuel Armstrong who was appointed to the Freedmen's Bureau to help in the effort to reform and reorganize the South, was called with the specific task to arrive at ways to reform and reorganize the recently freed African Americans (Anderson, 1988).

From this, surfaced a similar discourse as found in the Manumission Society, where African Americans were again constructed as lazy, idle and uncivilized. This period however, marked a different context for which African American education was conceptualized and employed. African Americans' civil rights as citizens were now supported by the constitution, even providing African American men the legal right to vote. While it is noted that white supremacist organizations employed extra legal efforts to repress African Americans civil rights, the school site also served as a space to challenge African Americans' participation in southern political life. For example, historian James D. Anderson (1988) notes that Armstrong felt that "freedmen should refrain from participation in southern political life because they were culturally and morally deficient and therefore unfit to vote and hold office in "civilized" society." (p. 38) African American education therefore, was constructed around ideological interests to repress African American political participation. As Anderson (1988) further states, Armstrong chose to develop a curriculum later called the Hampton Idea that focused on moral development rather than mental development as "the chief criterion for political enfranchisement." (p. 39)

Here again, education was provided to African Americans under the guise of white political interest. The effort of the Hampton vision was to depoliticize African Americans from active participation in the body politic. As Anderson (1988) explains:

> The Hampton-Tuskegee philosophy, which requested black southerners to eschew politics and concentrate on economic development, was as it had been hailed, a great compromise. It was the logical extension of an ideology that rejected black political power while recognizing that the south's agricultural economy rested on the black agricultural workers. (p. 44)

As Anderson (1988) illustrates, the push for African American education worked toward educating a multitude of African Americans devoted to focus on economic and moral development rather than equity politics. This convergence of interest is striking, because while thousands of African Americans were educated under this philosophy, it simultaneously set in place an ideology, which suggested that African American education could only exist when it provided greater returns to white power interests.

In this context, the notion of "citizen" was at the center of discussions about African American education. Similar to the efforts of manumission societies during the turn of the century, a select few of African Americans were given the privilege of literacy and numeracy, so long as political ambitions and social justice was silenced. The seemingly *quid pro quo* relationship where education is offered to African Americans in exchange for larger white interests would remain as an implicit philosophy and method for educational reform for African Americans through most of the twentieth century. In addition, this period would hold in place a deficit discourse that insisted on constructing African Americans as morally and socially underdeveloped to thoroughly engage as citizens in the body politic (Scott, 1997).

Brown, Interest convergence and Damaged Psyche

Throughout the first part of the twentieth century, numerous scholars and activists had actively challenged the Hampton Tuskegee model of education, insisting that education must reform the existing racial norms of society (Anderson, 1988). W.E.B. DuBois critical commentaries reflect his discontent with depoliticized educational models. Carter G. Woodson also adamantly argued that the curriculum and schooling for African Americans had to actively challenge the existing racial theories of that time (Brown, 2010). However, by the late 1940s and 1950s, much of the African American civil rights leadership insisted on challenging educational inequities via the courts, arguing for equal access to education— what political scientist Michael Dawson refers to as *radical egalitarianism.* Dawson (2001) defines *radical egalitarianism* as an ideology "typified by the coupling of a severe critique of racism in American society, an impassioned appeal for America to live up to the best of its values, and support for a radical egalitarian view of a multiracial democratic society." (pp. 15–16) The period from 1954 to 1965 clearly illustrates the most overt connection between education and citizenship.

The legislative victory of *Brown* clearly marked the most significant change in African Americans' status as citizens in U.S. since Reconstruction. Using schools as the context of which to dismantle the "separate but equal" doctrine outlined in the Supreme Court case *Plessy v. Ferguson*, the social engineers of *Brown* poignantly deliberated and changed the context for African American education (Guinier, 2004). The rationale for challenging the legal system of racism was both logical and straightforward. By dismantling *Brown*, opportunities historically excluded from African Americans were perceived to be readily available via the desegregation of schools and society. Yet, aside from the fact that *Brown* was not able to redress the historically entrenched inequities between whites and African Americans, legal scholars would come to realize that *Brown* emerged from historically situated white interests. (And the development of color blind racism as explained by Bonilla-Silva, 2006).

For example, Derrick Bell (1980) in his classic *Harvard Law Review* article argued that civil rights advances of *Brown* emerged amidst changing economic conditions and white elite interests. He hypothesized that government sentiment for *Brown* emerged because of a growing concern that African American servicemen had fought loyally under the principles of democracy, would potentially return to the U.S. discontent with their social status as second class citizens and "were unlikely to return willingly to regimes of menial labor and social vilification." (Delagdo & Stefancic, 2001, p. 19) As Delgado and Stefancic (2001) state: "For the first time in decades, the possibility of mass domestic unrest loomed" (p. 19).

Additionally, during this period the U.S. government was ideologically entrenched in the Cold War. During this period, government officials worried that stories about lynching, racist sheriffs and murders would potentially taint the U.S.'s international imagery as a democratic nation, and thus influence uncommitted Third World countries (mostly Asian and black) to ally with international communist nations. These two institutional interests clearly illustrate that African American education did not emerge from a growing American benevolence or consciousness about African American educational inequity. Here this illustrates again, how the contours of African American educational reform only emerged because of larger white power interests.

In addition to the implicit power interest that advanced *Brown,* this case also helped to set in place deficit discourses about African Americans, which has endured within contemporary discussions about African American education. Civil rights lawyers presented to the Supreme Court data taken from the famous "Doll Test Study" conducted by psychologists Mamie and Kenneth Clark, (Guinier, 2004) which described African American children in segregated school settings as psychologically damaged (Scott, 1997), for identifying white dolls as pretty and black dolls as ugly. The circulation of these findings from the Doll studies, helped to set in place decades of research concerned with how the psychological fragility or low self esteem of African Americans informed their academic achievement in schools as opposed to the effectiveness of schools or teachers in helping or hindering students success. As Guinier (2004) states:

> Linking responsibility for educational disadvantage to black self-loathing and connecting that to a psychological abstraction did little however, to disrupt powerfully negative views of blacks in public imagination. As Charles R. Lawrence III has written, many whites do not believe that racial discrimination is the principle cause of black inequality. The explanation lies instead in some version of black inferiority. (p. 110)

The history of *Brown* illustrates a consistent theme that situates the question about African American education within larger white interests and nation building. Similarly, the history of Mexican American education and citizenship in the U.S. includes historically racialized conceptions of citizenship. The next section of this chapter outlines significant themes in which Mexican American education and citizen rights emerged amid larger white interests.

RACIALIZATION, MEXICANS, AND MEXICAN AMERICANS IN THE U.S. IMAGINARY

The story of Mexican Americans and citizenship in the U.S. has always been interesting and contradicting. Latina/o people (Hispanics), especially Mexicans,

Mexican Americans and Puerto Ricans due to colonization and imperialism have been typically racialized, or categorized as a distinct "racial" group in U.S. society. Latinas/os, however, are very diverse in many aspects, including racially. Mexicans in particular, although largely *mestizo* (of mixed Native American, Spanish, and African ancestry), are not a single "racial" group. It was not until the 2000 Census that Latina/o people were allowed to choose a racial category in addition to "Hispanic." Given this racial ambiguity and the historical and current controversies over citizenship rights and immigration, we will attempt to locate how Mexican Americans, in particular, have been simultaneously granted and denied limited forms of citizenship rights in U.S. society since 1848. We use 1848 as a point of departure due to the U.S. invasion and continuous subsequent military occupation of Mexican and Native American territories since the signing of the Treaty of Guadalupe Hidalgo.

Manifest Destiny, Colonialism, and Mexican and Native Americans

The U.S. has been considered an internal colony by postcolonial theorists for colonizing its Native American, Alaskan Native, Hawaiian, Samoan, Mexican, and Puerto Rican populations and for actively contributing to the mass dislocation and genocide of people in the African Diaspora (Urrieta, 2004). Although some would argue that the U.S. could also be considered a "settler" colony, others would refute that claim because of the U.S. imperialist, neocolonial and global enterprise, which is another form of colonization (Ashcroft, Griffiths & Tiffin, 1995). In this section, we will discuss Manifest Destiny and the military invasion of Northern Mexico (the U.S. Southwest) in the 19th Century as a colonizing project. We believe this historical context is extremely important in understanding Mexican Americans and Mexican immigrants' current social, cultural, economic, and political relationship to the U.S., especially as it relates to labor exploitation and limited citizenship rights.

Prior to the military invasion and continuous occupation of over half of Mexico's territories (Acuña, 2000), the Anglo-Saxon imaginary had created Mexicans as racialized inferior people (Gutiérrez, 2001) due to the racial mixture that occurred in Mexican society because of *mestizaje*. Manifest Destiny, as a colonizing project, was thus justified by racial theories of Anglo-Saxon (later white) superiority (Menchaca & Valencia, 1990). In such white supremacist, pseudo-religious Anglo racist ideology, Mexicans, like Native Americans, were thought of as an un-industrious, unchristian, amoral, and genetically inferior, half-breed "Indian/savage" people not worthy of occupying vast amounts of presumably unused land (Horseman, 1981). Mexican men were especially dehumanized. Gutiérrez (2001) documents:

> Mexican men were typically portrayed as a breed of cruel and cowardly mongrels who were indolent, ignorant, and superstitious, given to cheating, thieving, gambling, drinking, cursing, and dancing. (p. 204)

This dehumanizing process justified the invasion and military take-over of Mexican America during the War of the North American Invasion, today known in the whitestream respectively as the Mexican American War and as the U.S. Southwest.

The Treaty of Guadalupe Hidalgo (1848) politically condoned the U.S. military invasion of Mexican and Native American people and lands. Although this treaty guaranteed Mexican nationals left on the U.S. side equality and full legal citizenship under the law, as with most treaties signed with Native Americans, the U.S. failed to uphold its side of the bargain (Menchaca, 1999). For example, according to Donato, Menchaca, and Valencia (1991) from its inception the California state government through "... the California state constitution [1849] prohibited 'Indian-looking Mexicans' from voting and only extended that privilege to 'white-looking Mexican' males" (33). Limiting voting rights reflects just one type of racialization Mexican indigenous and Native American people endured by being placed in subaltern political status and also in exploitative economic labor conditions in the U.S. (Gómez-Quiñonez, 1994; Zamora, 1993). This California example also shows the ambiguity that existed with regard to Mexicans as potential U.S. citizens depending on their European (white) ancestry; those that were lighter skinned and possessed wealth (land) were usually considered better suited to be citizens.

Mexican society generally also functioned under a *racial contract*, where the Spanish legacy had privileged *pureza de sangre*, which meant having direct Spanish lineage and the Catholic faith (*gente de razon*) (Urrieta, 2003). Racialized others, excluded generally from the body politic in Mexican society, where indigenous and African people and people with indigenous and African ancestors, to different degrees depending on their skin tone; thus creating a highly stratified racial order. In terms of religion, Muslims, Jews and Protestants were excluded and anyone with Jewish or Moorish ancestors. This racial contract in Mexican society, which also privileged whiteness, thus came together with the U.S. *racial contract* of Anglo (white) supremacy with the invasion of Northern Mexico (Southwest) (Menchaca, 1999).

For the newly acquired territories, it was not until there was an Anglo white majority that they were admitted into the Union as states with voting rights; voting rights being representative of democratic participation for states. New Mexico, for example, was not admitted as a state until 1912 because it originally had a majority Hispanic and Native American population. The California Gold Rush, some historians have argued was also largely a manufactured hysteria to lure white settlers into California, to outnumber the *Californio* and Native American populations (Pitt, 1966), and establish a white majority before 1850, when California became part of the Union.[1]

Although racial mixture in U.S. society was illegal through anti-miscegenation laws that punished inter-racial legal unions, inter-racial exploitative sexual relations were all too common throughout U.S. history. This was clearly the case with African American slaves and Native American women, which were derogatorily referred to as "squaws" (Brown, 1970). However, Mexican American women, especially light-skinned daughters of landed and elite rancheros, seemed to be exempt initially as marriage partners (Montejano, 1987). Through these "marriages," many of which were only for fortune-seeking/making, Anglo men acquired land and ranches throughout the Southwest. Anglo men also later acquired land by requiring that Mexicans produce legal documents (in English) that proved their ownership of land and also through direct squatting on communal and private property (Acuña, 2000).

Mexican and Spanish descent people, as well as Native Americans, had lived in their lands for centuries and could not always produce legal documents, or had the money to pay for English translations, and were subsequently "legally" deposed, or "bought out" of their lands.

By 1900, Mexican descent peoples in the U.S. were more completely racialized as inferior, regardless of their skin tone, and had lost possession of most of their political influence (Menchaca & Valencia, 1990) as well as of their economic wealth (Donato, 1997). Regardless of indigenous features, Mexicans and Mexican Americans were largely relegated into segregated quarters, *barrios*, throughout the Southwest, except those who were light enough to pass as white, or who had married into Anglo families. By means of social segregation, policing, and denied access to economic resources, the Mexican population in the "occupied territories" (Acuña, 2000), generally came to occupy subaltern status to whites' social, political, economic, and religious power. Many eventually became servants and "foreigners" in what were once their own homes and native lands (Pitt, 1966).

Mexican Americans and Colonial Education in the U.S.

Schooling was undeniably a part of the conquering enterprise in the Southwest where formal schooling sought to strip the colonized away from indigenous learning structures and toward the structures of the colonizers (Spring, 2004). Anglo knowledge models actively attempted to replace indigenous models, justified by white supremacist ideologies and the Christian tenets of "salvation" (Willinsky, 1998). The moral[2] project of formal schooling in occupied lands was part of the colonizing project (Ashcroft et al., 1995) especially in Protestant schools, but also in Catholic schools for Mexican children throughout the Southwest (San Miguel & Valencia, 1998).

Indigenous people, both Mexican and Native American, like African Americans, were constructed as genetically and, or culturally inferior to Anglos and therefore in "need" of being "controlled," "saved," or "trained," especially for labour in whitestream civilization (Baker, 1998). Mexican American children were taught in segregated schools or in Mexican rooms in schools where they were taught from a deficiency perspective and with the goal of Americanizing them (San Miguel, 1996). These deficit perspectives in schools justified the dehumanizing and disposability of human bodies in the colonizing process since agriculturalists often encouraged early school desertion by Mexican children to fill their need for manual labor in the fields (Donato, 1997; Rivera, 1992). In urban areas such as Los Angeles, Mexican children were directed into technical and vocational programs (Gonzalez, 1990).

Through schools, colonial governments attempted not only to physically control their subjects, but as Fanon (1967) teaches us, to mentally maintain their strongholds by encouraging a desire to assimilate. Assimilation and acculturation are one of the strongest tools in the colonizing process. According to Skutnabb-Kangas (2000), assimilation is always rationalized as a way to benefit the dominated by promoting the culture, language, institutions, and traditions of the colonizer as "superior." Skutnabb-Kangas (2000) further states that assimilation generally follows three steps: glorification, stigmatization, and rationalization[3]. Assimilation (a more sterilized word for Americanization) has generally been America's goal for Mexican American education (San Miguel, 1999); thus our claim that Mexican American schooling in the U.S. follows a colonialist model.

Two examples of colonial schooling as a result of the U.S. invasion of the Southwest were Native American boarding schools and subtractive, segregated education models for Mexican descent students. Native American boarding schools functioned to "strip"[4] indigenous children of their traditional cultures (Lomawaima, 1994; Miheshua, 1993). At these schools Native American children were forced to wear Anglo clothing, forbidden to speak their native languages, and were forced to learn whitestream culture in isolation from their communities.

Subtractive education models were used (and continue to be used see Valenzuela, 1999) to teach/control Mexicans in the Southwest. In this model, active attempts are made to encourage rapid and uncritical assimilation, to replace the primary language and culture with English and whitestream culture, and to pit U.S.-born Mexican American and Mexican immigrant students against one another (Valenzuela, 1999). The pitting of minority groups against one another is a common strategy and outcome in colonized contexts, such as brown and black tensions (Urrieta, 2004). In either situation, by stigmatizing subaltern cultures and languages as culturally deficient and counter-productive to the assimilation process (sometimes also called the process of "success") (Valencia, 1997), the active murder of primary languages and cultures (Skutnabb-Kangas, 2000) and inter-group aggression is promoted.

Today, Native American, Mexican American, and Mexican immigrant children in the U.S. are burdened with the distorted legacy of Manifest Destiny as a just and teleological process. The historical amnesia and sterilization of this brutal history of colonialism constructs both Native American and Mexican descent students as "problems," diseased (at-risk)[5] to low academic performance, as is the case with other colonized groups (such as African Americans). For example, the active lynching of Mexicans throughout the Southwest, but especially in Texas, by white mobs is historically often overlooked due to the documentation of these state sanctioned murders under the category of other whites (Carrigan, 2003).

Stereotypes of Native American and Mexican students continue to include that they are "lacking," "deficient," "slow learners," "illegal," not capable of literacy, from families that are not involved and do not care about education, or simply not expected to do well in schools (Urrieta & Quach, 2000). Historically, Mexicans have also been portrayed as outsiders, foreigners, aliens, enemies, or outlaws (bandits—*bandidos*)[6]. It is this historical colonial context, achieved through Manifest Destiny, we are attempting to analyze and theorize from to discuss education and citizenship for Mexican Americans.

The Scraps of Citizenship

Due to this colonial history, Mexicans and Mexican Americans have a special postcolonial relationship to the U.S. that even in its modern immigrant diasporic community context is different than for other U.S. "immigrant" groups. Throughout this history, Mexican Americans have been granted limited forms of citizen rights.

For example through early desegregation litigation in education, *Alvarez v. Lemon Grove* (1931) and *Méndez v. Westminister* (1947), Latina/o school segregation was outlawed in California, not on racial terms, but rather on the basis of language since language has always been and continues to be used a proxy for race with this group (Gutiérrez & Jaramillo, 2006). In these cases segregation of Latina/o children was outlawed on the basis that it "retarded" the assimilation (i.e. colonization) process. Inclusion came with the contradictory justification of a better way to colonize; thus, this also decision served white interests. Both the *Alvarez* and *Mendez* cases served as a backdrop for the *Brown v. Board of Education* case (Moreno, 1999).

The build up to *Brown v. Board of Education*, as was the case with African Americans, was also a time when Mexican American and Puerto Rican servicemen where returning from fighting for the U.S. oversees. World war II was a time of violent attacks against Mexican American communities, especially youth. Muñoz (1989) writes about the zoot-suit "riots" in Los Angeles:

> In 1943, World War II was at the height and thousands of soldiers of Mexican descent were dying on the battlefields, Tragically, their younger brothers were being attacked on the streets of Los Angeles by white sailors and marines on leave. Those confrontations, which became known as the 'zoot-suit riots,' were manifestations of a vulgar Mexican racism promoted by the Hearst newspapers, which publicly condoned and supported these racial attacks. (p. 37)

Upon their return to a country they fought bravely for Mexican American veterans were treated disrespectfully and unequally, although, through the American G.I. Bill of Rights (Gándara, 1995), limited educational opportunities did arise for some. The American G.I. Forum is an organization formed by Mexican American veterans after World War II to demand equal treatment in U.S. society (Muñoz, 1989).

Although the *Brown* decision (1954) ended legal school segregation, most school districts were slow to implement school desegregation plans and others tried to find ways to getting around its enforcement (Orfield, 2001). During the 1970s almost twenty years after *Brown*, Texas and Colorado legislators and school board members sometimes consolidated (integrated) primarily Mexican American schools with African American schools as a way to avoid desegregation. In this case, Mexican Americans were conveniently given the status of (Other) "whites" to avoid fulfilling the legal mandates of *Brown* (1954) and thus avoid integrating African American children with Anglo children; thus protecting white interests while giving Mexican Americans access to (Other) whiteness. This led to the legal cases, *Cisneros v. Corpus Christi Independent School District* (1970) and later to *Keyes v. School District Number One* (1973) in which the U.S. Supreme Court declared that Mexican Americans were an identifiable minority group and could not be paired up with African Americans in the desegregation process (San Miguel & Valencia, 1998).

In California, *Lau v. Nichols* (1973) granted citizen rights to primary language instruction to Chinese American students, however, this ruling was again used throughout the U.S. to re-segregate language minority students, including Latinas/os for whom language has always been used a proxy for race. This resegregation is in the form of separation within schools by language dominance and level of second language ability; thus justifying the separation of native English speakers, mostly whites, from non-native English speakers, mostly non-whites. In the late 1990s language was again used to target Latinas/os, especially immigrants, through the anti-bilingual education campaigns led by Ron Unz. Unz initiatives ended bilingual education programs in California, Arizona, and other states through a civic right to access discourse, which advocated for the right to learn English, which is precisely what bilingual education advocates for—the right to learn English in a safe and research supported effective method and pedagogy.

Amendment 31 (the anti-bilingual initiative), which attempted to end bilingual education in the state of Colorado in 2002, however, was defeated as an exception. Interestingly, this initiative was not defeated on the basis that Latina/o children deserve to have bilingual instruction in order to learn both English and Spanish, but on the basis that white voters feared that ending bilingual education programs would involve integrating Latina/o children with white children in their schools since language minority children were generally segregated within schools as a co-opted consequence of Lau. In such cases, the granting of citizen rights in education for Latinas/os, especially Mexicans, Mexican Americans and Puerto Ricans, was with contradictory ends and largely motivated by white interests.

DISCUSSION

The educational issues we present with regard to limited forms of citizen rights granted with contradictory ends to groups like African Americans and Mexican Americans is what we want to highlight as part of *racial contract* and *interest convergence* theory. In terms of racial contract, what we show is that early Anglo-Saxon domination/conquest/invasion and later white supremacy as a form of institutionalized political system, has always been at the root of who has access to full legal citizen rights in the U.S., including educational rights (Williams, 1991). Historians Stuart Hall and David Held argue that the history of citizenship is one of successive attempts to limit citizenship to certain groups (Hall & Held, 1989). In the U.S. African Americans and Mexican Americans have been among those groups with limited access to citizen rights.

Critical Race scholars, Ladson-Billings (2004) and Harris (1993), concur with Mills and Bell that race, gender, and class have been the criterion for citizenship in the U.S. since the 17th century. In the 3/5s Compromise, the twenty-year extension of the slave trade and the fugitive slave clause that concluded the Constitutional Convention in 1787 and laid the foundation for the new nation-state, the 'possession' of whiteness was constructed as the ultimate form of property. While the compromises listed above defined African Americans as subhuman (3/5 of a human) and as property, in a nation conceived and built on property rights, possessing whiteness automatically conferred to whites rights not available to others. In the case of Mexican Americans, those with more access to whiteness through European ancestry and land (property) were also allowed more access to legal citizen rights, while these were denied to non-white and poor Mexicans.

Harris (1993) describes the right to use and enjoy reputation and status and the absolute right to exclude as part of the property functions of whiteness. In this manner, Anglo culture became historically and institutionally normalized in schools as natural, and is imposed on all other forms of cultural capital as the standard to emulate (Appleton, 1983). This construction of whiteness as the criterion for citizenship and education, also presupposes Anglo conformity (assimilation) (Appleton, 1983) as a condition of fuller (yet not full) citizenship for all those designated as non-white— this is where limited and conditional forms of access are granted to non-whites (if they assimilate), but always serving the general interests of whites, *interest convergence*. Thus the limited forms of educational access and citizenship rights granted to black and brown communities in U.S. history have always been limited and contradictory in terms of gains for the entire community, but not in terms of how they have generally always benefitted whites. To cite an example often used against African Americans and Latinas/os, the primary beneficiaries of affirmative action programs were white women; thus, the limited gains achieved through such programs mostly benefitted white interests.

Generally, this type of historically informed, revisionist information is always omitted from meaningful discussion in social studies texts, and probably from most social studies classrooms in the U.S. (Loewen, 1996). Marciano (1997), based on an analysis of history textbooks, points out that most people in the U.S. are civically illiterate in general. We argue that when it comes to issues of race and citizenship, most of the students we teach, and the public in general, are far more ignorant of not only the history around these issues, but have also generally internalized the idea that the U.S. is no longer bound by a racial contract that privileges whites and serves the interests of whites. In general, people believe in the rhetoric of person-centered rights, but fail to see how in practice, property rights, including the property of whiteness overshadow person-centered rights (Williams, 1991).

Implications for Contemporary Issues in Education

We agree with Bell that we need to look to the past in order to understand the present and see how historical issues are tied to contemporary issues. In this section we would like to address some contemporary educational issues that also involve contradictory ends and often are used to lure African American and Latinas/os. Harris' (1993) legal analysis of whiteness as property is helpful to understand how whiteness functions to ascribe racial privilege and status to predominantly white schools. Historically and legally, only white possession and occupation of land was justified and whiteness was subsequently privileged as the basis for property rights. Because white identity and whiteness were sources of privilege they became exclusionary and legally protected.

An example in education is schools "integration" to enforce the *Brown v. Board of Education* decision of 1954. The legal mandates to desegregate were carried out in a way that did not disrupt the expectations and interests of whites (Harris, 1993). Schools of color generally were closed and their staff and students disbursed to white schools (Noblit & Dempsey, 1998), where they would acquire "minority" status, sustaining white supremacy. Equitable and equal school integration that included a systemic resource and population redistribution was never fully implemented. white flight to the suburbs and the redrawing of district boundaries subsequently led to persistent residential separation and school resegregation (Margonis & Parker, 1995). In fact Laosa (2001) finds that U.S. schools are undergoing a new segregation based not only on race/ethnicity, but also on language that results in *de facto* concentration of poverty and low academic achievement.

The 1980s initiated a conservative political movement pushing for privatization, standardization, high-stakes testing, and school choice (Marciano, 1997; Saltman, 2003). School choice, in particular is relevant in an analysis of charters. Margonis and Parker (1995) argue that choice proposals are an extension of white segregationist, middle class strategies that amount to policies of racial containment. Further, they add that school choice pushed by raceless metaphors such as *choice* effectively legitimate existing race-based inequalities and further privatize education. Margonis and Parker (1995) state: "… schools of choice are extensions of historical middle class movements to create economically and racially homogenous schools" (p. 385). In this section we highlight how charter schools, school vouchers, and not-for-profit schools often lure black and brown communities, but also serve primarily white interests.

Geske et al., (1997) attribute the rise of charter schools in 1991 to fall "somewhere on a continuum between public choice and private choice options" (p. 16), with choice remaining the main metaphor of equal access. As colorblind charter school laws are implemented using school *choice* rhetoric, charter school reform takes on diverse forms of implementation that result in unequal and inequitable resource distribution. Although charter schools with predominantly students of color might appear to have empowering potential, studies show that these schools generally do not have access to economic resources as do predominantly white schools (Wells et al., 1999; 2000; 2002; Goldhaber, 1999). This translates into charter schools with predominantly students of color being perceived as "bad schools," with unequal economic resources available to them as compared to predominantly white middle class schools (Urrieta, 2006).

CONCLUSION

Examining the history of citizenship for African Americans and Mexican Americans does not provide the most optimistic outlook for what the future holds. This history however, provides a historical foundation to the theoretical logics that have undergirded the closed and expanded definitions of citizenship and education for communities of color in the U.S. for centuries. In the U.S., brown and black people have been either completely left out of the body politic or "included" only under "contractual" conditions.

This however, presents a difficult quagmire for people color with limited resources. With the prominence of white supremacy and racial antagonism, its highly likely that both African American and Mexican American families, educators and activists will continue to find ways to buffer against this dual reality of "non-citizen" and/or "conditional citizen." For example, the racists and neo-nativist discourse around issues of immigration and the still common phrase "go back to Africa" when African Americans speak out on injustices, provide a clear indication of this dual reality of citizenship. This coupled with limited resources to thwart the legal, institutional and discursive ways the citizen is constructed and reproduced, may cause communities to reluctantly and sometimes naively "sign" and abide this "racial contract," with hopes of receiving in return resources (e.g. better schools, better housing, etc.) to change their material and educational realities. Given this historical context, it stands to reason that all discussions of citizenship in U.S. are defined, influenced and informed by race. Our hope then, is that the history provided from this chapter will result in future studies in social studies education that critically and carefully examine the nuanced and complex ways race encloses the legal and conceptual meanings of "citizen."

NOTES

[1] *Californio* (historic and regional Spanish for "Californian") is a term used to identify a Californian of Hispanic—and in some rare cases, of Portuguese, Brazilian, or other non-Hispanic Latin American—descent, regardless of race, during the period that California was part of the Viceroyalty of New Spain and Mexico. The territory of California was annexed in 1848 by the United States following the Mexican-American War. Californios included the descendants of agricultural settlers and escort soldiers from Mexico.

[2] Moral education was indeed anti-Catholic and based on the King James Bible. McDuffy readers emphasized patriotism and heroism while referring in racist ways to immigrants, while school texts described the poor as in need of regulation while extolling the moral virtue of the rich (Purpel, 2000).

[3] Glorification involves the active promotion of the colonizer's culture as superior. Subsequently, subaltern culture is stigmatized as "backward," language as "gibberish," religion as "evil" and institutions, and traditions are stigmatized as "unproductive." Colonization is rationalized as a good thing meant to benefit the natives. It is suggested that the natives should be thankful, for without European uplift, uncivilized savagery would persist.

[4] Strip is highlighted in quotations to accentuate that this meant a literal as well as metaphorical "stripping."

[5] Grady Johnson (2003) indicates that the term "at-risk" is borrowed from medical discourse and is used to focus on outbreaks of disease, epidemics—epidemiology. Grady Johnson (p. 191) states, "The locus of the disease in educational theories is primarily the family of the student labeled and *treated* (sic) as "At-Risk." ... What categorizes a student as "At-Risk" in this model is background characteristics—minority status, poverty, language differences, and family structure. Given that school and educators have historically been assigned the task of "fixing" children ... rather than altering the socioeconomic conditions—primarily intergenerational poverty—the child and her family are commonly viewed as carriers of social pathologies in need of preventive measures" (p. 191).

[6] The image of the Mexican as a bandit has always been prevalent in U.S. society from the image of Pancho Villa, to Joaquin Murrieta (Pitt, 1966), to Frito's Chips advertising using the Frito Bandito image, and current images in the news and law enforcement programs.

REFERENCES

Acuña, R. (2000). *Occupied America: A history of Chicanos* (4th ed.). New York: Longman.
Anderson, J. D. (1988). *The education of blacks in the South, 1860–1935*. Chapel Hill, NC: University of North Carolina.

Appleton, N. (1983). *Cultural pluralism in education: Theoretical foundations*. NewYork: Longman.
Ashcroft, B., Griffiths, G., & Tiffin, H. (1995). *The post-colonial studies reader*. London: Routledge.
Baker, L. D. (1998). *From savage to Negro: Anthropology and the construction of race, 1896–1954*. Berkeley, CA: University of California Press.
Bell, D. (1980). Brown v. Board of Education and the interest convergence dilemma, *Harvard Law Review, 93*, 518–533.
Berlin, I. (1974). *Slaves without masters*. New York: Pantheon.
Brown, A. L. (i2010). Counter-memory and race: An examination of African American Scholars' Challenges to Early 20th Century K-12 Historical Discourses. *Journal of Negro Education, 79*(1), 54–64.
Brown, D. (2001/1970). *Bury my heart at Wounded Knee: An Indian history of the American West*. New York: Holt.
Dawson, M. (2001). *Black visions: The roots of contemporary African-American political ideologies*. Chicago: University of Chicago.
Delgado, R., & Stefancic. (2001). *Critical race theory: An introduction*. New York: New York University Press.
Donato, R. (1997). *The other struggle for equal schools Mexican Americans during the Civil Rights era*. Albany, NY: State University of New York Press.
Donato, R., Menchaca, M., & Valencia, R. (1991). Segregation, desegregation, and integration of Chicano Students: Problems and prospects. In R. Valencia (Ed.), *Chicano school failure and success: Research and policy agendas for the 1990s*. Philadelphia: Falmer Press.
Epstein, T. (2009). *Interpreting national history: Race, identity, and pedagogy in classrooms and communities*. New York: Routledge.
Fanon, F. (1967). *Black skin, white Masks*. New York: Grove Press.
Foner, E. (2005). *Forever free: The story of emancipation and reconstruction*. New York: Knopf.
Geske, T. G., Davis, D. R., & Hingle, P. L. (1997). Charter schools: A viable public school option? *Economics of Education Review, 16*, 15–23.
Goldhaber, D. D. (1997). School choice: An examination of the empirical evidence on achievement, parental decision making, and equity. *Educational Researcher, 28*(9), 16–25.
Gómez-Quiñonez, J. (1994). *Mexican American labor, 1790–1990*. Albuquerque: University of New Mexico Press.
González, G. G. (1990). *Chicano education in the era of segregation*. Philadelphia: Balch Institute Press.
Grady Johnson, G. (2003). Resilience, a story: A postcolonial position from which to [re]view Indian education framed in "at-risk" ideology. *Educational Studies, 34*(2), 182–198.
Guinier, L. (2004). From racial liberalism to racial literacy: Brown v. Board of Education and the interest-divergence dilemma. *Journal of American History, 91*, 92–118.
Gutiérrez, K. D., & Jaramillo, N. (2006). Looking for educational equity: The consequences of relying on Brown. *Yearbook of the National Society for the Study of Education, 105*(2), 173–189.
Gutiérrez, R. (2001). Historical and social science research on Mexican Americans. In J. A. Banks & C. A. Banks (Eds.), *Handbook of research on multicultural education*. San Francisco: Jossey-Bass.
Hall, S., & Held, D. (1989). Citizens and citizenship. In S. Hall & M. Jacques (Eds.), *New times: The changing face of politics in the 1990s*. London: Lawrence & Wishart.
Harris, C. (1993). Whiteness as property. *Harvard Law Review, 106*(8), 1709–1791.
Horseman, R. (1981). *Race and manifest destiny: Origins of American racial Anglo-Saxonism*. Cambridge, MA: Harvard.
Howard, T. (2003). The dis(g)race of the social studies: The need for racial dialogue in social studies. In G. Ladson-Billings (Ed.), *Critical race theory perspectives on social studies: The profession, policies, and curriculum* (pp. 27–44). Greenwich, CT: Information Age.
Ladson-Billings, G. (2004). Culture versus citizenship: The challenge of racialized citizenship in the United States. In J. A. Banks (Ed.), *Diversity and citizenship education*. San Francisco: Jossey-Bass.
Loewen, J. W. (1996). *Lies my teacher told me: everything your American history textbook got wrong* (1st Touchstone ed.). New York: Simon & Schuster.

Marciano, J. (1997). *Civic illiteracy and education: The battle for the hearts and minds of America's youth*. New York: Peter Lang.

Margonis, F., & Parker, L. (1995). Choice, privatization, and unspoken strategies of containment. *Educational Policy, 9*(4), 375–403.

Menchaca, M. (1999). The treaty of Guadalupe-Hidalgo and the racialization of the Mexican Population. In J. Moreno (Ed.), *The elusive quest for equality, 150 years of Chicana/Chicano education* (pp. 3–29). Cambridge, MA: Harvard Education Press.

Menchaca, M. (1997). The early racist discourses: The roots of deficit thinking. In R. Valencia (Ed.), *The evolution of deficit thinking: Educational thought and practice* (pp. 13–40). New York: Routledge.

Menchaca, M., & Valencia, R. (1990). Anglo-Saxon ideologies in the 1920s–1930s: Their impact on the segregation of Mexican students in California. *Anthropology and Education Quarterly, 21*(3), 222–249.

Moreno, J. (1999). *The elusive quest for equality, 150 years of Chicana/Chicano education*. Cambridge: Harvard Education Press.

Muñoz, C. (1989). *Youth, identity, power: The Chicano movement*. London & New York: Verso.

Noblit, G., & Dempsey. (1998). *The social construction of virtue*. Albany, NY: State University of New York Press.

Pitt, L. (1966). *The decline of the Californios*. Berkeley, CA: University of California Press.

Purpel, D. (2000). Moral education. In D. Gabbard (Ed.), *Knowledge and power in the global economy* (pp. 247–254). Mahwah, NJ: Lawrence Erlbaum Associates.

Rivera, T. (1992). *Y no se lo tragó la tierra; And the hearth did not devour him*. Houston, TX: Arte Público Press.

Rury, J. (1985). Philanthropy, self help and social control: The New York Manumission Society and free blacks, 1785–1810. *Phylon, 46*, 231–241.

San Miguel, G. (1996). Education. In N. Kanellos (Ed.), *Reference library of Hispanic America* (Vol. II). Detroit, MI: Gale Research, Inc.

San Miguel, G. (1999). The schooling of Mexicanos in the Southwest, 1848–1891. In J. Moreno (Ed.), *The elusive quest for equality: 150 years of Chicana/Chicano education* (pp. 31–52). Cambridge, MA: Harvard Education Press.

San Miguel, G., & Valencia, R. R. (1998). From the treaty of Guadalupe Hidalgo to "Hopwood": The educational plight and struggle of Mexican Americans in the Southwest. *Harvard Educational Review, 68*(3), 353–412.

Scott, D. M. (1997). *Contempt & pity: Social policy and the image of the damaged Black psyche*. Chapel Hill, NC: University of North Carolina.

Skutnabb-Kangas, T. (2000). *Linguistic genocide in education-or worldwide diversity and human rights*. New Jersey, NJ: Lawrence Erlbaum.

Smith, R. (1993). Beyond Tocqueville, Myrdal, and Hartz: The multiple traditions in America, *American Political Science Review, 87*, 549–566.

Solórzano, D. G. (1998). Critical race theory, race and gender microaggressions, and the experience of Chicana and Chicano scholars. *Qualitative Studies in Education, 11*(1), 121–136.

Spring, J. (2004). *Deculturalization and the struggle for equality: A brief history of the education of dominated cultures in the United States*. Boston: McGraw Hill.

Tyson, C. (2003). A bridge over troubled water: Social studies, civic education and critical race theory. In G. Ladson-Billings (Ed.), *Critical race theory perspectives on social studies: The profession, policies, and curriculum* (pp. 15–26). Greenwich, CT: Information Age.

Urrieta, L. (2003b). Las identidades también lloran/identities also cry: Exploring the human side of indigenous Latina/o identities. *Educational Studies, 34*(2), 147–168.

Urrieta, L., Jr. (2004). Dis-connections in "American" citizenship and the post/neo-colonial: People of Mexican descent and whitestream pedagogy and curriculum. *Theory and Research in Social Education, 32*(4), 433–458.

Urrieta, L., Jr. (2006). Community identity discourse and the Heritage Academy: Colorblind educational policy and white supremacy. *International Journal of Qualitative Studies in Education, 19*(4), 455–476.

Valencia, R. (1997). *The evolution of deficit thinking: Educational thought and practice.* Washington, DC: Falmer Press.

Valenzuela, A. (1999). *Subtractive schooling: U.S.-Mexican youth and the politics of caring.* Albany, NY: State University of New York Press.

Wells, A. S., López, A., Scott, J., & Holme, J. J. (1999). Charter schools as postmodern paradox: Rethinking social stratification in an age of deregulated school choice. *Harvard Educational Review, 69*(2), 172–205.

Wells, A. S., Holme, J. J., López, A., & Cooper, C. W. (2000). Charter schools and racial and social class segregation: Yet another sorting machine? In R. D. Kahlenberg (Ed.), *A Notion at risk: Preserving public education as an engine for social mobility* (pp. 169–222). New York: The Century Foundation Press.

Wells, A. S., Slayton, J., & Scott, J. (2002). Defining democracy in the neoliberal age: Charter school reform and educational consumption. *American Educational Research Journal, 39*(2), 337–361.

Williams, P. (1991). *The alchemy of race and rights.* Cambridge, MA: Harvard University Press.

Willinsky, J. (1998). *Learning to divide the world: Education at empire's end.* Minneapolis, MN: University of Minnesota Press.

Zamora, E. (1993). *The world of the Mexican worker in Texas.* College Station, TX: Texas A&M University Press.

Anthony Brown
University of Texas, Austin

Luis Urrieta, Jr.
University of Texas, Austin

KEVIN D. VINSON, E. WAYNE ROSS AND MELISSA B. WILSON

6. "THE CONCRETE INVERSION OF LIFE"

Guy Debord, the Spectacle, and Critical Social Studies Education

1. THE WHOLE LIFE of those societies in which modern conditions of production prevail presents itself as an immense accumulation of *spectacles*. All that once was directly lived has become mere representation.

2. IMAGES DETACHED FROM every aspect of life merge into a common stream, and the former unity of life is lost forever. Apprehended in a *partial* way, reality unfolds in a new generality as a pseudo-world apart, solely as an object of contemplation. The tendency toward the specialization of images-of-the-world finds its highest expression in the world of the autonomous image, where deceit deceives itself. The spectacle in its generality is a concrete inversion of life, and, as such, the autonomous movement of non-life.

3. THE SPECTACLE APPEARS at once as society itself, as a part of society and as a means of unification. As a part of society, it is that sector where all attention, all consciousness, converges. Being isolated—and precisely for that reason—this sector is the locus of illusion and false consciousness; the unity it imposes is merely the official language of generalized separation.

4. THE SPECTACLE IS NOT a collection of images; rather, it is a social relationship between people that is mediated by images. (Debord, 1967/1995, p. 12–13)

So begins Guy Debord's most famous work, *The Society of the Spectacle*.[1] To a large extent ours is an age of spectacle in which many if not most of our social relationships are mediated by images—an age in which living largely has been replaced by representation.

It is an era of separation through connectivity and connectivity through separation. The social today means avatars, Facebook, YouTube (see, e.g., "Fred"[2]), Twitter, MySpace, Blackberrys, Skype, texting, blogging, and Wii. Of the iUniverse of ibeing. It is a "reality" of viewing and contemplation, one in which "human" interaction occurs electronically, not face-to-face. Above all else it means wirelessness, the apparent gold standard of the modern era. Games are played in real time but in virtual space. We offer on-line degrees and distance education. We keep in touch yet never really see—or even hear, in some cases—others; we don't need to. Today we present ourselves as we choose to be perceived. As, therefore, we will be perceived (unless we're photoshopped). Our Facebook pictures can be anything. For who would know otherwise? And who could do anything about it? Why would they? We are our representations.

We are increasingly in communication, on-line, separated and yet connected. We are members of more and larger communities than we have ever been before, albeit sometimes anonymous ones. Yet loneliness/aloneness has perhaps never been more prevalent or pervasive. Go figure.

As we bemoan the assault on privacy, we aspire to be public figures, "famous" potentially for all eternity and not merely a measly fifteen minutes. Increasingly we are all "reality" stars, or rather virtual reality stars.

Human beings, of course, have always developed new technologies for communication, maintaining contact, and entertainment. "Necessity" is, after all, the mother of invention. But Blackberrys, Wiis, iPods, and the Internet are not the telephone, radio, or TV (sort of). Today is different. In the past communication technologies (connectivity) made up for, temporarily, separation. They were a less desirable, though welcomed and even sometimes and regrettably necessary, alternative to face-to-faceness. They sufficed though they never replaced the immediacy and intimacy of the directly lived interpersonal. We engaged in them usually because we had no other acceptable choice.

Today we simply don't choose. Or we prefer not to choose. Or we choose the virtual over the direct, the mediated over the unmediated, the image over the real, unable to fathom why we would ever choose otherwise. We simply e-interact as if there were no other choice. We have to. This is Debord's "pseudo-world," his "autonomous movement of non-life." Where once we used connection to overcome separation, today we use it to maintain separation and separation to maintain—to rationalize—connectivity. The two are mutually reinforcing if not indistinguishable. As opposed to the communication technologies of the past, today's are instantaneous and all-encompassing, 24/7, absolute. We do not, or cannot, leave home without them. All representation, all mediation, all of the time. Connection and separation are substitutes, not complements, or perhaps both substitutes and complements. One is the same as the other. The spectacular world today, in essence, is multifaceted and increasingly convergent—interfaced. In the past, it was either/or, one or the other, sometimes simultaneously, but always independently. One watched TV or telephoned, even if one did so at the same time. In the present all is hybrid. Is a telephone not a TV? There is no such thing as connection, and no such thing as separation. Or, there's nothing but connection and, or *as,* separation. All is separation-connection, connection-separation. It makes no difference either way. Are we or are we not "bowling alone" (Putnam, 2000)?

This contemporary state is both positive and negative. We are not Luddites. Our purpose here is not to trash technology; we like technology very much. Our point is simply that advances in mediation bring consequences, sometimes good, sometimes bad. Maybe even mostly good. Who could argue, for instance, with being able to stay in contact with others if the alternative is not being able to do so? To Skype one's family from overseas? To making education available to those who might not be able to access it were it not for newer communication tools? Who would not

THE CONCRETE INVERSION OF LIFE

favor the speed, if not the intimacy and detail, of broadband over that of posting letters? Free wi-fi and mobile phoning over the cost and paper waste of postage stamps and landline long-distance charges? Flash drives over file cabinets? Cell phones when one's car breaks down? Of seeing and hearing simultaneously over either by itself? The frequent over the infrequent? That this may all represent progress is unquestionable, yet with progress something always is inevitably lost.

Our point instead is that it is not all good. With the advantages of these technologies come disadvantages. There are drawbacks to an era of cyberreality, virtual reality, and hyperreality. To our society of the spectacle. To the fact that what "once was directly lived has become mere representation," to a society in which social relationships between people have become increasingly mediated by images" (Debord, 1967/1995, p. 12–13). More specifically, the advent of the society of the spectacle brings with it implications for contemporary citizenship, and these implications for contemporary citizenship bring with them implications for education, most particularly, we argue, for social studies education and its emphasis on effective citizenship.

In much of our previous work we have sought to understand the relationships between schooling and society by exploring the contemporary convergence of spectacle and Foucauldian surveillance, principally as a means of critique.[3] We have considered this spectacle-surveillance merging as the context within which image comes to dominate reality; contemporary schooling develops as a reproductive mode of discipline and deterrence; and schooling becomes increasingly oppressive, antidemocratic, inauthentic, and counter to the collective good. We have pursued these ideas through interdisciplinary frameworks developed in such diverse yet connected fields as visual studies, cultural studies, media studies, and film studies, and through such conceptions as Bakhtin's *chronotope*, Barthes's "rhetoric of the image," Boorstin's *pseudo-event*, Baudrillard's *simulacra* and *simulation*, and McLuhan's "the medium is the message." We have situated the emergence of image-power via the postmodern desire to see and be seen—that is, the union of exhibitionism and voyeurism—and located the mechanisms according to which all of this must be critically interpreted within the complex and interrelated settings of "the will to standardize," "globalization," and "technological change" (Vinson & Ross, 2003).

Our purpose in this chapter is to more precisely explore the meanings of Debord's notion of "The Society of the Spectacle": its definitions, components, and implications. We address most importantly its potential relevance for contemporary social studies education. As such, this chapter is both an extension of our previous work and a narrowing of it. That is, although we treat only the idea of spectacle—as opposed to spectacle and surveillance combined, for example—we do so here in greater depth and breadth than we did in our earlier studies. While we continue to believe that spectacle and surveillance must be interrogated as conjoined characteristics of society, in this chapter we seek to provide some greater understanding of spectacle by focusing on it in isolation. As such, our specific questions are:
– What is the "society of the spectacle"? What are its key components and attributes? What are its implications as a critical concept in terms of making sense of contemporary society?

– How and to what extent might Debord's conception of "spectacle" be relevant to critical social studies education today?
– What does it mean to be a "good" or "effective" or "engaged" citizen within "the society of the spectacle" and what is the significance of these meanings for (critical) social studies education?

In this chapter we explore Debord's characterization of "the spectacle," drawing primarily on "Separation Perfected," the first chapter of *TSS*. Next we consider the spectacle's implications for critical social studies, relating it primarily to the framework established in *Expectations of Excellence: Curriculum Standards for Social Studies* (National Council for the Social Studies, 1994).[4] Lastly, we consider the potential implications of applying Debord's spectacle to critical social studies, specifically in terms of purpose, curriculum, and instruction.

DEFINING THE SPECTACLE

In the first chapter of *The Society of the Spectacle,* "separation perfected," Debord lays out several of the spectacle's most complex and necessary themes, many of which he develops further in subsequent chapters. At the very least, the spectacle means:
– the dominance of image over lived experience
– the privileged status of the commodity
– the promotion of abstract (exchange) value and labor
– alienation
– passive observation (by spectators) and contemplation (at the expense of living or experiencing)
– a specific economics and ideology (capitalism)
– isolation/separation/fragmentation/lack of community, and
– the denial of history. (Vinson & Ross, 2003; Debord, 1967/1995)

Further, Debord's treatment is different from Foucault's perhaps better known use of "spectacle" in his effort to characterize modern "surveillance" as a disciplinary technology distinct from the disciplinarity of antiquity. As Foucault argued:

> Antiquity had been a civilization of spectacle. "To render accessible to a multitude of men [*sic*] the inspection of a small number of objects": this was the problem to which the architecture of [ancient] temples, theatres and circuses responded. With spectacle, there was a predominance of public life, the intensity of festivals, sensual proximity. In these rituals in which blood flowed, society found new vigour and formed for a moment a single great body. The modern age poses the opposite problem: "To procure for a small number, or even for a single individual, the instantaneous view of a great multitude." In a society in which the principal elements are no longer the community and public life, but, on the one hand, private individuals and, on the other, the state, relations can be regulated only in a form that is the exact reverse of the spectacle: "It was to the modern age, to the ever-growing influence of the state, that was reserved the task of increasing and perfecting

its guarantees, by using and directing, towards that great aim the building and distribution of buildings intended to observe a great multitude of men [*sic*] at the same time." (1975/1979, p. 216)

Foucault's distinction is between ancient discipline grounded in spectacle, or the observation of the few by the many, and modern discipline grounded in surveillance, or the observation of the many by the few. While we do not necessarily disagree with this view, that is with Foucault's spectacle-surveillance distinction with respect to discipline (we have argued elsewhere that we see exploring the convergence of Foucauldian spectacle and surveillance as useful in explaining the disciplinary tendencies of contemporary society), Foucault's treatment of spectacle is in many ways less developed than, and incompatible with, Debord's. For, basically, Foucault and Debord were defining different concepts. This fact helps explain why for Foucault surveillance is fundamental to the structure of modern society, and why for Debord it is spectacle.

In order to better define Debord's unique conception of spectacle we turn first to Sadie Plant, Len Bracken, and Anselm Jappe, distinguished scholars of the Situationist International (SI) and interpreters of *The Society of the Spectacle*. We then present our own analysis, specifically drawing on "separation perfected" as a central theme in Debord's theorizing.

Plant, Bracken, Jappe

According to Sadie Plant (1992), for Debord the spectacle is the characteristic structure of "modern capitalist society ... a frozen moment of history in which it is impossible to experience real life or actively participate in the construction of the lived world" (p. 1). In this Debordian view, that of society as "organisation of spectacles," spectacle suggests that

> The alienation fundamental to class society and capitalist production has permeated all areas of social life, knowledge, and culture, with the consequence that people are removed and alienated not only from the goods they produce and consume, but also from their own experiences, emotions, creativity, and desires. (Plant, 1992, p. 1)

Here, "People are spectators of their own lives, and even the most personal gestures are experienced at one remove" (Plant, 1992, p. 1). As Plant (1992) summarizes,

> Above all the notion of the spectacle conveyed the sense in which alienated individuals are condemned to lives spent effectively watching themselves. It suggested that, far from being inevitable attributes of the human condition, the boredom, frustration, and powerlessness of contemporary life are the direct consequence of capitalist social relations ... [The spectacle means that] the only possible relation to the social world and one's own life is that of the observer, the contemplative and passive spectator [situated within a] tautological world in which the appearance of real life is maintained in order

> to conceal the reality of its absence. Bombarded by images and commodities which effectively represent their lives to them, people experience reality as second-hand ... (p. 10)

The society of the spectacle, then, is one of separation and alienation, passivity, representation, non-life, and mere observation, one of mediation by images and commodities.

Len Bracken (1997), in *Guy Debord: Revolutionary,* stresses the Marxian character of Debord's spectacle, and argues that Debord "explicitly ties his concept of the spectacle to Marx's critique of the commodity" (p. 129). As Bracken rightly notes, Debord's opening of *The Society of the Spectacle*— "the whole life of those societies in which modern conditions of production prevail presents itself as an immense accumulation of spectacles" (p. 12) is a play on Marx's (1867/1887) introduction to *Capital*— "The wealth of those societies in which the capitalist mode of production prevails, presents itself as 'an immense accumulation of commodities'" (Chapter 1, Section 1). Bracken suggests that by "the spectacle" Debord means the "spectacle-commodity" and that spectacle is "shorthand for the *society of the spectacle-commodity*" (p. 129). In essence, the spectacle is the totality of capitalism, alienation, and isolation self-maintained and self-perpetuated by way of separation masquerading as connection or unification.

> For Debord, the spectacle is the tyrant that thwarts the natural human situation of acting and speaking together; not merely using crude, time-tested means of orchestrating isolation such as mutual fear, but with the multifaceted methods of separation of the modern political economy that go to the heart of existential alienation ... [In effect], Debord is making a Marxist critique of the economy that highlights the production of "image-objects" and the way this process subjugates workers. [For] Debord, the spectacle isn't the world of vision, it is the vision of the world promoted by the powers of domination. (Bracken, 1997, pp. 129–130)

Further, Bracken (1997) understands the spectacle as Debord's update of Lukacs' (1923/1967) interpretation of reification and fetishism. From this perspective, the clearest and most effective way of making sense of what the spectacle means "is to equate the society of the spectacle-commodity with the entire economic ecology that none of us can escape: the spectacle as the economy and its self-representation" (p. 131). In the spectacle, "as people consume the object-images that circulate in a society governed by ... meaning-making machinery, they become part of the spectacle. Indeed, they become the spectacle" (p. 131).

Anselm Jappe's (1999) take on the Debordian spectacle, most notably in his biography *Guy Debord,* parallels to some extent the interpretations of Bracken. Like Bracken, Jappe suggests that too frequently the spectacle is misunderstood *solely* as the powerful workings of the contemporary and "neutral" mass media. In Jappe's judgment, this view is too simplistic and incomplete; it is a misreading of Debord. As Jappe (1999) argues:

> Invasion by the means of mass communication is only seemingly a deployment of instruments that, even when badly used, remain essentially neutral; in reality

the operation of the media perfectly expresses the entire society of which they are a part. The result is that direct experience and the determination of events by individuals themselves are replaced by a passive contemplation of images (which have, moreover, been chosen by other people). (p. 6)

This point is that the mass media are not themselves the spectacle, but are rather one political and politicized aspect or expression of the entirety of the society of the commodity-spectacle—in Debord's (1967/1995) words, "its most stultifying superficial manifestation" (p. 19). Or, as Bracken (1997) writes:

... people [too often] narrowly identify Debord's concept of the spectacle with media images ... Debord very explicitly states that ... the "mass media" is only a "glaring superficial manifestation" of the spectacle. (pp. 130–131)

In Jappe's (1999) reading of Debord, central to understanding the spectacle is making sense of separation, or the "fragmentation" of life "into more and more widely separated spheres, and the disappearance of any unitary aspect of society" (p. 6). Here Jappe takes on Debord's famous conception of spectacular alienation—an outgrowth of Marx's view. Where alienation meant historically "an obvious downgrading of *being* into *having* ... the present stage, in which social life is completely taken over by the accumulated products of the economy, entails a generalized shift from *having* to appearing" (Debord, 1967/1995, p. 16). Here, spectacular alienation/ separation is where the importance of image comes into play.

The spectacle consists in the reunification of separate aspects at the level of the image. Everything life lacks is to be found within the spectacle, conceived of as an ensemble of independent representations. (Jappe, 1999, p. 6)

This, for Debord, was a *reunification in separateness,* one that worked toward the specific ends and interests of the spectacle, of its strengthening and reproduction. Within the context of the hegemony of appearance, "everywhere we find reality replaced by images. In the process, images end up by becoming real, and reality ends up transformed into images" (Jappe, 1999, p. 7).

As Jappe (1999) argues, however, the problem is not with images or representations per se, but rather it "resides in the independence achieved by representations" (p. 8). Such representations, though "born of social practice, behave as independent beings" (p. 8), existing outside of human control, speaking to human beings monologically, and requiring only passive contemplation and spectatorship to maintain their dominance and their ability to fragment and to reunite in separation to the spectacle's own politico-economic advantage.[5] This, in essence, is the ontology of what today we call viral.

From Plant, Bracken, and Jappe, then, we are left with a fairly straightforward view of the spectacle. It is as Ford (2005) states: "In *The Society of the Spectacle* Debord describes in 221 theses a society devastated by the shift from use-value and material concreteness to exchange value and the world of appearances" (p. 102). Or as Debord (1988/1998) himself wrote in *Comments on the Society of the Spectacle*:

In 1967, in a book titled *The Society of the Spectacle,* I showed what the modern spectacle was already in essence: the autocratic reign of the market economy which had acceded to an irresponsible sovereignty, and the totality of new techniques of government which accompanied this reign. (p. 2)

Overall, then, the society of the spectacle is modern capitalist existence extended throughout the entirety of social and individual life. It is alienation, as we are separated—fragmented—from one another and from ourselves via autonomous, mediating images and commodities that present, in effect, our lives to us. Being is appearing, as living and experiencing have been reduced to the consumptive and passive contemplation and mere observation that the society of the spectacle necessitates. The spectacle, dictatorial politico-economic capitalism, leads to spectatorial non-life, which in turn strengthens and perpetuates, through its totalizing unification-in-separation tendencies, the spectacle—that is, itself. At its most simplistic we are the spectacle and the spectacle is us.

Our Interpretation

In "Separation Perfected" Debord (1967/1995) presents the society of the spectacle— or, simply, "the spectacle"—according to four defining and overlapping themes: (a) separation versus unity and unity within separateness; (b) the expansion of capitalism into all aspects of social life; (c) the replacement of living and experiencing by representation or the mediation of social life by images; and (d) appearance-based passivity, contemplation, observation-spectatorship, and falsity.

Separation versus unity/unity within separateness. Debord (1967/1995) calls separation "the alpha and omega of the spectacle" (T25)[6]; separation in fact is both the spectacle and the spectacle's cause and effect. Grounded in the power of the self-perpetuating economic order and in the mediation of the social by images, separation (and the related phenomena of isolation, alienation, and fragmentation) becomes not only separation from the products of one's labor (historical alienation) and separation from others via representation (isolation), but also separation from self (fragmentation).

> The spectacle is hence a technological version of the exiling of human powers in a 'world beyond'—and the perfection of separation *within* human beings. (T20)

The spectacle *appears,* however, as a means of unification, not one of separation, and it is this, for Debord, that reveals its ultimate deceit. "As a part of society, [the spectacle] is that sector where all attention, all consciousness converges" (T3). Though the spectacle also appears "as society itself" (T3), when seen as only a part, a specific focal point, the emptiness of the spectacle's apparent unity becomes clear. "Being isolated—and precisely for that reason—this sector is the locus of illusion and false consciousness; the unity it imposes is merely the official language of generalized separation" (T3), or unity within separateness. For Debord this is crucial, for "the origin of the spectacle lies in the world's loss of unity" (T29). The spectacle's falseness is its seeming ability to authentically reunify when in fact it divides. What unification there is rests simply on a linkage through isolation— workers from the products of their labor, "spectators" from one another, self from self. The spectacle indeed does "unite what is separate, but it unites it only *in its separateness*" (T29). It is this truth, according to Debord, upon which the modern economy, which is produced by and produces isolation, and the modern ascendancy of non-life, "the spectator's alienation from and submission to the contemplated object" (T30), both depend.

The expansion of capitalism into all aspects of social life. Debord's second theme, the expansion of the economy—of capitalism—into all aspects of social life, illuminates his notion of "the spectacle [as] both the outcome and the goal of the dominant mode of production" as it comes to rule, as it comes to be—as it "epitomizes"— "the prevailing mode of social life" (T6). The economic becomes the social and the social becomes the economic, ad infinitum. Thus, "what the spectacle expresses is the total practice of one particular economic and social formation; it is ... that formation's agenda" (T11). It is also, therefore, our formation and our agenda.

The spectacle is, moreover, "the perfect image of the ruling economic order" (T14) and its—society's—*"chief product"* (T15). It produces and is produced by the social/economic sphere; it is "simply the economic realm developing *for itself*" (T16), with no other ends, such that the spectacle's "triumph," "founded on separation, leads to the *prolitarianization of the world*" (T26). The economy and the spectacle and separation merge—they become indistinguishable. This is because "the spectacle's function in society is the concrete manufacture of alienation ... the alienation that has inhabited the core of the economic sphere from its inception" (T32) and that fundamentally "cuts people off from their lives" (T33). For in the end, "the spectacle is *capital* accumulated to the point where it becomes image" (T34), mediation, and non-life.

The replacement of living and experiencing by representation. According to Debord (1967/1995), "The whole life of those societies in which modern conditions of production prevail presents itself as an immense accumulation of spectacles. All that once was directly lived has become mere representation" (T1). Representation, however, is not in itself the spectacle. For "The spectacle is not a collection of images; rather, it is a social relationship between people that is mediated by images" (T4). It is our mode of (non)life, therefore, not representations or images per se, that defines the spectacle. In other words, whatever the particular image and whatever the particular mechanism of mass mediation, the spectacle as spectacle is "a visible negation of life ... a negation of life that has invented a visual form for itself" (T10) in which "all activity is banned, all *real* activity has been forcibly channeled into the global construction of the spectacle" (T27). The spectacle, thus, is not image or representation, but life as representation, social relationships mediated by images; it is a construction of social life which "in its generality is a concrete inversion of life, and, as such, the autonomous movement of non-life" (T2). To the extent that life is representation and social relationships are image-mediated, and granting the totalizing power of such modern inventions as capitalism and the mass media, then, Debord concludes, life itself has become and is *appearance-life* rather than *real-life,* and there is no longer any experience, any unmediated social, any unified or genuine being.

Finally, this spectacular world of non-life reaches it "highest expression in the world of the autonomous image, where deceit deceives itself" (T2).

> For one to whom the real world becomes real images, mere images are transformed into real beings—tangible figments which are the efficient motor of trancelike behavior ... The spectacle is by definition immune from human activity, inaccessible to any projected review or correction ... Wherever representation takes on an independent existence, the spectacle reestablishes its rule. (T18)

The power of the spectacle to elevate the unreal to the real—the image-life—is then its life's blood, its peculiar mechanism of reproductive and self-serving maintenance.

Appearance-based passivity, contemplation, and spectatorship. In the society of the spectacle appearance comes to matter more than anything else that transforms life into *non*-life—passivity, contemplation, spectatorship. Or, rather, appearance and alienation. Within the spectacle being equals appearing, and "everything that appears is good; whatever is good will appear" (T12). In fact, "the spectacle proclaims the predominance of appearances and asserts that all human life, which is to say all social life, is mere appearance" (T10). Here there is nothing else but passivity, contemplation, and spectatorship—watching. The spectacle is "modern passivity" (T13) and modern unreal reality, modern non-life. It is the mediation of all relationships, being, experience, and existence by image-objects and the modern politico-economic (capitalist) commodity-image; it is the spectacular complex that dominates humanity and denotes the entirety of what it is to be—to appear—human.

For Debord (1967/1995) *non*-life is *appearance*-life; as "the spectacle turns reality on its head" (T8) life and non-life are inverted. "Lived reality suffers the material assaults of the spectacle's mechanisms of contemplation ..." (T8). Life becomes non-life, experience becomes contemplation, and unity in separateness—the spectacle itself—becomes the contemplated. It is precisely here, in spectacular "society's real unreality" (T6), that "truth is a moment of falsehood" (T9), and that life actually becomes non-life, a "reality" of appearing and seeing, "a universe of speculation" (T19). It is, further, within this realm of non-life, of appearance-life, that (1) the spectacle operates, both as producer and produced and cause and effect, and (2) the sovereign economy, the autonomous image, passive contemplation, and appearance form and are formed by the spectacular "perfection" of separation.

Overall, then, considering the explications offered by Plant, Bracken, and Jappe as well as our own interpretations, we are left with a general conception of the Debordian spectacle as a phenomenon characterized by both an inherent critical complexity and a gestalt-like architecture in which its whole is created out of the interaction of its several and diverse essential elements. In sum, the society of the (commodity) spectacle—*the spectacle*—is the totality of contemporary, postmodern social life: alienation, isolation, fragmentation; the sovereign and encroaching power of the economic sphere; the mediating, autonomous image-object/commodity-image; spectatorship, passivity, contemplation (of ourselves, of others, of images); appearance; and the false, deceitful, unreal reality of "separation perfected," (re)unity within separateness.

In the next section we begin our critical examination of the relation between the Debordian spectacle and radical social studies education by providing a perspective on contemporary social studies education drawing principally on the NCSS's (1994, 2008) *Expectations of Excellence*.

CIVIC COMPETENCE AND SOCIAL STUDIES EDUCATION

According to the National Council for the Social Studies social studies is

> the integrated study of the social sciences and humanities to promote civic competence ... Its purpose ... is to help young people make informed and reasoned decisions for the public good as citizens of a culturally diverse, democratic society in an interdependent world. (NCSS Task Force on Standards for Social Studies [TFSSS], 1994, p. 3; NCSS Curriculum Review Task Force [CRTF], 2008, p. 6)

NCSS defines "civic competence" both as "the knowledge, intellectual processes, and dispositions required of students to be active and engaged participants in groups and public life (CRTF, 2008, p. 6) and as "the knowledge, skills, and attitudes required of students to be able to assume 'the office of citizen' (as Thomas Jefferson called it) in our democratic republic" (TFSSS, 1994, p. 3). For the NCSS this purpose of promoting civic competence is one of the distinguishing features of social studies; the second, that social studies "integrate[s] knowledge, skills, and attitudes within and across disciplines" (TFSSS, 1994, p. 3) supports the first. Both require, in the vision of the NCSS, an understanding of and a commitment to "the inclusion of all students" and "diversity" (CRTF, 2008, pp. 6–7). In the *Expectations of Excellence* (TRSSS, 1994; CRTF, 2008) "thematic strand" most clearly connected to civic competence—Strand Ten, "Civic Ideals and Practices"—NCSS maintains that "Social studies programs should include experiences that provide the study of the ideals, principles, and practices of citizenship in a democratic republic" (TRSSS, 1994, p. 30; CRTF, 2008, p. 21).

Overall, then, the NCSS's approach to citizenship can be characterized as one in which (a) citizenship education as informed and reasoned decision-making for the public good is the fundamental purpose of social studies education; (b) effective citizenship is civic competence; and (c) civic competence results from social studies education that involves teaching and learning those knowledges, intellectual skills and processes, attitudes, and dispositions that are most consistent with or relevant to understanding and strengthening democracy and "democratic" global interconnectedness. In the next section we attempt to make sense of this view of social studies education vis-à-vis the spectacle and critical pedagogy.

THE SPECTACLE, CRITICAL PEDAGOGY, AND CRITICAL SOCIAL STUDIES EDUCATION

The social studies are understood to be those whose subject matter relates directly to the organization and development of human society and to [the human being] as a member of social groups. (Committee on Social Studies, 1916, p. 9)

Our purpose in this section is twofold. First we attempt to construct a definition of critical social studies education by applying the principles and characteristics of contemporary critical pedagogy to the conception of social studies education outlined by the NCSS. Second, we consider how and to what extent Debord's notion of the spectacle might contribute to the theory and practice of contemporary critical social studies education. Our focus throughout is upon the theory and practice of both the organization of society and the individual as a member of society, as a member of social groups, a theme emphasized in social studies education at least as far back as 1916.

Critical Social Studies Education

Although contemporary critical social studies education is grounded in the closely related though broader and more multifaceted realm of critical pedagogy, its roots go back at least to the works of Karl Marx.[7] In its modern form it evolved most obviously from the writings of John Dewey (1916/1966, 1938/1963, 1956), social reconstructionists such as George S. Counts (1932) and Harold Rugg (1923), and the scholarship of such early critical pedagogues as Paulo Freire (1970) and Samuel Bowles and Herbert Gintis (1976).

In the social studies proper, much of the initial critical framework was developed by authors such as William B. Stanley and Jack L. Nelson (1986). More recent efforts to define and create critical social studies can be found in the work of Bickmore (2008), Gibson (2007), Hursh and Ross (2000), Kincheloe (2001), Malott and Pruyn (2006), Marciano (1997), Marker (2000), Ross (2000a, 2006), Ross and Queen (2010), and Vinson (1999, 2006).

Defining the means and ends to be pursued in critical social studies is not something that can or should be done once and for all, or separated from the experience of everyday life in a particular context. There is no monolithic program, plan, or approach that encompasses critical social studies and any attempt to characterize it must necessarily be at least somewhat imprecise and incomplete. That said, critical social studies education is typically recognized as left-leaning social and pedagogical opposition to "traditional," "dominant," or "mainstream" social education, however each of these is defined (e.g. Ross, 2000a). It is often characterized as social studies for social justice and participatory democracy. Critical social studies most often is linked to teaching and learning that takes seriously the causes and effects of racism, classism, sexism, heteronormativity, ableism and other technologies of oppression. It explores questions of power, culture, and difference, incorporating both theoretical and activist orientations, and it seeks in the process the construction of some mode of socio-pedagogical praxis committed to some form of emancipatory/resistance-directed social reconstruction.[8]

Our view of critical social studies education is fixed most directly in the theoretical and practical principles of contemporary critical pedagogy. As a complex field of study, critical pedagogy is inclusive; its tenets and influences are wide-ranging so that no two "critical pedagogues" likely agree entirely on every point or issue. In its contemporary constructions critical pedagogy draws upon a range of radical perspectives, including but not limited to neo-Marxism, feminist theory, critical race theory, postmodernism/poststructuralism, cultural studies (and related disciplines such as film and media studies), queer studies, postcolonial studies, and anarchism.[9]

Perhaps the most distinguishing element of critical pedagogy is its aim to empower people to transform their world. There is no uniform definition of critical pedagogy as educators and theorists have transformed the concept over the years as they deployed new approaches to understanding the world and changing it.

Critical pedagogy usually refers to educational theory, teaching, and learning practices that aim to raise learners' critical consciousness regarding oppressive social conditions. Critical pedagogy focuses on the development of critical consciousness for both "personal liberation" and collective political action aimed at overcoming oppressive social conditions and to create a more egalitarian, socially just world. Pedagogy that is critical encourages students and teachers to understand the interconnected relationships among knowledge, culture, authority, ideology, and power. Understanding these relationships in turn facilitates the recognition, critique, and transformation of existing undemocratic social practices and institutional structures that produce and sustain inequalities and oppressive social relations.

Critical pedagogy is particularly concerned with reconfiguring the traditional student/teacher relationship, where the teacher is the active agent, the one who knows, and the students are the passive recipients of the teacher's knowledge. The critical classroom is envisioned as a site where new knowledge, grounded in the experiences of students and teachers alike, is produced through meaningful dialogue. In short, critical pedagogy aims to empower students by: (1) engaging them in the creation of personally meaningful understandings of the world and (2) providing opportunities for students to learn that they have agency, that is their actions can enable social change.

Lastly, according to Kincheloe (2007), critical pedagogy today involves a new synthesis of critical principles. He identifies the "key dimensions of this critical synthesis" as:
– The development of a socio-individual imagination;
– The reconstruction of the individual outside the boundaries of abstract individualism;
– The understanding of power and the ability to interpret its effects on the social and the individual;
– The provision of alternatives to the alienation of the individual;
– The cultivation of a critical consciousness that is aware of the social construction of subjectivity;
– The construction of democratic community-building relationships between individuals;
– The reconceptualization of reason—understanding that relational existence applies not only to human beings but concepts as well; and
– The production of the social skills necessary to active participation in the transformed, inclusive democratic community. (pp. 35–39)

Taken together, these principles and characteristics present a reasonably good portrait of contemporary critical pedagogy—its commitments, its key concepts, and its theoretical alignments. When applied to the depiction of citizenship education offered by NCSS, they suggest insights into what a meaningful understanding of critical social education *might* look like.

For instance, what would "civic competence" mean from a critical pedagogical perspective? What knowledges, skills and intellectual processes, attitudes and dispositions would it require? What would define the "public good" toward which citizens are to make "informed and reasoned decisions"? What kinds of decisions would these be?

The knowledge component of civic competence might include, for example, an interdisciplinary understanding of concepts or ideas such as marginalization, disenfranchisement, class, gender, race, ideology, hegemony, critical consciousness, and resistance and their relationships to social justice and equality—their complexities, contextualizations, histories, and present-day enactments (Darder, Baltodano, & Torres, 2003; Kincheloe, 2005). These concepts, from a critical perspective, could not be reduced, say, to a set of vocabulary terms to be memorized and multiple-choiced. An in-class or school-based curricular effort might involve, as but one example, a "thematic unit" on oppression, perhaps following Iris Marion Young's (1992) broad and multidisciplinary "five faces of oppression" framework.

As advanced by Kincheloe (2005), of course, such an approach would be "interested in maintaining a delicate balance between social change and cultivating the intellect—developing a rigorous education in a hostile environment that accomplishes both goals" (p. 21). So with respect to civic competence, critical knowledge would certainly include such "traditional" content as the principles and structures of the Constitution, the Declaration of Independence, and the Bill of Rights.

Further, a critical civic competence might incorporate such requisite skills and intellectual processes as reading the world, social critique, resistance, authentic dialogue, imagination, interpretation, community-building, reasoning, and the social skills necessary to active participation in democracy that would contextualize and characterize the purposes of critical social education. On this last point, Kincheloe (2007) is particularly helpful:

> As a result of an evolving critical pedagogy, teachers and students will gain the ability to act in the role of democratic citizens. Studying the ideological in relation to self-development, socially educated individuals begin to conceptualize the activities of social life. Viewing their social actions not only through the lenses of the political but also the economic, the cultural, the psychological, the epistemological, and the ontological, individuals analyze the forces that produce apathy and passivity. In this manner, critical pedagogy [and critical social studies education] comes to embody the process of radical democratization, the continuing effort of the presently excluded to gain the right and ability to have input into civic life. As individuals of all stripes, ages, and backgrounds in contemporary hyperreality search for an identity, critical pedagogy provides them an affective social and individual vision in which to invest. Making connections between the political, the economic,

the cultural, the psychological, the epistemological, the ontological, and the educational, individuals gain insight into what is and what could be as well as the disposition to act. Thus, as political agency is cultivated, critical pedagogy becomes a democratic social politic. Once again, social consciousness and the valorization of the individual come together to produce an emancipatory synergy. (p. 39)

The attitudes and dispositions relevant to a critical civic competency might include, among others (a) a commitment to justice and equality (perhaps obviously); (b) an understanding of human activity (including education) as inherently political; (c) a dedication to the alleviation of human pain and suffering (physical, emotional, psychological, and so on); (d) a commitment to empowerment and anti-oppressiveness; (e) taking seriously the issues surrounding identity, culture, and diversity; (f) anti-conformity; (g) a dedication to authentic democracy and community; and (h) an opposition to alienation, marginalization, and silencing/voicelessness.

Informed and reasoned decision-making would be grounded in what Kincheloe (2007) called "the reconceptualization of reason—understanding that relational existence applies not only to human beings but concepts as well" (p. 38). This reconceptualization—or reconstruction—begins both with the understanding of the "irrationality of what has sometimes passed for reason in the post-Enlightenment history of Western societies" and with the formulation of "relational reasoning" (p. 38).

> A relational reason understands conventional reason's propensity for conceptual fragmentation and narrow focus on abstraction outside of a lived context. The point here is not to reject rationality but to appreciate the limits of its conventional articulation in light of its relationship to power ... [I]t analyzes the importance of that deemed irrational by dominant Western power and its use-value in sociopolitical affairs and the construction of a critical consciousness. Such alternative ways of thinking are reappropriated via the realization of conventional decontextualization ... All things are a part of larger interactive dynamics, interrelationships that provide meaning when brought to the analytical table. Indeed, our evolving critical pedagogy finds this relational reason so important and so potentially transformative that we see the interaction between concepts as a living process. These relational dynamics permeate all aspects of not only our social education but also of critical consciousness itself. (pp. 38–39)

The ends, the "public good," toward which these knowledges, skills and intellectual processes, attitudes and dispositions would be applied would, of course, be one of a social and educational vision of justice and equality. From a critical pedagogical point of view, this is a vision that "demands a fundamental rethinking, a deep reconceptualization of," for example:
- what human beings are capable of achieving
- the role of the social, cultural, and political in shaping human identity
- the relationship between community and schooling
- ways that power operates to create purposes for schooling that are not necessarily in the best interests of the children that attend them

- how teachers and students might relate to knowledge
- the ways schooling affects ... students from marginalized groups [and]
- the organization of schooling and the relationship between teachers and learners.

Further, with respect to the good, the public, and society:

> A critical pedagogical vision grounded as it is in social, cultural, cognitive, economic and political contexts understands schooling as part of a larger set of human services and community development ... In this context, educators deal not only with questions of schooling, curriculum, and educational policy but also with social justice and human possibility ... In this context teachers draw on their larger vision to help them determine what types of human beings they want to graduate from their schools ... If we are unable to articulate this transformative, just, and egalitarian critical pedagogical vision, then the job of schooling will continue to involve taming, controlling, and/or rescuing the least empowered of our students. Such students do not need to be tamed, controlled, and/or rescued; they need to be respected, viewed as experts in their interest areas, and inspired with the impassioned spirit to use education to do good things in the world. (Kincheloe, 2005, pp. 6–8)

This is critical pedagogy directed toward a socially just social transformation, a pedagogy in opposition to dominant, mainstream, and disconnected or reproductive schooling that serves, in this critical view, primarily the interests of the powerful.

So, a cautious and preliminary definition of critical social studies education, one grounded in civic competency and critical pedagogy, might be that

> critical social studies education is education for critical citizenship, that is civic competence, built upon (a) *critical knowledge* (e.g., knowledge of such concepts or ideas as marginalization, disenfranchisement, class, gender, race, ideology, hegemony, critical consciousness, and resistance, (b) *critical skill and intellectual processes* (e.g., reading the world, social critique, resistance, authentic dialogue, imagination, interpretation, community-building, reasoning, and the social skills necessary to active democratic participation), and (c) *critical attitudes and dispositions* (e.g., a commitment to justice and equality; an understanding of human activity as inherently political; a dedication to the alleviation of human pain and suffering; a commitment to empowerment and anti-oppressiveness; taking seriously the dynamics of identity, culture, and diversity; anti-conformity; a dedication to authentic democracy and community; and an opposition to alienation, marginalization, and silencing/voicelessness).

It is such a definition that would orient, that would serve as the heart of, the theory and practice of any critical or radical social studies education.

Although we believe that these should be central to any social studies education, they typically are not, at least with respect to most mainstream social studies programs in this age of standards-based educational reform.

In the next section we consider what contributions Debord's notion of spectacle might make to contemporary critical social studies education.

Critical Social Studies Education and the Spectacle

Essentially, our conceptual and problematic goal in this section is to combine our initial definition of critical social studies education with our understanding of Debord's construction of the spectacle. To reiterate, we see critical social studies education as, perhaps too obviously, an education for critical citizenship, an education that takes seriously the demands of civic competence and, therefore, emphasizes critical knowledge, critical skills and intellectual processes, and critical attitudes and dispositions. Our understanding of the spectacle rests on what we see as the four foundational themes Debord pursues in "separation perfected,"
– separation versus unity and unity within separation;
– the expansion of capitalism into all aspects of social life;
– the replacement of living and experiencing by representation (the mediation of social life by images); and
– appearance-based passivity, contemplation, spectatorship, and falsity.

Our main effort here is to consider what each of these themes means with respect to critical knowledge, critical skills and intellectual processes, and critical dispositions.

Critical knowledge. Against the backdrop of the society of the spectacle, a contemporary critical citizenship education would focus upon critical knowledge in terms of addressing the following questions:
– How, if at all and to what extent, is contemporary society one of unity within separateness? What does this mean? What are the implications and consequences of this possibility?
– How, if at all, and to what extent, has capitalism—the dominant mode of modern production—infiltrated *all* other aspects of modern society and modern social life/social relations? To what effects?
– What is the significance of the increasingly mediated nature of social interaction—for instance, through Facebook, Twitter, MySpace, YouTube, smart phones, texting and so on? Is this significance positive or negative?
– To what extent is society today more passive/contemplative/appearance-based / spectatorial than it was in the past? How has this affected what it means to be a good or effective citizen?
– What does/might/should any or all of this mean with respect to social justice, equality, and the rights and responsibilities of citizens—*civic competence?*

The sources of information relevant to such critical knowledge would be both broad and deep, and would include the personal, the "official," the dominant, and the marginalized; it would be knowledge that is fundamentally political, economic, cultural, social, historical, and contextualized, and it would be knowledge that takes the issues of race, gender, sexuality, ability, and class etc. seriously with respect to separation, capitalist oppression, representation, appearance, and passive contemplation (among other considerations).

Critical skills and intellectual processes. The critical skills and intellectual processes consistent with a Debord-inspired critical social studies education are similar to those of any other critical education. Thus they include: reading the world, social critique, resistance, authentic dialogue, imagination, interpretation, community-building, reasoning, and the social skills necessary to active and critical democratic participation. The principal differences, which we discuss in the next section, encompass those behaviors and constructions specifically delineated by Debord and the Situationist International themselves, namely the "construction of playful situations," the *dérive,* and *détournement* (e.g., Debord, 1956, 1957; Marcus, 1989; Merrifield, 2005; Situationist International, 1958a, 1958b).

Critical attitudes and dispositions. As is the case with critical skills and intellectual processes, the critical attitudes and dispositions of a Debordian critical social education are similar to those most consistent with a critical pedagogically-constructed citizenship education more generally. Again, these include: a commitment to justice and equality; an understanding of human activity as inherently political; a dedication to the alleviation of human pain and suffering; a commitment to empowerment and anti-oppressiveness; taking seriously the dynamics of identity, culture, and diversity; anti-conformity; a dedication to authentic democracy and community; and an opposition to alienation, marginalization, and silencing/ voicelessness. What would perhaps, however, distinguish the critical attitudes and dispositions of a critical citizenship education designed specifically with the society of the spectacle in mind would be its connection to what we identify in the next section as the fundamental principle of Debordian critical theory, which is its view of social change. As we describe in the next section, it is this principle that distinguishes the Debordian vision of citizenship.

A DEBORDIAN VISION OF CRITICAL CITIZENSHIP

We begin this section with our attempt to reconstruct a "Debordian" vision of critical citizenship. We then consider the implications of such a vision for contemporary critical social studies education.

Any notion of a Debordian critical citizenship must be grounded in a single basic idea that underlies much of the SI's thinking: "First of all we think the world must be changed. We want the most liberating change of the society and life in which we find ourselves confined. We know that this change is possible through appropriate actions" aimed toward "a superior organization of the world" (Debord, 1957, p. 17).

We base our specific understandings of a Debordian critical citizenship on three fundamental components of the SI's agenda, each developed in opposition to the various aspects of the spectacle we defined in previous sections, and each consistent with Debord's interpretation of social change, appropriate action, and a superior organization of modern life. These components are (a) "constructing situations," (b) the *dérive,* and (c) *détournement.* Each of these principles reflects both a theoretical and applied orientation, and taken together they constitute the principal Situationist program, its praxis, and its revolutionary strategies and tactics.

Constructing Playful Situations

The Situationist International (1958a) defined a "constructed situation" as "a moment of life concretely and deliberately constructed by the collective organization of a unitary ambience and a game of events" (p. 45). It involves "the concrete construction of momentary ambiences of life and their transformation into a superior passional [sic] quality (Debord, 1957, p. 22). A constructed situation, therefore, includes at least three primary characteristics: (a) it is unitary rather than separated or fragmented; (b) it is a game, and thus playful; and (c) it is superior to those situations which are presented to us by and as the commodity-spectacle.

Debord's understanding of a constructed situation relates to and implies another of the SI's key conceptualizations, that of "unitary urbanism." For the SI (1958a), unitary urbanism is "the theory of the combined use of arts and techniques for the integral construction of a milieu in dynamic relation with experiments in behavior" (p. 45). It is the creation of a setting—the milieu or ambience—in which Debordian praxis—critical citizenship—is enacted and with which it interacts. Unitary urbanism is "dynamic" as often the outcome and "nature" of constructed situations and the specific traits of "experimental behavior" cannot be predetermined.

In general, Debord (1957) defines the essence of this behavior—the action side of a constructed situation—"as the invention of games ... of an essentially new type" whose "most general goal must be to extend the nonmediocre part of life, to reduce the empty moments of life as much as possible" (pp. 23–24). For Debord (1957):

> The situationist game is distinguished from the classic conception of the game by its radical negation of the element of competition and of separation from everyday life. The situationist game is not distinct from a moral choice, the taking of one's stand in favor of what will ensure the future reign of freedom and play. (p. 24)

This unique emphasis on play sprang from Debord's critique of the "industrializing of leisure," its commodification and spectacularization, and its stultifying effects on the working classes. Thus, the Debordian game demands the intentional reunification of leisure in the service of the most radical forms of freedom and liberation. To Debord, then, play, as a radical component of constructed situations, was at its heart a permanent revolutionary art and technology of life (see Marcus, 1989; Merrifield, 2005).

In sum, Debord and the SI (1958b) saw constructed situations as comprising two inseparable and reciprocating features, a unitary ambience or milieu *and* a set of experimental behaviors directed toward a revolutionary and superior recreation of contemporary life; both the ambience/milieu and behaviors were crucial.

> Our conception of a "constructed situation" is not limited to a unitary use of artistic means to create an ambience, however great the force or spatiotemporal extension of this ambience may be. The situation is also a unitary ensemble of behavior in time. It is composed of gestures contained in a transitory decor. These gestures are the product of the decor and of themselves. And they in their turn produce other forms of decor and other gestures ... The really

experimental direction of situationist activity consists in setting up, on the basis of more or less clearly recognized desires, a temporary field of activity favorable to these desires. This alone can lead to the further clarification of these primitive desires, and to the confused emergence of new desires whose material roots will be precisely the new reality engendered by ... situationist constructions. (SI, 1958b, p. 43)

For Debord and the SI, two of the most important modes of experimental behavior were the *dérive* and *détournement.*

The dérive. For the SI (1958a), *dérive*—literally "the drift" or "drifting"—was defined as "a mode of experimental behavior linked to the conditions of urban society; a technique of transient passage through varied ambiences" (p. 45). In some ways, as a critical act, it is related but not identical to Baudelaire's (1863/1964) and Benjamin's (2006) conceptions of the *flâneur* (more or less urban "stroller"; see also Merrifield, 2005; Tester, 1994; White, 1994). For Debord (1956), it is

a technique of transient passage through varied ambiences. It entails playful-constructive behavior and awareness of psychogeographical effects ... which distinguishes it from ... classical notions of the journey and the stroll. (p. 50)

Its intentionality, then, its concern with *psychogeography*— "the study of the specific effects of the geographical environment, consciously organized or not, on the emotions and behavior of individuals" (SI, 1958a, p. 45; see also Self & Steadman, 2007)— is what makes it a qualitatively different concept from that of the *flâneur.*

In a *dérive* one or more persons during a certain period drop their usual motives for movement and action, their relations, their work and leisure activities, and let themselves be drawn by the attractions of the terrain and the encounters they find there. The element of chance is less determinant than one might think: from the *dérive* point of view cities have a psychogeographical relief, with constant currents, fixed points and vortexes which strongly discourage entry into or exit from certain zones. (Debord, 1956, p. 50)

This diminished role of chance, therefore, also distinguishes one who engages in *dérive* from the *flâneur.*

A *dérive* is fundamentally about the emotional "natures" of various "quarters" of a city; it is essentially urban, a walking or "wandering" tactic, usually nocturnal and lasting for several hours. In a *dérive* those involved seek to "identify ... [the] subtle moods and nuances of neighbourhoods ... documenting [the] odours and tonalities of the cityscape, its unconscious rhythms and conscious melodies; ruined facades ... [and] foggy vistas" (Merrifield, 2005, pp. 30–31). According to Merrifield (2005), "*Dérive* sought to reveal the idiocy of separation, trying to stitch together—by highlighting the gaping holes—what was spatially rent" (p. 48). It is, further, what "paved the way" for the SI's understanding of unitary urbanism (Merrifield, 2005).

The idea of the *dérive* was to reveal and challenge the status of separation and fragmentation, non-life/appearance-life/commodity-life—the spectacle itself. As an experimental behavior within a constructed (and playful) situation, the unitary urban *dérive* was to be a "living critique ... reuniting physical and social separations" (Merrifield, 2005, p. 48). It was, as praxis, the anti- or counter-spectacle.

Détournement. Related to the *dérive,* and like it "at the core of unitary urbanism" (Merrifield, 2005, p. 50), *détournement* was a second experimental behavior that worked within constructed situations to challenge the peculiar power of spectacular society. For the SI (1958a), *détournement* was

> Short for: *détournement* of preexisting aesthetic elements. It necessitates the integration of present or past artistic production into a superior construction of a milieu. In this sense there can be no situationist painting or music, but only a situationist use of these means. In a more primitive sense, *détournement* within the old cultural spheres is a method of propaganda, a method which testifies to the wearing out and loss of importance of those spheres. (pp. 45–46)

Détournement. is a mode of subverting the normal, of contradicting or negating accepted behavior in order to "create light, to *disalienate,*" to connect and to unify (Merrifield, 2005, p. 50). It is a means to "make life richer" (Merrifield, 2005, p. 50). Classic examples, according to Merrifield (2005), are "squatting, building and street occupations ... graffiti and 'free associative' expressionist art" (p. 50). Such strategic tactics

> ... turn things around, lampoon, plagiarize and parody, deconstruct and reconstruct ambience, unleash revolutions inside one's head as well as out on the street with others ... They force people to think and rethink what they once thought ... [*Détournement* operates as] an instrument of propaganda, an arousal of indignation, action that stimulates more action. (p. 50)

As the spectacle turns life and reality on their heads, *détournement* turns the spectacle on its head, forcing it to confront the anti- or counter-spectacular and to make room for, or to get out of the way of, living, experiencing, and unity.

As acts of unified living, as counter-mediation, as counter-appearance and counter-separation, the *dérive* and *détournement* work together within the overall context of constructed playful situations and as enacted according to the milieu/ambience of the anti-commodity-image/image-object. As Greil Marcus (1989) describes this project, this artistic technology of critique and revolution, Situationist praxis would demand that we:

> practice détournement—write new speech balloons for newspaper comic strips, or for that matter old masters ... insist simultaneously on a "devaluation" of art and its "reinvestment" in a new kind of social speech, a "communication containing its own criticism," a technique that could not mystify because its very form was a demystification ... [It would demand as well that] we pursue the dérive—give up to the promises of the city, and then to find them wanting—to drift through the city, allowing its signs to divert, to "detourn," steps, and then to divert those signs, forcing them to give up routes

that never existed before—there would be no end to it. It would be to begin to live a truly modern ... life, made out of pavement and pictures, words and weather: a way of life anyone could understand and anyone could use. (p. 170)

As we understand it a Debordian vision of critical citizenship is a twofold and dialogical project. It first pursues the creation of superior situations—ambiences and milieus—in opposition to those imposed by the spectacle. Second it advocates the practice of uniquely experimental behaviors, the *dérive* and *détournement,* for example, that are necessarily linked not only to one another but also to the contextual and constructed situations within which they are actualized and with which they interact. The resulting complex is organic and constitutes a mutually productive, innovative, and reciprocating mechanism of resistance and critique. This praxis, both strategic and tactical, aims at the complete destruction or negation of the totality of practices that define the society of the spectacle.

Implications of Debordian Critical Citizenship for Contemporary Social Studies Education

In our view critical citizenship education should be the centerpiece of any effort to construct a radical, social justice-oriented program of social studies education. And while there may be broad agreement on this point among critical social educators in principle, the devil, as always, is in the details. For there are undoubtedly many possible and reasonable visions of a radical social studies.

Our goal in this section is, in a sense, one of "putting it all together." What are the implications of a Debordian critical citizenship education for contemporary social studies education? What would a Debord-inspired radical social studies education look like in terms of purpose, curriculum, and instruction?

Most simply, and with the understanding that the point of critical social studies education would be critical citizenship education, the purpose of critical social studies, then, would be the promotion of critical citizenship. Again this implies (a) a critical civic competence organized around the teaching and learning of certain critical knowledge, critical skills and intellectual processes, and critical attitudes and dispositions (in other words the spectacle-based critical citizenship education we described earlier in this chapter); and (b) an emphasis on Debord's (and the SI's) fundamental premise, that "the world must be changed," that this must mean "the most liberating change of the society and life in which we find ourselves confined," and "that this change is possible through appropriate actions" (e.g., *dérive* and *détournement*) toward and in interaction with "a superior organization of the world" (i.e., "constructed [playful] situations"; Debord, 1957, p. 17). Ultimately this would be a citizenship education grounded in resistance to the workings of the spectacle, to separation, fragmentation, isolation, alienation, the capitalization of social life, non-life, the dominance of appearance, and contemplation-passivity-spectatorship.

From this perspective, the curriculum of a critical social studies education would first seek to abolish school-society distinctions as well as any distinctions among the formal, the informal, the enacted, the null, and the hidden curricula. Everything would be on the table. The specifics of this curriculum would involve the particulars of a Debordian-inspired critical competence—critical knowledge, critical skills and intellectual processes, and critical attitudes and dispositions. It would, therefore, include the application of certain critical skills and behaviors, for example dialogue, imagination, reading the world, and resistance (among others) and the SI-specific behaviors of *dérive* and *détournement,* toward the acquisition of particular critical knowledge, including that relevant to the meaning and purpose of constructed situations and to our questions regarding the spectacular nature of modern, techno-capitalist society.

What is perhaps most important is what all this might mean for instruction. For we are suggesting, in effect, a pedagogical practice grounded in constructed situations, the *dérive,* and *détournement.* From this view, teachers and students would embrace the notion that constructing superior milieus and ambiences is appropriate to a critical social studies—to a revolutionary theory and practice (a *praxis*) of the social.

The first implication of this would be the blurring, even the destruction, of the boundaries that exist or are perceived to exist between the school and the larger society. Ideally then instruction would be no more or less likely to occur "in the world" than it is to occur in the classroom. Schooling really would become living. Social studies teachers and students would be engaged in the *dérive,* exploring the psychogeographical effects of their communities, constructing situations, playfully experiencing in a unified way both the banalities and the "nonmediocre aspects" of the world and of life.

A second possibility might involve teachers and students treating schools and classrooms like Debord and his SI colleagues treated the urban streets of Paris. Teachers and students might re-imagine the school/classroom environment and recreate it as a set of "playfully" and "deliberately constructed," evolving and new—unified and superior—ambiences and milieus, ones aimed toward "the most liberating change of the society and life in which [they, teachers and students] find [themselves] confined" (Debord, 1957, p. 17). One can only imagine what this might suggest within the present conformative and restrictive age of *No Child Left Behind*, Race To The Top, and other standards-based education reforms.

The *dérive,* of course, is as possible within schools as it is outside them, and certainly teachers and students could examine the unique psychogeographical relief(s) of each of the often hidden spaces of and within schools. Wandering through hallways, in and out of classrooms and offices, being drawn into or away from particular points, being instead of appearing, engaging in passionate rather than passive, active rather than contemplative, playful and unified behavior. Why not?

The construction of situations and engaging in the *dérive,* of course, take on new meanings when enacted within the age of separation-connection we described in the introduction to this chapter. For, plausibly, the utilization of playful situations and the *dérive* could work against, could resist and counter, whatever fragmenting and isolating tendencies exist within today's mediated and representational social world. Students and teachers might jointly, whether in "real reality" or cyberreality, reconstruct the milieus of such technological spaces as Facebook and Twitter—what would Facebook or Twitter look like if reconstituted as "superior" and passionate ambiences? What would define superior? How might students and teachers make these "situations" better, more life than non-life—perhaps as more critical tools of effective citizenship? What kinds of curriculum would be necessary to support this? Is hacking a legitimate technique, perhaps as a sort of nonviolent disobedience? (It is important to note here that true harm does not have to occur. One point of such activities is play and experimentation. These practices are aimed in the direction of social justice and unsettling and/or disrupting the political and economic power of the spectacle; and the practice of constructing situations is by its very definition temporary.

The second experimental behavior, *détournement,* would encourage teachers and students to reconstruct "preexisting aesthetic elements" into new and superior meanings; its practices might include graffiti, parody, lampoon, and satire, even plagiarism in a way. Distributing newspapers or standardized tests, for example, with reinvented headlines and questions and answers; touching-up—"improving"— news broadcasts or photographs or websites (think *The Onion, The Daily Show,* or Dada). As Merrifield (2005) describes it, the purpose of this kind of *détournement* would be to "force people to think and rethink what they once thought" and to "turn things around … to stimulate action" so as to "unleash revolutions inside one's head as well as out on the street with others" (p. 50). As is the case with constructing situations and the *dérive,* with *détournement* contemporary technologies may be used against themselves to challenge their potentially isolating/ separating/ fragmenting and appearance/mediation/representation-dominated tendencies. All of these artistic techniques, these strategic tactics—constructed situations, the *dérive,* and *détournement*—are aimed at overthrowing the commodity-spectacle and the autonomous reign of image-objects in the interests of a maximized status of social justice, liberation, and "truly" living and experiencing. This is a humanist and anti-capitalist project *par excellence,* a project of not only critical social studies but also one of "effective" and authentic citizenship, and one that not only values and advocates a critical schooling for social justice, but one that takes seriously both an intellectual and an activist education.

SUMMARY AND CONCLUSIONS

In this chapter we have explored the connections between Guy Debord's conception of the society of the spectacle and contemporary critical social studies education. We have grounded our work within the modern context of social networking and technological interconnectivity—separated connectedness or connected separation. We have offered our own interpretative definition of the spectacle and of critical social studies education, one that builds on a specific combination of the fundamental principles of contemporary critical pedagogy and the NCSS's mainstream conception of civic competence. Most importantly, perhaps, we have constructed a Debordian "vision" of critical citizenship and considered its implications for a critical social studies curriculum and instruction. Our overall effort has been to look at the interrelationships among Debord's understanding of the spectacle, modern "social" life, critical pedagogy, and critical social studies education. While ours is merely an initial and speculative study, we hope that this chapter will stimulate not only a renewed and reinvigorated dialogue about the meanings of citizenship and citizenship education, but also a re-examination of the theory and practice of critical social studies education and contemporary critical pedagogy more broadly.

NOTES

1. It is beyond the scope and purpose of this chapter to provide any degree of in-depth biographical or interpretive introduction to Guy Debord, the Situationist International (SI), or the vast body of Debord's work beyond *The Society of the Spectacle*. Readers interested in this literature, however, should see, for example, Debord's (2004) own *Panegyric: Volumes 1 & 2*, Len Bracken's (1997) *Guy Debord: Revolutionary*, Andrew Hussey's (2001) *The Game of War: The Life and Death of Guy Debord*, Anselm Jappe's (1993/1999) *Guy Debord*, Greil Marcus's (1989) *Lipstick Traces: A Secret History of the Twentieth Century*, Andy Merrifield's (2005) *Guy Debord*, Sadie Plant's (1992) *The Most Radical Gesture: The Situationist International in a Postmodern Age*, Simon Ford's (2005) *The Situationist International: A User's Guide*, and McKenzie Wark's (2008) *50 Years of Recuperation of the Situationist International* (among others). A great deal of information, including translations of Debord and other situationists' texts (the SI was anti-copyright) are available on a number of excellent websites. See especially those of The Bureau of Public Secrets (www.bops.org), Not Bored! (www.notbored.org), and nothingness.org (www.nothingness.org).
2. We thank our junior colleague Miriam Pellegrino for the reference to "Fred".
3. See, for example, Ross, 2000b; Ross & Vinson, 2003; Vinson, 1999, 2001a, 2001b, 2002, 2005, 2006; Vinson, Gibson, & Ross, 2001; Vinson & Ross, 2001, 2003, 2007; Welsh, Ross, & Vinson, 2009.
4. While there are a number of reasonable approaches to social studies education we could have chosen to emphasize, we selected *Expectations of Excellence* for two principal reasons: (1) its prominence as representative of the thinking of NCSS, the largest organization of social studies educators in the United States; and (2) its *general* resemblance to mainstream social education. In previous work (e.g., Vinson, 2001) we have also explored the Center for Civic Education's (CCE) *CIVITAS: A Framework for Civic Education* (CCE, 1991) and its *National Standards for Civics and Government* (CCE, 1994). We do not mean to imply that *Expectations of Excellence* is *inherently* any better or worse than other similar standards documents. See also the "Draft Revision" by the NCSS Curriculum Review Task Force (2008).
5. Like Bracken's, Jappe's analysis emphasizes capitalism and the critique of the commodity, a subject Debord takes up most directly in "The Commodity as Spectacle," the second chapter of *The Society of the Spectacle*. In that we are focusing foremost on Debord's notion of "separation perfected," we will not concentrate on Debord's theory of the commodity here but will instead refer readers to Debord, Bracken, and Jappe.
6. In this section we cite direct quotes to Debord's (1967/1995) *The Society of the Spectacle* by thesis (T) number so that readers can refer to any published or on-line edition of the work. Our quotations are from the translation by Donald Nicholson-Smith (Debord, 1967/1995). Thus "(T1)" is a citation of a direct quotation taken from Thesis 1 in *The Society of the Spectacle*.
7. For an excellent introduction to the historical foundations of critical pedagogy see Darder, Baltodano, and Torres (2003, esp. pp. 1–10), who trace the origins of modern critical pedagogy through "twentieth century educators and activists" such as Dewey, Myles Horton, Herbert Kohl, Jonathan Kozol, Maxine Greene, Bowles and Gintis, Martin Carnoy, Michael Apple, and Ivan Illich; Brazilian authors such as Freire and Augusto Boal; Foucault and Antonio Gramsci; and the Critical Theory of the Frankfurt School.
8. In this chapter we treat critical social studies and critical citizenship education as synonyms.
9. The following paragraphs are drawn from Ross (2008).

REFERENCES

Bakhtin, M. (1984). *Problems of Dostoevsky's poetics* (C. Emerson, Ed., & Trans.). Minneapolis, MN: University of Minnesota Press.
Bakhtin, M. M. (1981). *The dialogic imagination: Four essays* (M. Holquist & C. Emerson, Eds., & Trans.). Austin, TX: University of Texas Press.
Barthes, R. (1977). *Image/music/text* (S. Heath, Trans.). New York: Hill and Wang.
Baudelaire, C. (1964). *The painter of modern life*. New York: Da Capo Press. (Original work published 1863)
Benjamin, W. (2006). *The writer of modern life: Essays on Charles Baudelaire* (M. W. Jennings, Ed., H. Eiland, E. Jephcott, R. Livingstone, & H. Zohn, Trans.). Cambridge, MA: Harvard University Press.
Bracken, L. (1997). *Guy Debord: Revolutionary*. Venice, CA: Feral House.
Baudrillard, J. (1987). *Forget Foucault*. New York: Semiotext(e).
Baudrillard, J. (1995). *Simulacra and simulation* (S. F. Glaser, Trans.). Ann Arbor, MI: University of Michigan Press.
Bickmore, K. (2008). Social justice and the social studies. In L. S. Levstik & C. A. Tyson (Eds.), *Handbook of research in social studies education* (pp. 155–171). New York: Routledge.
Boorstin, D. J. (1992). *The image: A guide to pseudo-events in America*. New York: Vintage Books. (Original work published 1961)
Bowles, S., & Gintis, H. (1976). *Schooling in capitalist America: Educational reform and the contradictions of economic life*. New York: Basic Books.
Center for Civic Education. (1991). *CIVITAS: A framework for civic education*. Calabasas, CA: Author and National Council for the Social Studies.
Center for Civic Education. (1994). *National standards for civics and government*. Calabasas, CA: Author.
[Committee on Social Studies]. (1916). National Education Association. *The social studies in secondary education*. Washington, DC: United States Government Printing Office.
Counts, G. S. (1932). *Dare the schools build a new social order?* New York: John Day.
Darder, A., Baltodano, M., & Torres, R. D. (2003). Critical pedagogy: An introduction. In A. Darder, M. Baltodano, & R. D. Torres (Eds.), *The critical pedagogy reader* (pp. 1–21). New York: Routledge Falmer.
Debord, G. (1956). Theory of the *dérive*. In K. Knabb (Ed. & Trans.), *Situationist International anthology* (pp. 50–54). Berkeley, CA: Bureau of Public Secrets.
Debord, G. (1957). Report on the construction of situations and on the International Situationist tendency's conditions of organization and action. In K. Knabb (Ed. & Trans.), *Situationist International anthology* (pp. 17–20). Berkeley, CA: Bureau of Public Secrets.
Debord, G. (1995). *The society of the spectacle* (D. Nicholson-Smith, Trans.). New York: Zone Books. (Original work published 1967)
Debord, G. (1998). *Comments on the society of the spectacle* (M. Imrie, Trans.). New York & London: Verso. (Original work published 1988)
Debord, G. (2004). *Panegyric* (J. Brook & J. McHale, Trans., Vols. 1 & 2). London & New York: Verso. (Original works published 1989 & 1997)
Dewey, J. (1956). *The child and the curriculum/The school and society*. Chicago & London: University of Chicago Press. (Original works published 1902 and 1899)
Dewey, J. (1963). *Experience and education*. New York: Collier. (Original work published 1938)
Dewey, J. (1966). *Democracy and education: An introduction to the philosophy of education*. New York: Macmillan. (Original work published 1916)
Foucault, M. (1979). *Discipline and punish: The birth of the prison* (A. Sheridan, Trans.). New York: Pantheon. (Original work published 1975)
Ford, S. (2005). *The Situationist International: A user's guide*. London: Black Dog Publishing.
Freire, P. (1970). *Pedagogy of the oppressed*. New York: Continuum.

Gibson, R. (2007). Paulo Freire and revolutionary pedagogy for social justice. In E. W. Ross & R. Gibson (Eds.), *Neoliberalism and education reform* (pp. 177–215). Cresskill, NJ: Hampton Press.

Hammer, R., & Kellner, D. (Eds.). (2009). *Media/cultural studies: Critical approaches*. New York: Peter Lang.

Hursh, D. W., & Ross, E. W. (Eds.). (2000). *Democratic social education: Social studies for social change*. New York: Falmer.

Hussey, A. (2001). *The game of war: The life and death of Guy Debord*. London: Jonathan Cape.

Jappe, A. (1999). *Guy Debord* (D. Nicholson-Smith, Trans.). Berkeley, CA: University of California Press. (Original work published 1993)

Kincheloe, J. L. (2001). *Getting beyond the facts: Teaching social studies/social sciences in the twenty-first century*. New York: Peter Lang.

Kincheloe, J. L. (2005). *Critical pedagogy primer*. New York: Peter Lang.

Kincheloe, J. L. (2007). Critical pedagogy in the twenty-first century: Evolution for survival. In P. McLaren & J. L. Kincheloe (Eds.), *Critical pedagogy: Where are we now?* (pp. 9–42). New York: Peter Lang.

Lukacs, G. (1967). *History and class consciousness* (R. Livingstone, Trans.). London: Merlin Press. (Original work published 1923)

McLuhan, M. (1994). *Understanding media: The extensions of man*. New York: McGraw-Hill. (Original work published 1964)

Malott, C., & Pruyn, M. (2006). Marxism and critical multicultural social studies. In E. W. Ross (Ed.), *The social studies curriculum: Purposes, problems, and possibilities* (3rd ed., pp. 157–170). Albany, NY: State University of New York Press.

Marciano, J. (1997). *Civic illiteracy and education: The battle for the hearts and minds of American youth*. New York: Peter Lang.

Marcus, G. (1989). *Lipstick traces: A secret history of the twentieth century*. Cambridge, MA: Harvard University Press.

Marker, P. M. (2000). Not only by our words: Connecting the pedagogy of Paulo Freire with the social studies classroom. In D. W. Hursh & E. W. Ross (Eds.), *Democratic social education* (pp. 135–148). New York: Falmer.

Marx, K. (1887). *Capital, volume one: The process of production of capital* (S. Moore & E. Aveling, Trans.). Moscow, USSR [Russia]: Progress Publishers. (Original work published 1867). Retrieved March 20, 2009, from http://www.marxists.org/archive/marx/works/1867-c1/

Merrifield, A. (2005). *Guy Debord*. London: Reaktion Books.

National Council for the Social Studies Curriculum Review Task Force. (2008, Fall). *Expectations of excellence: Curriculum standards for social studies* (draft revision). Washington, DC: National Council for the Social Studies. Available on-line: http://www.socialstudies.org/system/files/standards Draft10_08.pdf

National Council for the Social Studies Task Force on Standards for Social Studies. (1994). *Expectations of excellence: Curriculum standards for social studies*. Washington, DC: National Council for the Social Studies. Retrieved February 26, 2010, from http://www.socialstudies.org/standards/curriculum

Plant, S. (1992). *The most radical gesture: The Situationist International in a postmodern age*. London: Routledge.

Putnam, R. D. (2000). *Bowling alone: The collapse and revival of American community*. New York: Simon & Schuster.

Ross, E. W. (2000a). Redrawing the lines: The case against traditional social studies instruction. In D. W. Hursh & E. W. Ross (Eds.), *Democratic social education* (pp. 43–63). New York: Falmer.

Ross, E. W. (2000b). The spectacle of standards and summits. *Z Magazine, 12*(3), 45–48.

CHAPTER 6

Ross, E. W. (2006). Remaking the social studies curriculum. In E. W. Ross (Ed.), *The social studies curriculum: Purposes, problems, and possibilities* (3rd ed., pp. 319–332). Albany, NY: State University of New York Press.
Ross, E. W. (2008). Critical pedagogy. In S. Mathison & E. W. Ross (Eds.), *Battleground schools* (pp. 156–161). Westport, CT: Greenwood.
Ross, E. W., & Queen, G. (2010). Globalization, class, and the social studies curriculum. In D. Kelsh, D. Hill, & S. Macrine (Eds.), *Class in education: Knowledge, pedagogy, subjectivity* (pp. 153–174). New York: Routledge.
Ross, E. W., & Vinson, K. D. (2003). Controlling images: The power of high stakes testing. In K. J. Saltman & D. Gabbard (Eds.), *Education as enforcement*. New York: Routledge.
Rugg, H. O. (1923). *The social studies in the elementary and secondary school* (22nd Yearbook of the National Society on the Study of Education, Part II). Bloomington, IL: Public School.
Self, W., & Steadman, R. (2007). *Psychogeography: Disentangling the modern conundrum of psyche and place*. New York: Bloomsbury USA. (Original work published 2003)
Situationist International. (1958a). Definitions. In K. Knabb (Ed. & Trans.), *Situationist International anthology* (pp. 45–46). Berkeley, CA: Bureau of Public Secrets.
Situationist International. (1958b). Preliminary problems in constructing a situation. In K. Knabb (Ed. & Trans.), *Situationist International anthology* (pp. 43–45). Berkeley, CA: Bureau of Public Secrets.
Stanley, W. B., & Nelson, J. L. (1986). Social education for social transformation. *Social Education, 50*, 532–534.
Tester, K. (1994). *The flâneur*. New York: Routledge.
Vinson, K. D. (1999). National curriculum standards and social studies education: Dewey, Freire, Foucault, and the construction of a radical critique. *Theory and Research in Social Education, 27*, 295–327.
Vinson, K. D. (2001a). Image, authenticity, and the collective good: The problematics of standards-based reforms. *Theory and Research in Social Education, 29*, 363–374.
Vinson, K. D. (2001b, April). *Pursuing image: Making sense of popular pedagogical representations*. Poster session presentation at the annual meeting of the American Educational Research Association (Media, Culture, & Curriculum SIG), Seattle, WA.
Vinson, K. D. (2002, April). *The end of the panopticon? Baudrillard & Debord—A critique of Foucault's disciplinarity*. Paper presented at the annual meeting of the American Educational Research Association (Foucault & Education SIG), New Orleans, LA.
Vinson, K. D. (2005). Social studies in an age of image: Surveillance-spectacle and the imperatives of "seeing" citizenship education. In A. Segall, E. Heilman, & C. Cherryholmes (Eds.), *Social studies—The next generation: Re-searching in the postmodern* (pp. 27–45). Peter Lang Publishing.
Vinson, K. D. (2006). Oppression, anti-oppression, and citizenship education. In E. W. Ross (Ed.), *The social studies curriculum: Purposes, problems, and possibilities* (3rd ed., pp. 51–75). Albany, NY: SUNY Press.
Vinson, K. D., Gibson, R., & Ross, E. W. (2001). *High-stakes testing: The threat to authenticity* [John Dewey Project on Progressive Education]. Burlington, VT: University of Vermont. Retrieved February 26, 2010, from http://www.uvm.edu/~dewey/monographs/ProPer3n2.html
Vinson, K. D., & Ross, E. W. (2001). Education and the new disciplinarity: Surveillance, spectacle, and the case of SBER. *Cultural Logic, 4*(1). Retrieved February 26, 2010, from http://eserver.org/clogic/4-1/vinson%26ross.html
Vinson, K. D., & Ross, E. W. (2003). *Image and education: Teaching in the face of the new disciplinarity*. New York: Peter Lang.
Vinson, K. D., & Ross, E. W. (2007). Education and the new disciplinarity: Surveillance, spectacle, and the case of SBER. In E. W. Ross & R. Gibson (Eds.), *Neoliberalism and educational reform*. Cresskill, NJ: Hampton Press.
Wark, M. (2008). *50 years of recuperation of the Situationist International*. New York: Princeton Architectural Press.

Welsh, J. F., Ross, E. W., & Vinson, K. D. (2009). To discipline and enforce: Surveillance and spectacle in state reform of higher education. *New Proposals: Journal of Marxism and Interdisciplinary Inquiry*, 3(2), 25–39. Retrieved February 26, 2010, from http://ojs.library.ubc.ca/index.php/newproposals/issue/view/80/showToc

White, E. (1994). *The flâneur: A stroll through the paradoxes of Paris.* New York: Bloomsbury USA.

Young, I. M. (1992). Five faces of oppression. In T. E. Wartenberg (Ed.), *Rethinking power* (pp. 174–195). Albany, NY: SUNY Press.

Kevin D. Vinson
University of West Indies

E. Wayne Ross
University of British Columbia

Melissa B. Wilson
University of Texas, San Antonio

BRAD J. PORFILIO AND MICHAEL WATZ

7. CRITICALLY EXAMINING THE PAST AND THE "SOCIETY OF THE SPECTACLE"

Social Studies Education as a Site of Critique, Resistance, and Transformation

During the late-19th and early-20th centuries, US political, economic, and academic leaders charted the nation on a course to embrace the new industrial age and to associate "progress" with the white Anglo-Saxon race creating an overseas economic empire, predicated on the ideals of rugged individualism, on the acceptance of social hierarchy, and on the alleged power of technology and science to *a priori* make the future better than the past (Blee, 2005; Frisch, 2001; Rydell, 1981; Rydell, Findling, & Pelle, 2000). The US powerbrokers utilized world's fairs as a chief cultural medium to garner support for their industrial practices, imperialistic policies, and jaded worldviews. Rather than being viewed as merely benign forms of entertainment that provided leisure for over 100 million fairgoers who explored the exhibits and ventured along the midways in numerous cities across the United States, when the inaugural fair was launched in Philadelphia in 1876 to just prior to the US's entry in World War I, America's fairs, as noted by many cultural historians and sociologists, ought to be viewed as educative sights or "object lessons," which attempted to inculcate the public to support whole cloth hegemonic ideologies, assumptions, and institutional arrangements (Frisch, 2001, p. 197). However, despite the fact that the political, economic and academic elite held the power to give shape to the displays, events, and practices embedded within the fairs, some female, African American, and working-class activists launched counter-hegemonic movements to position fairgoers and citizens to recognize the unjust byproducts, such as poverty, violence, racism, and ethnocentrism, associated with the elite's notion of "progress," industrialization, imperialism, unfettered capitalism, and Social Darwinism.

The importance of fostering a critical view of world's fairs during the Victorian Era in the United States cannot be underestimated. These events served as contentious sites that ultimately aided the country's economic, political, and academic elite in their quest to promote their vision of "progress" and achieve their desire to promulgate policies bent on extracting labor power and resources across the globe, and quell counter-hegemonic movements generated by working-class citizens against the visions and practices associated with the new industrial age. Teachers who guide and encourage students to go beyond viewing these and similar cultural events purely as entertainment and come to view world's fairs as a set of cultural texts, which need to be scrutinized for "hidden messages or underlying messages and power differentials" (Stevens & Bean, 2007, p. xiv), are developing students' critical literacy skills. It is through developing a critical attitude toward history that students are enabled to interrogate the socially constructed nature of their own worlds. That is, students can create understandings of the inextricable relationship between power and knowledge, the socially constructed nature of their identities and experiences, and the institutions and arrangements that perpetuate social inequalities in their communities, and across the global landscape (Johnson, 2007; Shor, 1999). Echoing Freire (1998), having the power to "read the word and the world" is also an essential ingredient in formulating counter-hegemonic movements against the structures of power, unjust practices, and debilitating discourses that fuel greed, hate, hostility, and oppression today. Critical pedagogues who encourage students to question the nature of their social worlds also attempt to foster a sense of hope and optimism that it is, indeed, possible to join other transformative intellectuals and concerned citizens in an effort to redefine themselves and remake society "through alternative rhetoric and dissident projects" (Shor, 1999). Therefore, critical literacy is a form of language use that "challenges the status quo in an effort to discover alternative paths for self and social development" (Shor, 1999).

When we assess the state of social studies education in the US, we sense a pressing urgency for social studies teachers to remake their classroom practices in an effort to foster critical literacy skills. Since the *No Child Left Behind Act* (NCLB) was implemented in the United States in 2001, there has been a steep decline in the amount of time devoted to social studies instruction (O'Conner, Heafner, & Groce, 2007, p. 255). School districts across the US, particularly school communities who are considered "low-performing," have been forced to focus time and resources on subject areas that are tied to high-stakes, standardized forms of assessment. For instance, at the elementary level, schools have focused their instruction on language arts and science because if students' test scores "do not meet an arbitrary, quantitative hurdle," teachers may face reprisals and schools may lose federal funds (O'Conner et al., 2007, p. 255).

Even in schools where teachers have the professional autonomy to create classroom environments that encourage students to question power differentials in society and the "received interpretations of our history and dominant worldview" (Case & Clark, 1997, p. 20), they often create boring and meaningless classrooms, where students are required to learn irrelevant facts from textbooks about the history of "dead white males" and their military conquests (Kornfeld, 1998, p. 306). Not coincidentally, most K-12 students, regardless of their race, class, or gender, dislike the social studies, find it meaningless, and perceive it to be one of the most difficult subjects in the school curriculum (Kincheloe, 2001; Kornfeld, 1998).

The purpose of this chapter is to outline how a critical evaluation of world's fairs during the Victorian Era in the United States (and similar modern-day political and economic spectacles) have the potency to revitalize the social studies so that students (1) develop the critical literacy skills necessary to make sense of what constitutive forces give rise to their experiences and the experiences of Others; (2) learn to interrogate the hidden agendas proffered in various discursive sites by political, economic, and intellectual leaders; and (3) recognize the urgency to remake themselves and institutions and culture as part of an effort to build a society free from hate, hostility, and injustice.

The first part of the Chapter deconstructs the political, intellectual and economic elite during the late-19th and early-20th centuries utilized world's fairs as a form of propaganda. In the process, we also examine the cultural work of groups who did not have the power to play a predominant role in how the exhibits were organized and the functions they served. We believe the bourgeois white women's, African American activists', and working-class citizens' activities surrounding the Victorian Era's world's fairs have the power to assist today's teachers and students in the pursuit of becoming cognizant of the forces that create injustice in schools and society.

The second part of the chapter is designed to capture how the same critical reading of expositions in the past can be done with modern-day political and economic spectacles. We capture how today's elite leaders engage "in the systematic production of images, events and institutional infrastructure of commodities" (Cruickshank, 2009, p. 89) to a keep the vast majority of citizens in the Western world from taking inventory of how modern-day neoliberal capitalism—seeped in consumerism, technology, commodities, images, and slogans—is responsible for controlling more of the globe's labor power, extracting the earth of its resources, exponentially intensified suffering and pain inflicted on most global citizens. The chapter concludes with several contemporary examples of teachers, teacher educators, activists, and youths joining collectively to challenge the hidden agendas proffered by the political and economic elite in various newscasts, podcasts, sporting events, talk shows, blogs, and websites.

CRITICALLY EXAMINING VICTORIAN WORLD'S FAIRS IN THE UNITED STATES: STRUGGLES FOR ECONOMIC AND IDEOLOGICAL SUPREMACY

From the late-19th century through the early-20th century, Victorian world's fairs in the United States were held throughout various regions of the country, including New Orleans, Chicago, Buffalo, Atlanta, Nashville, Jamestown, Portland, St. Louis, and Omaha (Badger, 1979; Downey, 2002; Fojas, 2005; Marling, 1992; Pepchinski, 2000; Rydell, 1983a; Rydell & Kroes, 2005). On the surface, the fairs were magnificent displays of beauty, ingenuity, accomplishment, and hope. Incredible sums of money, labor, and media attention generated optimism amongst many fairgoers that industrialization, science and technology would usher peace and prosperity for US society (Fojas, 2005; Frisch, 2001; Rydell & Kroes, 2005). The world's fairs looked as if they provided an outlet for the nation to clarify the social and economic disparities of the past and configured a worldwide stage for social growth and reconciliation in the future.

However, when we look beyond the fairs' gleaming exteriors and exuberant media coverage, we find that the cultural events promoted the US political and economic leaders' imperialistic policies, visions of "progress," and the nation's burgeoning industrial and commercial culture. The leaders' mandates were responsible for the harsh realities present in the US and its colonized territories during the Victorian Era, such as racism, sexism, subjugation, domination, and poverty. In essence, the Victorian world's fairs can be viewed as "cultural windows," illuminating life in the United States during the age of new industrialism, immigration, and imperialism. By critically analyzing primary and secondary materials pertaining to several world's fairs during the Victorian Era, it becomes possible to detect how US political and economic leaders' worldviews, policies, and practices coalesced to negatively impact the lives of women, minorities, and working-class citizens. Moreover, through this analysis, it is possible to gain insight in relation to how certain indomitable individuals, despite being located within the incredibly hostile fair cultures, were able to confront the social actors and institutions responsible for their own marginalized subject positions as well as responsible for the poverty, violence, and oppression permeating life outside the cultural exhibitions.

Evaluating Women's Cultural Work and Displays: Promoting and Resisting the Imperatives of Empire, Industrialism, and Social Hierarchy

The world's fairs that took place in Victorian America marked a significant, if somewhat enigmatic, role in the lives of women. Badger (1979) paralleled the highly complex and ambiguous role that women played within society to the similarly uncertain role that they played at the exhibitions. During the Victorian Era, the nature of womanhood was in a constant state of flux, especially for the many white bourgeois women who were valued fair workers and fairgoers. For instance, some white bourgeois women challenged hegemonic notions of femininity—that is, women being perceived as domestic agents, wives, and caregivers—by engaging "in remunerative work and political activity or choosing independence and careers over marriage and procreation" (Pepchinski, 2000). Even though the women who challenged socially accepted notions of womanhood faced a negative backlash from many white male and female fairgoers, the women's buildings located at the fairs as well as female produced artifacts held more resonance and repeatedly reinforced that white bourgeois women could perform socially acceptable forms of womanhood outside of the home, so long as they were engaged in stereotypical feminine activities, such as caring for children, the weak, and the unfortunate (Pepchinski, 2000). Unfortunately, the impact of displaying white women's philanthropic endeavors ubiquitously at the world's fairs reinforced the ideal that racialized immigrants and 'Other' downtrodden subjects were intellectually and socially inferior subjects who could only be "saved" by embracing the practices, worldviews, and ideals of the dominant society. As a result, fairgoers did not connect the suffering and misfortune experienced by the millions of new immigrants arriving to the United States and racialized minorities who lived in a nation founded upon social hierarchy, to the imperialistic and industrialized policies and practices implemented by white female philanthropic fair organizers' husbands, brothers, or sons.

By examining women's contributions at the US Victorian Exhibitions, we witness firsthand how the white, middle-class, male organizers ensured that white middle-class women would neither launch a significant challenge to their subjugated position within the wider US society nor challenge white America's imperialistic, industrial, and civilizing domestic and overseas agenda. For instance, white middle-class women who were given permission to speak at the fairs generally supported the racialized rhetoric that US imperial and industrial policies would seemingly produce economic prosperity for US citizens as well as ensure that white America "civilized" the Other in line with the dominant culture's ideals, beliefs, and values (Hoganson, 2001).[1] Whereas the minority voices of white middle-class citizens who recognized the racist nature girding US political, economic, and foreign policies, the violence and injustice inherent in the aforesaid policies, and the impact patriarchy had on all women across the globe, were purposely kept from sharing their alternative narratives with fairgoers.

The political and economic leaders, in a seemingly progressive gesture that had not been seen in other world's fairs, awarded women a separate building of their own at the Chicago Exhibition (Downey, 2002). The Women's Building did little, however, to change fairgoers' perception of womanhood or reconfigure the relationship between the sexes in US Victorian society. The Woman's Building was the smallest hall and was constructed next to the Children's Building to propagandize the rightful place of women within society (Downey, 2002). Similarly disturbing, at the Pan-American Exhibition, which was held in 1901 in Buffalo, New York, classes were offered in the Woman's Building that included, "household work," "the washing of flannels," "scouring woodwork, cleaning knives and silver household utensils," "table setting and window washing," and, "bed making" ("Women workers meet," 1901, p. 3). Even most female organizers tried to participate in and reinforce this vision of domestic oppression (Downey, 2002). This attitude was easily unveiled when considering the International Council of Women at the Chicago Exposition. Here, Adelaide Hunter Hoodless discussed, among other conservative domestic ideologies, the inadequacies of women as governmental leaders and suggested that women should move more slowly and partake in training instead of attempting to compete with more competent male counterparts ("Women of other lands," 1901). Other prominent associations such as the Board of Lady Managers and the Women's Christian Temperance Union offered similar viewpoints.

Some female-centered organizations that partook in the fairs not only sought to further the agenda of the ruling elite, but also to lull fairgoers into the fictitious notion that critical social issues such as poverty, racism, and crime could be cured through women's charitable work. Downey (2002) discussed the notion of the "proper" role of Victorian women as those who gave of themselves in order to help marginalized members of society. The media also facilitated this ideology through articles, which praised the establishment of such groups ("Women workers: National League," 1901). The irony seems harshly evident as ever-increasing numbers of middle and upper-class white women signed up to bravely battle the capitalistic-created ills of society, such as joining the Anti-Imperialistic League when the US began its overseas imperial plot by way of defeating the Spaniards in Cuba, while many white middle-class women perpetuated the very existence of such issues by creating erroneous distractions of an improved society through their generous support of a small number of unfortunates (Hoganson, 2001).

Overall, it was strangely incongruous, that through separate women's spaces and exhibits, freedom, growth, and acceptance by the white male elite was not only discouraged, it was isolated within a space separate from men's (Downey, 2002). Or perhaps this was not so surprising considering the women fair organizers' exhibits and spaces were not a real threat to the male-centered power existing in US society. Most fairgoers accepted the characterization of women as "less logical than men and less able to take part in the national administration owing to the fact that at some remote period their development was arrested" ("Women of other lands," 1901, p. 3). Thus the notion of women as token, mindless servants was woven through the fairs from the planning stages, through the creation of architecture, and ending in the discussions and events that occurred every day. Millions of visitors were subjected to this illogical and punitive view of feminine existence. It is not surprising that Pepchinski (2000), who evaluated exhibition architecture at several world's fairs during the Victorian Era, concluded Women's Buildings and their vast displays "did not challenge prevailing feminine ideals, but repeatedly reinforced traditional female roles" (para. 2).

In spite of the powerful forces that worked against the acceptance, inclusion, and modernization of women into American society, certain women used the fairs as an opportunity to stage resistance against their roles as Victorian caregivers. This indicated that despite the actions of the dominant culture, new roles for women were emerging. Society could not ignore the growing proportion of women who did not fit into traditional Christian ideals. Downey (2002) observed that some women were choosing to remain single; others were less fortunate victims of abuse and divorce; still others sought to integrate equally into the workforce. These women were charting a new course, a course that many times came into conflict with the status quo at the world's fairs.

Individuals, such as Susan B. Anthony, Elizabeth Cady Stanton, and Lucy Stone, used the fairs as opportunities to mount important economic and political reform from the perspective of most feminists in this era (Downey, 2002). An example of this form of reform is noted in the concerns for women in the workplace that were highlighted in the *Buffalo Express* ("Of mutual benefit," 1901; "Women workers: National League," 1901). Suffrage, equal rights, fair working conditions, and independence were undercurrents that radiated throughout the fairs. Occasionally, these issues made it into the wider culture through newspapers or music. From token gestures, such as the creation of the completely female Board of Lady Managers who were graced with the notion of showing women's roles in sculpture, art, and music, through much more radical enterprises, such as the World's Congress of Representative Women, which provided genuine outlets for marginalized voices, the fairs did provide limited opportunities for reform. The short-sighted volunteer opportunities provided to white women to "uplift" the poor, along with the conglomeration of women who traversed the fairgrounds from numerous countries, feminists who generated hundreds of newspaper articles concerning equal rights, and white bourgeois women who designed exhibits that influenced millions of fairgoers, threw into flux what constituted socially acceptable notions of femininity in the Victorian Era (Rydell, 1983a).

THE "SOCIETY OF THE SPECTACLE"

Creating White America: Trivializing, Demonizing and Erasing the Other at Victorian World's Fairs

The world's fairs were frequently hotbeds for promoting US imperialism and industrialization through the exultation of the white Anglo-Saxon race and culture and the concurrent demonization and trivialization of the Other. Woven into messages of national pride, modernism, and cultural enlightenment, subtle as well as boldly intolerant contexts of capitalistic, religious, and racial superiority abounded. The most incredulous example of this occurred when minoritized cultures were put on display to maximize their radical departure from "civilized" Western culture.[2] Powerful additional examples can be seen in the disturbing absence of minority accomplishment and participation at the fairs. In similar fashion to the plight of women, minorities were also discriminated against by the *whiteness* fairs, influential women, and also by other minoritized individuals.

As many scholars have noted, world's fairs reflected the desire of powerful white American leaders to usher in an age based on industry, imperialism, science, and technology (Badger, 1979; Downey, 2002; Fojas, 2005; Marling, 1992; Rydell, 1983a; Rydell, 1983b). Truthfully, in their fervor to establish the fledgling power of the American nation, fair administrators used every means at their disposal, including science, technology, religion, and the media, to shock and amuse the millions of visitors who passed through the fairgrounds with the barbarism, ignorance, and wretched existence that allegedly characterized "uncivilized" peoples in the United States and around the globe. World fair organizers and sponsors, with the assistance of some of the world's leading ethnographers, created ethnological villages, which, "featuring live displays of predominately non white people, were intended to give living and visible proof to the proposition that human beings could be divided into categories of civilization and savagery" (Rydell & Kroes, 2005). Backed with scientific "credibility," most fairgoers felt comfortable supporting the notion that white American society was the most "advanced" civilization because it embraced scientific initiatives, modern technology, social hierarchy, competition, and industrialization (Fojas, 2005; Rydell & Kroes, 2005). Exhibition leaders to demonstrate the superiority of white Anglo-Saxon American culture put various minoritized groups on display. However, First Nation and African cultures were especially targeted for various political, social, and religious reasons.

Frisch (2001) discussed this dramatic difference of white and Other at Buffalo's Pan American Exposition, and noted the manipulation of the dominant culture to portray the "dark" cultures as being "primitive," and ripe for imperial and Christian forces to exploit. Entertainment for fairgoers included "Darkest Africa," the "Old Plantation," as well as the wild, and incarcerated, Indian, Geronimo (p. 197). Therefore, the midway "entertainment" showcased to fairgoers the dominant power of the white elite and provided a modern excuse and direction for furthered actions of "civilization" throughout the world.

At the Chicago Exposition of 1893, "modern science" was used to enlighten and amuse the public about the Darwinistic superiority of Western civilization while concurrent actions of the fair administration and viewing public polluted the every-day existence of the "backward villagers" with intolerable injustice (Downey, 2002). The media also willingly participated in the atrocities that led to the dehumanization of minoritized peoples. Written coverage was polluted with blatantly racist articulations such as, "savages," "hideous," "guttural," and "pigs" (p. 77). All of this rhetoric lent credence to the religious zeal of the day, namely that Christianity needed to be spread throughout the world (Badger, 1979). Although most fairgoers thought that the exposition-created city was named for its incredible and modern use of electricity, Downey (2002) accurately highlighted the not-so-subtle nickname of the Chicago Exposition, the "White City."

Similarly, Rydell (1983b) discussed the portrayal of the Other at the Philippines Exhibit during the Seattle 1905 world's fair. Here, Igorote villagers were displayed at a primitive village for the amusement of the fair visitors, while the media dared audiences to visit the "dogeaters," and the fair administrators offered exotic pictures of fairgoers with the savages (pp. 52–54). The Seattle fair offered snapshots of additional "uncivilized" cultures as well, including Japan, Egypt, Alaska, and the more commonplace, "southern negroes" (p. 55). Each of these inaccurate, racist, and oppressive sideshows flaunted not only the opportunity, but also the obligation, for the American people to transform the world into a place of enlightenment and modernization. This represented raw imperialism in its most blatant form.

In addition to the shocking creations that were displayed at the fairs to highlight the differences between cultures, the plight of minoritized peoples can be seen in an equally disturbing way when we consider the materials and information that was purposefully ignored concerning minority involvement in the broader American culture. Throughout the fairs, multifaceted accounts of the progress of the American homeland were lauded. Numerous displays were established to highlight the advancement of many different peoples. Unfortunately, these accounts failed to identify the minoritized cultures of the country. Several transformative scholars have identified an utter lack of recognition when it came to the accomplishments of African American and Native American peoples (Blee, 2005; Downey, 2002; Frisch, 2001; Rydell, Findling, & Pelle, 2000). Even in the compilation of data, important minoritized individuals and achievements were completely ignored (Downey, 2002 p. 114). It was also not helpful for minoritized groups that some of the few mainstream and popular minority leaders lent credence to the false power of white, European superiority. For example, at the World's Fair of 1900, W.E.B. Du Bois was chosen to help create a display that pictorially represented the lives of African Americans. Osborne and Virga (2003) critically challenged this account by noting the false sense of tranquility between races, an incorrect account of the societal and employment status of African Americans, an utter lack of realistic photographs that might traumatize the public, and an unrealistic representation of African Americans who were chosen for the pictures based upon their light skin and European clothing.

In similar fashion to the incredible women who had managed to resist being pulled down by the plight of women at the fairs, certain progressive entities as well as a few chosen, valorous individuals forged a passage toward recognition and equality that marked an extreme departure from the norm. At the Chicago Exposition, the Congress Auxiliary, clearly against the wishes and financial support of the mainstream fair culture, included numerous lectures pertaining to, and given by, minority factions (Downey, 2002). From an individual standpoint, Mary Logan, wife of Senator John Logan, valiantly fought with multiple boards, on several occasions, for the rights of African Americans to be involved and recognized for their accomplishments within the broader society. Perhaps most remarkable was the involvement of Frederick Douglass. Not only did Douglass passionately and realistically address audiences about the "Race Problem in America," he also assisted in the publication of thousands of pamphlets that were distributed to decry the problems of racism not only in society, but also at the fair itself (Downey, 2002).

Cementing a New Industrial America at World's Fairs: Industrial Capitalists Subduing the Labor Movement

Not only did the industrial elite during the Victorian Era perpetuate its wealth and power through imperialistic pursuits overseas, but it exploited the labor power of millions of US immigrants and workers, who facilitated industrial expansion by constructing thousands of miles of railroad tracks, digging shafts and portals and engaging in tunnel-blasting to provide power for various commercialized pursuits, and toiling in sweatshops to produce textiles and various pieces of clothing in the US's ever-expanding garment industry (Liebhold & Rubenstein, 1998; Porfilio & Hall, 2005). Badger (1979) alluded to this when he discussed the incredible expansion of the railroad system, a system that brought untold thousands to work and play at the fairs and concentrated wealth and power into the hands of US industrial "robber barons." He noted,

> ... by the 1890s the results of that expansion seemed less to increase the freedom and prosperity for the many than to make millionaires out of a corrupt few, whose power appeared so great as to enslave the democracy itself. (Badger, 1979, p. 117)

The US world's fairs were also reflective of how corporate leaders asserted their power to corral a cheap pool of labor as well as to extinguish the growing unrest of labor unions in the US, who raised their opposition to the fact that industrial capitalists' growing wealth and power were tied to working-class citizens having poor working and living conditions and low wages. At the Portland fair of 1905, fair administrators asserted their power over labor by garnering union support through the malicious promise to retain organized labor for the construction of every aspect of the fair (Badger, 1979). Not only did the fair organizers betray their agreement with the unions, through the media and in an effort to break the unions, they advertised throughout the Portland area that there were jobs in abundance available for any working man, which kept the labor cheap and the working conditions incredibly unpleasant in the best of situations (Badger, 1979).

At the Alaska-Yukon-Pacific Exposition, which was held in Seattle in 1909, the tactics were even more extreme. Here, fair administrators falsely advertised heavily on the East coast causing thousands of workers who could not possibly afford the cost of a return trip to flood the Seattle area. Then, when unions and supporters attempted to hold a rally to protest the actions and conditions of the fair managers, the influential managers went so far as to halt and re-route public transportation in order to suppress the gathering (Badger, 1979).

Even under conditions of extreme duress, resistance was apparent in the form of organized labor, which sometimes did manage to make a difference (or at least a statement). In Portland, Oregon unions participated in a strike that impacted the fair construction to such an extent that the administration was willing to negotiate for an eight-hour workday. This represented a tremendous victory for working individuals who had been, and would continue to be, constantly exposed to extremely difficult and potentially lethal conditions. In Seattle, thousands of union workers and their supporters managed to organize and carry out a Labor Day parade (Badger, 1979). This parade drew supporters and attention even though one of the most riveting events in history was simultaneously occurring, a world's fair.

MODERN-DAY SPECTACLES IN THE AGE OF NEOLIBERALISM

Turning the trajectory to today's socio-historical moment, we are also able to witness how hegemonic ideologies, arrangements, and practices are perpetuated within various social contexts by critically examining cultural artifacts that are prevalent in all aspects of social life. However, since the Victorian Age, the transnational capitalist class has continually organized society through "consumption, media, information, and technology," rather than controlling bodies chiefly through the production process (Kellner & Best, 1999). Echoing French Situationist Guy Debord,[3] this has lead to a consumerist and entertainment-based society predicated on the production and the consumption of spectacles (Kellner & Best 1999; Cruickshank, 2009; Vincent et al., 2009).

Yet, we would be lax not to mention that the working class is still alive and well in the current manifestation of capitalism. In fact, we have more workers across the globe today because workers are not only those who produce value the way an industrial worker produces value (McLaren, in press). Today's workers tend not to own land or work for themselves. Rather, their labor is often tied to the corporate structure. Arguably, by organizing society on corporately-produced discourses, images, services, slogans, and entertainment, the form of domination exerted against the populace in the age of consumer capitalism is more detrimental than the form of domination exerted against the populace during the Victorian Age. Rather than experiencing firsthand the deleterious impact of industrial capitalism, the majority of citizens in 'First World' regions have become stupefied through their consumption of spectacles. They have lost sight of how techno-capitalism is inextricably linked to the swelling of abject poverty, suffering and misery, environmental degradation, the US's permanent "War on Terror," and the Western world's prison-education-industrial complex (Giroux, 2004, p. XVII; Kellner, 2007). Clearly, over the past thirty years, corporate giants have harnessed various forms of technology, such as computers, televisions, cell phones, DVDs, and videogames, to name a few, to position individuals to "consume a world fabricated by others rather than producing one of their own" (Kellner & Best, 1999).

THE "SOCIETY OF THE SPECTACLE"

Modern-day Sporting Events as Spectacles

In similar fashion to the historical marginalization of women, minorities, and impoverished members of the dominant culture at the Victorian world's fairs, modern-day sporting events have, in many ways, become ubiquitous media spectacles that continue to subvert equality and further engrain the status quo. Vinson, Ross, and Wilson (in this volume) discuss the development and power of spectacles and how they do, and might, impact social studies education in the arena of citizenship. From these authors, an understanding of spectacles emerges as, which, through powerful media outlets, rewrite history and reality to become history and reality. Purposefully constructed, these images are controlled by the dominant, the wealthy, and the elite, to garner social, political, and economic advantage. Whitelegg (2000) discussed the tremendous financial resources that are staked and reaped through the cooperative dealings of business, media, and sports. It is, therefore, not surprising that these forces work tirelessly to create spectacle fantasies. The World's Fairs were all about the perception, rather than the reality, of world cities as places of enlightenment, education, modernization, equality, and wonder. Historically, spectacles worked, in many ways, against societies and promoting citizenship. Unfortunately, modern spectacles, most notably sports spectacles, now controlled by the elite through vast networks of media influence and social and economic power, continue to subvert, subject, and rewrite history and reality, thus working against societies generally and social studies education in particular.

Sports spectacles in general provide a platform for continued inequity. In addition, some of the most popular sports spectacles, the Olympic Games most notably, but also the World Cup, the Super Bowl, the Tour de France, NASCAR, the PGA and many other sporting venues enshrine corporatist values, such as consumption, greed, cronyism and competition (Milton-Smith, 2002). They also allegedly illustrate how corporatism improves social and economic conditions for all citizens, while purposefully excluding how the events, in reality, further concentrate power in the hand of the privileged few. The events also instill a passive form of citizenship, as millions of fans consume endless hours of media-saturated entertainment.

For instance, numerous researchers have unveiled the contradictions that occur between how Olympic cities are framed by the media and the everyday forms of oppression that unfold in the communities outside the entertainment spectacles (Billings, 2007; Ely, 2008; McCallum, Spencer, & Wyly, 2005; Milton-Smith, 2002; "Religious restrictions," 2008; Thompson, 2008; Tuggle, Huffman, & Rosengard, 2002; Whitelegg, 2000). When considering the 1996 Atlanta Summer Olympic Games, Whitelegg (2000) noted the misrepresentative process in which the city of Atlanta vied for and carried out the Olympic games. The Atlanta Committee for the Olympic Games (ACOG) sought to portray Atlanta as a 'modern city,' presumably a social context free from the historical legacy of racism, where city residents are prospering from corporate involvement in the community, and where social conditions improve through the continued leadership of the corporate elite. This false front would, undoubtedly, help create an image that would sell tickets to the event as well as allow the city's business leaders to benefit from the public expenditures and increased economic activity within retail and service sectors (McFarland, 1998).

Looking beyond the media-constructed discourses surrounding the event, the entertainment spectacle further marginalized many of the city's residents. The city's elite used militaristic initiatives to create a pristine image of the community, illustrating to millions of spectators across the globe how neoliberal capitalism allegedly ushers prosperity and happiness for those who embrace the economic system. They 'eliminated' poverty and homelessness by closing homeless shelters, by purchasing one-way transportation tickets to remove the most socially vulnerable occupants, and by retaining private security firms to lock up anyone who had the potential to sap the profit-making potential of the spectacle (Whitelegg, 2000). In all, "an estimated 35,000 people were displaced. Thousands of homeless, mostly blacks, were arrested and jailed during the Summer Games, while some nine thousand more were given one-way bus tickets out of the city (dubbed 'Project Homeward Bound')" (No2010.com, 2009). They also exerted their power to close and relocated small business that might cut into their profits.

Preparations and follow-through for the 2008 Beijing Summer Olympic Games were strikingly similar if not more substantiated in the media as a sports spectacle. The image of Beijing was so environmentally fabricated that lawns were spray painted green to give the appearance of lush conditions, traffic and factories were halted to control the horrendous air quality, and Chinese scientists seeded rain clouds to provide dry conditions for the games (Ely, 2008). In addition, the city planted millions of trees and relocated numerous factories to combat air pollution, as well as set up dedicated food supplies for Olympic athletes to mitigate the probable occurrences of food contamination (Thompson, 2008). All of this was happening while citizens were being relocated to other areas of Beijing and to the countryside and losing their homes and jobs. The bid for, and preparations for, the Olympics were also concurrent with the direct and indirect manipulation of the Chinese government in Burma, Darfur, and Tibet, which resulted in a ghastly loss of life, mass dispersing of populations, and tremendous political unrest (Ely, 2008).

In similar fashion, McCallum (2005) highlighted the bid for the 2010 Vancouver Winter Olympic Games. On a macro-media level, the Vancouver Olympic Committee, throughout several years, played upon several positive images associated with Canada across the globe, such as being the world's only multicultural society, a nation of peacekeepers, and the "best country on earth" in terms of education and health, to make the global community believe that the Olympics would improve social and economic conditions for all citizens (McCallum, 2005; No2010.com, 2009). Unfortunately, the corporate and political leaders behind this spectacle, just like other dominant social actors who have colonized and subjugating non-white and aboriginal people during Canada's past, used the event to amass wealth and power, while concurrently further oppressing minoritized citizens and inflicting more damage on the environment. For instance, since Vancouver launched the Olympic bid in 2003, homelessness in Vancouver has increased drastically. In fact, from 2002 to 2008 there was a 372 percent increase in number of homeless people, a figure that approached three thousand residents (No2010.com, 2009). A chief factor in the rise of homelessness was the corporate elite's policy of demolishing or closing low-income Single Room Occupancy Units (SRO). The elite procured this property to build and renovate upscale hotels, which was designed to attract Olympic goers and other tourists (No2010.com, 2009). The creation of this spectacle not only destroyed sections of rural areas outside of Vancouver, increased pollution with rampant consumerism and travelling, and endangered wildlife, it also ushered a "new era of development" on territory that is tied to the intellectual, spiritual, and emotional development of First Nation's people (Hern & Johal, 2010).

The Olympics also exposed Canadians to how the corporate and political elite often align themselves with draconian security apparatuses to amass wealth and power. For instance, the public spent almost one billion dollars on security equipment, the hiring of police officers and military personnel, and anti-terrorist training (Hern & Johal, 2010; No2010.com, 2009). Finally, Christopher Shaw reminds us that although there were a few contractors, high-end hotels, and some business leaders in the entertainment zone who reaped an economic windfall from the spectacle, there were other additional "losers" of the Vancouver Olympics:

> You and me, and our kids and our grandkids. This is going to be the Big Owe: we're going to be paying this for 30 years. The Olympic adventure has cost Vancouver a considerable amount of money, and some of it will never come back. The operating budget is a $60-million deficit, and there's no way the city can keep the 250 units [of the Athlete's Village] that were going to be social housing. They have to sell them. Basically, the province is paying for Vancouver's party. (Simpson, 2010).

The 2000 Sydney Summer Olympic Games were as sensationalized as any other Olympics, with sold-out hotels, capacity seating, and tremendous media coverage. Tuggle, et al., (2002) investigated the media coverage of the Olympics on NBC television. From a macro-media perspective, the Olympics were a tremendous success. For example, with simply the announcement that Sydney had been awarded the 2000 Summer Olympics, stock prices for a number of Australian businesses, including, "building materials, developers and contractors, engineering and miscellaneous services," improved tremendously (Berman, Brooks, & Davidson, 2000).

From a micro-media perspective, a disturbing pattern in relation to gender inequity can be uncovered. The coverage of the event was male-centered, not only in the coverage of the athletes, but also in the voices of those covering the athletes. Media coverage of female athletes dropped 2.6% from 1996 to 2000 (Tuggle et al., 2002). Furthermore, 35 on-air NBC broadcasters were male compared with 15 female broadcasters (Tuggle et al., 2002). Some additional shocking inconsistencies are also revealed. Men's soccer received twice the coverage of women's soccer even though the men did not win a medal and the women took silver; men's rowing received three times the coverage of women's rowing even though the men took one medal and the women earned two; men's weightlifting was well televised and women's weightlifting was not televised despite the men earning no medals and the women taking two, including a gold (Tuggle et al., 2002). All of this reveals the gender inequities that were occurring beneath the media spectacle. A similar story also occurred during the 2004 Athens Summer Olympic Games, where media coverage of women was again lacking in time and quality and women were portrayed as "second-class athletes" (Billings, 2007).

The World Cup is another spectacle generated by corporate and political leaders to increase corporate profits, to promote consumerist logics and practices, and to inculcate global citizens to believe that social relationships across the globe can become symmetrical by merely understanding the Other through the participation in competitive sporting events, instead of through the collective efforts of concerned citizens to overturn the policies, forces, and structures that oppress most citizens at today's socio-historical moment.

The World Cup has come to dominate soccer, which is the most popular sport in the world. The macro-media perspective allows hundreds-of-millions of viewers to experience the sport of soccer and gain a pedestrian understanding of, and appreciation for, the hosting nations around the world. Viewers gain a "tourist" view of the hosting nations and their athletes, as the announcers detail some of their favorite landmarks to visit, places to dine, or tell the viewers more about where the athletes were raised, about their family members, or about their favorite pastimes. In no way does coverage mention what forces drive conflicts within hosting nations, or the historical legacy of how certain Western powers have controlled the political and economic infrastructure of various nations taking part in this spectacle. Of course beneath the macro-media perspective, and ignoring the untold billions of euros circulating in tourism, sporting products, broadcast fees, sponsorship, and energy, an alternate reality emerges. This reality consists of personal tragedy, domination, and subjugation each year wherever the World Cup travels. From a tremendous increase in the trafficking of women in Germany during the World Cup ("Trafficking of women," 2006) to outrage, disgust, hatred, and violence against women in Iran during the World Cup (Byrne, 2002), the micro-media stories are virtually ignored and intentionally killed. This is not surprising to many female athletes, however, who are constantly portrayed by the media as inferior to male athletes. They are labeled as "lesbians" (Knight & Giuliano, 2003) or portrayed as sexual objects for the purpose of pleasing the events' male-centered audience.

MODERN-DAY POLITICAL SPECTACLES

Western political and economic leaders have also used television, radio, and cyberspace to sensationalize events that occur in 'First World' and in so-called 'Third World' regions. The elite orchestrate the events to play upon the fears, emotions, and concerns of their audience. Not only does the politicized spectacles enable them to sell, market, and promote goods and services to customers who are emotionally drawn to the images, slogans, and sound bites generated in newscasts, podcasts and talk radio shows, but they enable them to lull the public to support initiatives and practices bent on controlling labor power and extracting resources across the global landscape. For instance, the Bush administration preyed upon the fear generated by the 9/11 terrorist attacks on US soil by not only launching "The War on Terror" against Muslim people in the Middle East, but also by generating opportunities for private companies to take part in ventures that either supplied weapons, provided services, extracted oil abroad, or provided services or equipment for the $200 billon homeland security industry, which was supposedly created after September 11, 2001 to eliminate evil abroad and eradicate terror at home (Klein, 2007, p. 12).

Just as the business, academic, and government leaders during the Victorian Era used the world's fairs as media vehicles to garner support from fairgoers by trivializing and demonizing the Other, today's elite control television and radio airwaves and large portions of cyberspace to configure Muslim people in the Middle East as fantastical terrorists who can only be repelled from committing additional acts of violence on US soil by the presence of US's imperial armed forces in the Middle East.

The corporately-sponsored media in the United States has ensured that the general populous in the US believe US military forces have the power to rid the world of Muslim terrorists because it configures the US military as an altruistic organization designed to liberate people who are shackled under oppressive dictatorships, such as the Afghanistan people living under the draconian Taliban regime (McLaren & Jaramillo, 2007). Therefore, the US mainstream media has given a new face to the form of imperialism promoted by US political and economic leaders. There is no need to hide their interest in extricating a country's labor power, oil, or resources, when the US media effectively placates "the public's ontological anxiety about feeling vulnerable to terrorist attacks and sustains the image of the United States as global savior and purveyor of freedom and liberty" (McLaren & Jaramillo, 2007, p. 69). Consequently, the media's manipulation has culled support for the US government to "go ye forth into the world as Christian soldiers to bring God, freedom, and free market capitalism to the heathens around the world" (Kincheloe, 2006, p. XV). Indeed, this is witnessed most recently in President Obama's continuation of the US's "War on Terror" in Afghanistan, as he has called for additional 40,000 US troops to engage in imperial politics, the rearranging of the map and its (the Middle Eastern) people to serve Washington's interests (Smith, 2009).

Political and economic supporters of neoliberalism have also utilized dominant media outlets to generate inaccurate and sensational accounts of dispossessed populations in the United States. The spectacles are designed to convince the US populace that the social and economic maladies present in North America are result of an individual's lack of intelligence or motivation to succeed, deficit in character, or a lack of family values, rather than stemming from the inherent injustice in an economic system based upon greed and exploitation. These politicized spectacles have blocked many US's citizens from seeing the structural dynamics behind poverty, unemployment, and joblessness. They feel that impoverished, unemployed, and elderly citizens are "unnecessary burden on state coffers" and ought to be "consigned to fend for themselves" (Giroux, 2006, para. 23). For instance, supporters of "bootstrap" capitalism vilified and blamed impoverished African Americans, the elderly, and impoverished members of the dominant culture for their trauma and for the devastation that uncoiled during Hurricane Katrina. Ewscasters, newspaper columnists, and right-wing talk show hosts across the United States created spectacles of the disaster, replete with images of impoverished African Americans, supposedly to illustrate that they used event as an opportunity to steal property, commit acts of violence, and sell drugs. The media's untrue horror stories of African American "'wildings' gang-raping women and children, looting stores of liquor and drugs, shooting at ambulances, police patrols, and rescue helicopters, and throwing the city into a vortex of violence and anarchy" (McLaren & Jaramillo, 2007, p. 9) were similar to how neoliberal supporters in the 1980s generated media spectacles out of the images of the young black male "gansta" and the black female "welfare queen." By creating sensationalized and racist portraits of black citizens, US politicians and business leaders inculcated members of the dominant society to believe that minoritized citizens were to blame for social and economic ills. The public's fear and hatred of the Other made them ripe to support neoliberal policies, such as the need to dismantle "the welfare state, ushering in an era of unprecedented deregulation, downsizing, privatization, and regressive taxation" (Giroux, 2006).

To gain footholds in areas of life that were once considered social goods until the late-20th century, the ruling elite has, once again, utilized the media to gain public support for its profit-making agenda. For example, Hursh (2008) notes that since No Child Left Behind Policy was enacted in 2001, US politicians have enacted debilitating discourses in media outlets to make the public fear that the US will "lose jobs to economically competitive countries," unless its public school system enacts commercialized pedagogies and arrangements, such as high-stakes testing, scripted curriculum, accountability measures, vouchers, and charter schools. Unfortunately, the power of media-generated discourses blocks the public from recognizing that the implementation of commercialized practices in US schools has no power to prevent corporate leaders from outsourcing labor, corporate practices, and corporate logics from North America to so called "Third World" regions, where US multinational corporations find cheaper sources of labor, often in the form of young women and impoverished working-class citizens, to manufacture products or to sell services (Hart-Landsberg, 2002).

What has been left out of politicized characterization of NCLB is that the legislation has further exacerbated the marginalization of students who are oppressed on the structural axes of race and class. For example, this legislation is responsible for some of the most qualified teachers leaving urban schools because they are forced to implement "drill and kill" curriculum to help ensure their students and schools do well on corporately-produced standardized examinations, for more and more urban students failing to graduate on time or dropping out of school entirely, and for creating militarized school zones, where army recruiters are given free rein to cajole minority and poor students, who are desperate for funds to attend college, to join the imperial armed forces (Kozol, 2007; Mathison & Ross, 2008; McLaren & Jaramillo, 2007). The politicized reports of NCLB also fail to highlight the "real winners" of the implementation of NCLB: corporations. For the past several years, corporations have acquired the power to provide textbooks, test preparation services and materials, curriculum guides for schools, to take taxpayers' dollars to run charter schools, and to hire test polluted, high school graduates who are blinded from thinking about how the world functions outside of the orbit of social relations predicated on greed and on inequity (McLaren, 2005). Currently, the Obama administration is espousing that implementing commercialized policies and practices in schools will keep jobs in North America and will eliminate the opportunity gaps that plague the US's educational system. President Obama "has used the fiscal emergency and executive discretionary funds to bludgeon states into expanding the number of charter schools" and has supported high-stakes testing to improve the educational performance of youth as well as improve the performance of teachers in US schools (Hursh, 2009, para. 1).

CONSTRUCTING NEW REALITIES AND IDENTITIES: COUNTER-HEGEMONIC MOVEMENTS TO CHALLENGE SPECTACLE-BASED DOMINATION

Like the women's groups, African Americans, and other working-class fairgoers who succeeded in infiltrating their counter-message during the turn of the last century World's Fairs, some youths, teachers, and activists have found emancipatory fissures amid the neoliberal status quo. They have generated alternative formations and narratives to challenge the hidden agendas girding modern-day political and economic spectacles as well as policies and practices responsible for today's increasingly morally bankrupt world. For instance, over the past two years, thousands of students, teachers, and teacher educators have "rallied against racism in Jena, LA" (Au, 2007/2008) as well as staged walkouts in schools to end the economic exploittation of over 11 million illegal immigrants who serve as cheap source of labor for US business leaders (McFadden, 2006). In addition, in opposition to the Iraq War, to the dismantling of public education, and to military recruitment in schools, students and teachers across the US have forged protests, sit-ins and walkouts. For example, recently in Seattle, several hundred demonstrators, organized by Youth Against War and Racism, a student-led group founded by Socialist Alternative, an organization that opposes "the global capitalist system," halted traffic and forced a military recruitment center to close for an afternoon, when they targeted former President Bush, racism, the US involvement in Iraq, and big business (Iwasaki, 2007).

Many other teachers and teacher educators across the US, who have witnessed firsthand how corporate-driven mandates have taken the joy out of teaching and learning, and consequently, positioned marginalized youth into "mindless little robots" (Kozol, 2007, para. 6), have initiated social justice and study groups and have held "strategy talks about resisting standardized testing and pacing guides. They are no longer looking for ways to teach between the cracks of scripted curriculum. They are putting the scripts down and writing their own" (Au, 2007/2008, para. 7). Outside of the classroom, groups of public school educators, like New York Collective of Radical Educators (NYCoRE), have "worked with community, parent, and student organizations" ("New York Core," 2008). They have attempted to bring about social justice and equity in schools by developing curricula, holding events, and launching workshops, which collectively have educated teachers and the public about how neoliberal policies, such as high-stakes examinations, military recruitment, and zero-tolerance initiatives, as well as racism, sexism, and homophobia hinder the social and academic development of K-12 students.

Other educators and activists have brought awareness to the hidden political and economic agendas driving the creation of spectacles. For instance, they have connected how the Olympic Games foster some of the same values as globalization, "including winning at any price, commercial exploitation by MNCs (multinational companies), intense national rivalry, cronyism, cheating and corruption and the competitive advantage of advanced nations" (Milton-Smith, 2002, p. 131). An excellent example of how activists and community members have brought awareness to the deleterious impact of the corporatized spectacles occurred recently in Vancouver. Anti-Olympic organizers and other concerned citizens of Vancouver joined the Olympic Tent Village, the people who were criminalized by police officials and lost their homes due to large-scale gentrification of Downtown Vancouver. The groups held rallies, organized speakers, and held protests to oppose consumerism, militarism, and criminalization of the poor as well as to demand the state to provide adequate shelter and food to all citizens. The progressive citizens have also called for corporations to halt the continued appropriation of First Nation's land and resources and for concerned citizens to engage in acts of civil disobedience to halt the military and corporate takeover of the Olympics and other segments of daily life (Tent Village Voice, 2010).

Clearly, the cultural work generated by teachers, youth, and social activists to eradicate corporate imperatives in US schools, and to stop "The US from invading more countries" (McLaren & Jaramillo, 2007, p. 56), are important for ameliorating some of the deleterious effects emanating from the hegemony of neoliberal globalization. However, social movements formulated to eliminate a particular form of injustice or a specific set of unjust policies or practices are not capable of building sustained institutional arrangements, which are predicated on building life forms resting upon the ideals of equity, love, justice, and fairness. To build a new social world free of oppression, concerned citizens', teachers', and activists' cultural work must attempt to eliminate neoliberal capitalism, since it's *the raison d'être* behind the proliferation of social maladies and institutional forms of oppression pervading social contexts across the globe. Neoliberal capitalism is also responsible for "a crisis of overproduction, a crisis of legitimacy of democratic governance, and a crisis of overextension that has dangerously depleted the world's material resources" (McLaren & Jaramillo, 2007, p. 47).

Just as many railroad workers, coal miners, and lumberjacks in the US at the turn of the 20th century forged social movements to overturn the economic system that was at the root cause of social inequalities, some working-class citizens across the globe have spoken out and taken action to free the world from capitalists' social relations. For example, several hip-hop artists have been vociferous in naming neoliberal capitalism as the culprit behind the suffering and oppression spanning the global landscape as well as trenchant in their support of a socialist universe. Oakland-based hip-hop artist, Boots Riley, of the Coup, has followed in the footsteps of former Oakland Black Panther activists. Since the early-1990s, he has been involved in organizing youth to vote, spearheading movements to eliminate racism in schools, and joining labor unions to fight for a living wage in various service-oriented industries. He has also been a firm advocate for building movements to provide a socialist alternative to capitalism. Not coincidently, he has spoken out against US imperialist military incursions in Iraq, and has problematized the "obscure provision of the No Child Left Behind Act that forces public schools to supply high school students' names and private contact information to military recruiters" ("Boots Riley of the Coup," 2006, para. 2). He believes that "Public schools can't, out of one side of their mouth, tell students that they want them to have a bright future after high school and out of the other side of their mouth tell them that it's okay for them to go kill and die for a profit-making war machine" ("Boots Riley of the Coup," 2006, para. 3).

On a global scale, several hip-hop and punk pedagogues have similarly expressed their rage and built a worldwide movement against the unjust by products emanating from neoliberalism such as racism, classism, police brutality, homelessness, unemployment, political prisoners, imperialism and corporate control of knowledge. They have used the same technology employed by the elite to engender structured, coded, and predetermined sense of reality for citizens, to "create alterative spaces that can attack and subvert the established culture" (Best & Kellner, 1999, para. 66). For example Rap Conscient (2008) is a French website that highlights the music, lyrics, and videos of rap and punk pedagogues who link global capitalism to suffering and environmental degradation across the globe. The site also provides information on other global social activists and groups who are committed to building a society free from repressive globalist capitalist relationships.

Outside of the virtual realm, youth also get beyond the fragmenting and isolating tendencies that "exist within today's mediated and representational social world" (Vinson, Ross, & Wilson, this volume) by forming alternative communities. The social contexts are committed to promoting shared power relationships and embracing the values of democracy, justice, fairness and equity. For instance, some punk pedagogues have launched Temporary Autonomous Zones (TAZs) where they support each other socially and intellectually in order to develop collective identities and design revolutionary pedagogies. These alternative social sites illustrate the power we have to "live, interact, and establish human relationships, tactics, and a DIY (Do It Yourself) praxis. They defy global-capitalist hegemony" generally as well as challenge the elite defining our reality through political and economic spectacles specifically (Malott & Carrol-Miranda, 2003).

CALLING TEACHER EDUCATORS AND SOCIAL STUDIES TEACHERS: RESUSCITATING SOCIAL STUDIES VIA CRITICAL LITERACY PROJECTS

Through our critical reading of the US world's fairs of the late-19th and early-20th centuries, we find that US political, academic, and political leaders were able to lull most of the US populous to embrace their worldview, imperialist pursuits for creating an overseas empire, and a new industrial age. Their agenda led to the exploitation of workers, intensification of poverty, and an extraction of wealth and resources from dependant territories in the Pacific, in Latin America, in Asia, and Western lands of North America. As our social world has increasingly become defined by consumerism, technology, consumption, and the visual image, more and more people fail to see how the construction and consumption of political and economic spectacles have been instrumental in the economic and cultural domination of various people across the globe. For instance, in the United States, neoliberal policies and practices have undermined the ability of workers to unionize, reduced workers' benefits, gutted social programs and entitlements for the impoverished and elderly, intensified the workday, and fueled mass incarceration of minoritized populations, while concomitantly aiding and abetting the country's richest families in their quest to concentrate their wealth and power (Crow & Albo, 2005; McLaren, 2005; Nolan & Anyon, 2004; Scipes, 2007). Outside Western nations, the ruling elites' pro-capitalist agreements and organizations have pushed more and more working peoples to live in the throes of poverty, pollution, and hopelessness. Since their labor-power is often worthless from the boss' perspective, they are often left with grim prospects, such as "selling their organs, working the plantations or mines, or going into prostitution" (McLaren, 2005, p. 5). The political and economic leaders' drive to conquer the world's resources, labor power and privatize life is also responsible for America's "War on Terror," which has left over one million Iraqi men, women, and children dead, and left thousands of US soldiers as capitalism's "collateral damage."

The Neoliberal ordering of schooling is the key reason why the social studies are failing to provide youth in North America a rigorous examination of past historical events. The growing intensification associated with preparing K-12 students to pass an array of corporate-generated examinations leaves social studies educators without the time, opportunity or knowledge to guide students to possess a critical perspective of how social and economic institutions function at today's sociohistorical moment, of how power mediates their lived experiences and social relationships, and of how political, economic, and academic leaders configure cultural texts to propagate their interests and worldviews and to stymie oppositional thoughts or movements capable of challenging their privileged positions. We believe our critical examination of US Victorian World's Fairs and modern-day political and economic spectacles provides direction to K-12 teachers and teacher educators, particularly individuals, such as those mentioned above, who are committed to resisting corporate and government mandates to help learners "challenge disciplinary borders, to create a borderland where new hybridized identities might emerge, to take up in a problematic way the relationship between language and experience, and to appropriate knowledge as part of a broader effort at self-definition and ethical responsibility" (Giroux, 1997, p. 176). It will help them guide our youths to "read the word and the world" and understand the importance of struggling against the globalization of capital. [4]

We now call on other teacher educators and social studies teachers to provide similar critical readings of the past and a reflexive understanding of how technology, consumerism, knowledge, and the mass media merge together at the present to formulate the "society of the spectacle." This will resuscitate social studies education, untangling the discipline from perpetuating the status quo. It will finally become a pedagogical cornerstone of guiding youths to become agents of change and social transformation.

NOTES

[1] As Hoganson (2002, p. 11) notes, it is only in recent years that scholars have critically assessed the cultural work put forth by white middle-class women suffragists during the Victorian era. These women frequently tapped racist rhetoric to make their case that they should be given the right to vote. Not only did they argue they were more "qualified" to vote than men of color, but they aligned themselves with the "colonizing objectives of the state and claim[ed] power on the basis of race, class, and nationality." Many White bourgeoisie women also supported the imperialistic and industrial policies developed by economic and political elite leaders in the United States because their families had an economic stake in America becoming a modern industrial overseas empire. They were also complicit in supporting "US commercial empire and expansion" through purchasing goods from US overseas markets (Hoganson, 2002, p. 60). By decorating their homes with goods produced across the globe, white middle-class women were able to "convey their economic standing" and their unearned power to connect with the wider world (Hoganson, p. 61).

[2] The term "minoritized" is borrowed from Solomon et al. (2005, p. 166) to document that whites "are a member of a racial group [;] however their racialization affords them benefits that are seldom available to minority groups."

[3] Please see Best & Kellner (1999) to examine how Guy Debord and the Situationist International came to examine the impact of consumer-oriented capitalism, seeped in the production images, commodities, and slogans, on social life in Post World War II France. Since Debord disbanded the Situationist International during the 1970s, there has only been a proliferation of political and economic spectacles in the Western world, which collectively impact how people in Western societies perceive the Other, constitute their own identities, and make sense of the events that transpire inside and outside their own social worlds.

[4] We would like to thank E. Wayne Ross and Abraham Deleon for their suggestions in relation to how conceptualize the role modern spectacles play in promoting passive citizenship, in promulgating neoliberal policies and practices in all areas of social life, and in rewriting history in ways that marginalize critical social studies education in K-12 schools and in schools of education.

REFERENCES

Au, W. (2007/2008). Editorial: Winds of change. *Rethinking Schools Online, 22*(2). Retrieved July 31, 2008, from http://www.rethinkingschools.org/archive/22_02/edit222.shtml

Blee, L. (2005). Completing Lewis and Clark's westward march: Exhibiting a history of empire at the 1905 Portland World's Fair. *Oregon Historical Quarterly.* http://www.historycooperative.org/journals/ohq/106.2/blee.html

Badger, R. R. (1979). *The great American fair: The world's Columbian Exposition & American culture.* Chicago: Nelson-Hall.

Best, S., & Kellner, D. (1999). *Debord, cybersituations, and the interactive spectacle.* Retrieved November 23, 2009, from http://www.drstevebest.org/Essays/DebordCybersituations.htm

Berman, G., Brooks, R., & Davidson, S. (2000). The Sydney Olympic Games announcement and Australian stock market reaction. *Applied Economics Letters, 7*, 781–784.

Boots Riley of The Coup schedules a series of politically-charged speaking dates! (2006, March 15). Retrieved July 31, 2008, from http://www.epitaph.com/news/news/2544

Billings, A. (2007). From diving boards to pole vaults: Gendered athlete portrayals in the "BigFour" sports at the 2004 Athens Summer Olympics. *Southern Communication Journal, 72*(4), 329–344.

Byrne, N. (2002, Summer). In Iran, it's called progress. *Middle East Quarterly, 9*(3), 38.

Case, P., & Clark, R. (1997). Four purposes of citizenship education. In R. Case & P. Clark (Eds.), *The Canadian anthology of social studies* (pp.1–2). Vancouver, Canada: Pacific Educational Press.
Crow, D., & Albo, G. (2005). Neoliberalism, NAFTA, and the state of the North American labor movements. *Just Labour, 12*(6 &7), 12–21.
Cruickshank, R. (2009). Distinction, spectacle and symbolic violence in *journal du dehors and la vie exterieure*. *Nottingham French Studies, 48*(2), 80–93.
Dei, G. (2008). Equity and the economics of schooling in the context of a neo-liberal educational agenda. In B. Porfilio & C. Malott (Eds.), *The destructive path of neoliberalism: An international examination of urban education* (pp. 195–210). Rotterdam: Sense Publishers.
Downey, D. B. (2002). *A season of renewal: The Columbian Exposition and Victorian America*. Westport, CT: Praeger.
Ely, S. (2008). Circus in China. *New Presence: The Prague Journal of Central European Affairs, 11*(2), 35–37.
Fojas, C. (2005). American cosmopolis: The World's Columbian exposition and Chicago across the Americas. *Comparative Literature Studies, 42*(2), 267–287.
Freire, P. (1998). *Pedagogy of freedom*. Lanham, MD: Roman & Littlefield.
Frisch, M. (2001). Prismatics, multivalence, and other riff on the millennial moment: Presidential address to American Studies Association, 13 October 2000. *American Quarterly, 53*(2), 193–231.
Giroux, H. A. (1997). *Pedagogy and the politics of hope: Theory, culture, and schooling*. Boulder, CO: Westview Press.
Giroux, H. A. (2004). *The terror of neoliberalism: Authoritarianism and the eclipse of democracy*. New York: Paradigm Publishers.
Giroux, H. A. (2006). The politics of disposability. *Dissent Voice* (September 1, 2006). Retrieved on July 31, 2008, from http://www.henryagiroux.com/online_articles/Pol_Disposibility.htm
Hart-Landsberg, M. (2002). Challenging neoliberal myths: A critical look at the Mexican experience. *Monthly Review, 54*(7). Retrieved on July 31, 2008, from http://www.monthlyreview.org/1202hartlandsberg.htm
Hern, M., & Johal, A. (2009, December 16). Ten reasons to holler profanities at the television in February. *ZNET*. Retrieved February 17, 2009, from http://www.zcommunications.org/ten-reasons-to-holler-profanities-at-the-television-in-february-by-matt-hern
Hoganson, K. (2001). "As badly off as the Filipinos": U.S. women suffragists and the imperial issue at the turn of the twentieth century. *Journal of Women's History, 13*(2), 9–33.
Hoganson, K. (2002). Cosmopolitan domesticity: Importing the American Dream, 1865–1920. *The American Historical Review, 101*(1), 55–83.
Hursh, D. (2008). Raising false fears: Hijacking globalization to promote neoliberal education policies. In B. Porfilio & C. Malott (Eds.), *The destructive path of neoliberalism: An international examination of urban education* (pp. 23–40). Rotterdam: Sense Publishers.
Hursh, D. (2009). Obama's educational polices: More of the same. Retrieved November 3, 2009, from http://warner.rochester.edu/blog/warnerperspectives/?p=295
Iwasaki, J. (2007). High school students march against the Iraq war. *Seattlepi.com/*. Retrieved November 16, 2007, from http://seattlepi.nwsource.com/local/340003_peace17.html
Johnson, E. C. (2007). Critical literacy and the social studies methods course: How pre service social studies teachers learn and teach for critical literacy. *Social Studies Research and Practice, 2*(2). Retrieved July 31, 2008, from http://socstrp.org/issues/PDF/2.2.1.pdf
Kellner, D. (2007). *Globalism, terrorism, and democracy: 9/11 and Its aftermath*. New York: Springer.
Kincheloe, J. (2006). Foreword. In P. McLaren (Ed.), *Life in schools: An introduction to critical pedagogy and the foundations of education*. Boston: Allyn and Bacon.
Kincheloe, J. (2001). *Getting beyond the facts: Teaching social studies/social sciences in the twenty-first century* (2nd ed.). New York: Peter Lang.
Klein, N. (2007). *The shock doctrine: The rise of disaster capitalism*. New York: Metropolitan Books.
Knight, J., & Giuliano, T. (2003). Blood, sweat, and jeers: The impact of the media's heterosexist portrayals on perceptions of male and female athletes. *Journal of Sport Behavior, 26*(3), 272.
Kornfeld, J. (1998). Melting the glaze: Exploring student to responses to liberatory social studies. *Theory into Practice, 37*(4), 306–313.

Kozol, J. (2007). Why I am fasting: An explanation to my friends. *The Huffington Post.* Retrieved July 31, 2008, from http://www.huffingtonpost.com/jonathan-kozol

Liebhold, P., & Rubenstein, H. (1998). *Between a rock and a hard place: A history of American sweatshops, 1820-present.* http://historymatters.gmu.edu/d/145

Malott, C., & Miranda-Carol, J. (2003). Punkore scenes as revolutionary pedagogy. *Journal of Educational Policy Studies, 1*(2). Retrieved June 1, 2007, from http://www.jceps.com/index.php?pageID=article&articleID=13

Marling, K. A. (1992). Writing history with artifacts: Columbus at the 1893 Chicago Fair. *The Public Historian, 14*(4), 13–30.

Mathison, S., & Ross, E. W. (Eds.). (2008). *The nature and limits of standards-based reform and assessment.* New York: Teachers College Press.

McCallum, K., Spencer, A., & Wyly, E. (2005). The city as an image-creation machine: A critical analysis of Vancouver's Olympic bid. *Yearbook of the Association of Pacific Coast Geographers, 67,* 24–46.

McFadden, R. D. (2006, April 12). Across the United States, growing immigration rallies. *International Herald Tribune.* Retrieved August 4, 2008, from http://www.iht.com/articles/2006/04/10/america/web.0410.march.php

McLaren, P. (in press). THIN PEDAGOGY (Imitator of an Imitator): Response to Ellison. *Educational Theory.*

McLaren, P. (2008). Capitalism's bestiary: Rebuilding urban education. In Brad J. Porfilio & C. Malott (Eds.), *The destructive path of neoliberalism: An international examination of urban education* (pp. vii–xvi). Rotterdam: Sense Publishers.

McLaren, P., & Jaramillo, N. (2007). *Pedagogy and praxis in the Age of Empire.* Rotterdam: Sense Publishers.

McLaren, P. (2005). *Capitalists and conquerors: A critical pedagogy against empire.* New York: Roman and Littlefield.

Milton-Smith, J. (2002). Ethics, the Olympics and the search for global values. *Journal of Business Ethics, 35*(2), 131–142.

New York Core. (2008). Retrieved August 4, 2008, from http://www.nycore.org/

No2010.com. (2009). *Anti-2010: Information against the Olympic industry.* Retrieved February 15, 2010, from http://no2010.com/Resources/Anti-2010%20Booklet.pdf

Nolan, K., & Anyon, J. (2004). Learning to do time: Willis's model of cultural reproduction in an era of postindustrialism, globalization, and mass incarceration. In N. Dolby, & G. Dimitriadis (Eds.), *Learning to labor in new times* (pp. 133–150). New York: Routledge.

O'Conner, K. A., Heafner, T., & Groce, E. (2007). Advocating for social studies: Documenting for the decline and doing something about it. *Social Education, 71*(5), 255–260.

Of mutual benefit: Women's exchange helps employers and employees. (1901, August 20). *Buffalo Express,* p. 3.

Osborne, L. B., & Virga, V. (Eds.). (2003). *A small nation of people: W.E.B. Du Bois & African American portraits of progress.* New York: The Library of Congress.

Pepchinski, M. (2000). *The women's building and the world's exhibitions: Exhibition architecture and conflicting feminine ideals of European and American world's exhibitions, 1873–1915.* Retrieved July 31, 2008, from http://www.tu-cottbus.de/Theo/Wolke/eng/Subjects/001/Pepchinski/pepchinski.htm

Porfilio, B., & Malott, C. (2008). Introduction: The neoliberal social order. In B. Porfilio & C. Malott (Eds.), *The destructive path of neoliberalism: An international examination of urban education* (pp. xvii–xxiii). Rotterdam: Sense Publishers.

Porfilio, B., & Hall, J. (2005). Power city politics and the building of a corporate school. *Journal for Critical Education Policy Studies, 3*(1). Retrieved August 26, 2008, from http://www.jceps.com/index.php?pageID=article&articleID=38

Religious restrictions tightened ahead of Olympics: Youth trained to condemn Dalai Lama. (2008). *Tibetan Review: The Monthly Magazine on all Aspects of Tibet, 43*(3), 5.

Rydell, R. W. (1981). The trans-Mississippi and international exhibitions: "To work out the problem of universal civilization." *American Quarterly, 33*(5), 587–607.

Rydell, R. W. (1983a). *All the world's a fair: Visions of empire at American international expositions, 1876–1916.* Chicago: The University of Chicago Press.

Rydell, R. W. (1983b). Visions of empire: International exhibitions in Portland and Seattle, 1905–1908. *The Pacific Historical Review, 52*(1), 37–65.

Rydell, R. W., Findling, J. E., & Pelle, K. D. (2000). *Fair America: World's fairs in the United States.* Washington DC: Smithsonian Institute Press.

Rydell, R. W., & Kroes, R. (2005). *Buffalo Bill in Bologna: The Americanization of the world, 1869–1922.* Chicago: University of Chicago Press.

Saunois, T. (2006, June 29). Latin America in revolt against neoliberalism. *Socialistworld.net.* Retrieved July 31, 2008, from http://socialistworld.net/eng/2006/06/29latam.html

Scipes, K. (2007). Neo-liberal economic policies in the United States: The impact on American workers. *ZNET.* Retrieved June 1, 2007, from http://www.zmag.org/content/print_article.cfm?itemID=12018&sectionID=1

Shor, I. (1999). What is critical literacy? *The Journal of Pedagogy, Pluralism & Practice, 4*(1). Retrieved June 3, 2007, from http://www.lesley.edu/journals/jppp/4/index.html

Simpson, C. (2010, January 11). Olympic countdown: Interview with 2010 Watch's Christopher Shaw. *This Magazine.* Retrieved February 10, 2009, from http://this.org/magazine/2010/01/11/olympics-christopher-shaw-no2010/comment-page-1/

Smith, W. (2009). It's Obama's war and his tactics are criminal and his tactics are making us less safe. Retrieved December 8, 2009, from http://www.opednews.com/articles/It-is-Obama-s-war-and-his-by-winston-091209-283.html

Solomon, R. P., Portelli, J. P., Daniel, B.-J., & Campbell, A. (2005). The discourse of denial: How white teacher candidates construct race, racism and "white privilege". *Race Ethnicity and Education, 8*(2), 147–169.

Spivak, L. (2005). The Conservative marketing machine. *AlterNet* (January 11, 2005). Retrieved July 31, 2008, from http://www.alternet.org/mediaculture/20946/?page=2

Stevens, L. P., & Bean, T. W. (2007). *Critical literacy: Context, research and practice in the K-12 classroom.* New York: SAGE Publications.

The Tent Village Voice. (2010, February 20). *Newsletter of the Olympic Tent Village: Issue 1.* Retrieved February 26, 2010, from http://olympictentvillage.files.wordpress.com/2010/02/village-voice-issue1-final2.pdf

Thompson, D. (2008). Beijing Olympics: More at stake than gold medals. *China Business Review, 35*(1), 40–44.

Trafficking of women is a health issue. (2006, June). *Lancet,* 1954.

Tuggle, C., Huffman, S., & Rosengard, D. (2002). A descriptive analysis of NBC's coverage of the 2000 Summer Olympics. *Mass Communication & Society, 5*(3), 361–375.

Vinson, K., Ross, E., & Wilson, M. (2009). "The concrete inversion of life": Guy Debord, the spectacle, and critical social studies education. In A. P. DeLeon & E. W. Ross (Eds.), *Critical theories, radical pedagogies, and social education: Towards new perspectives for social studies education.* Rotterdam: Sense Publishers.

Whitelegg, D. (2000). Going for gold: Atlanta's bid for fame. *International Journal of Urban & Regional Research, 24*(4), 801–817.

Women of other lands: Several nations represented at council conference. (1901, August 22). *Buffalo Express,* p. 3.

Women workers meet: Many interesting speeches at opening session. (1901, August 28). *Buffalo Express,* p. 3.

Women workers: National League to meet here in August. (1901, July 8). *Buffalo Express,* p. 3.

Brad J. Porfilio
Lewis University

Michael Watz
Buffalo State College, SUNY

DAVID HURSH

8. THE LONG EMERGENCY

*Educating for Democracy and Sustainability during
Our Global Crisis*

If one of the goals of social studies is to enable students to think about the relationship between the individual and society, and what society should look like, then we in the United States have failed miserably. The dominant approach to social studies seems to have been the assumption that we live in the best of all possible worlds, the political system and capitalism for the most part works or at least is better than any alternative, and that at most a little tweaking is all that is necessary to improve our world.

However, I will argue, if we and much of the world are to survive very far into the future, if we are to live on a planet similar to the one on which we now live, we must radically transform our economic system, the impact we have on the environment, and the ways in which we relate to and care for one another (McKibben, 2006; Orr, 2009; Speth, 2008). We must also radically transform how we teach the social studies so that real questions about our environmental and our political future become central to the curriculum, and that social studies become central to an interdisciplinary approach to examining social and environmental problems.

Therefore, I begin this chapter by arguing that we face two monumental crises, one environmental and one economic, that, because they are inescapably intertwined, must be confronted together. Moreover, crises that are specific to each, such as the environmental crises regarding food, energy, global warming, and the political crises regarding global trade, and the rise of individualism and the decline of the common good, are also all intertwined in such a way that tackling any one issue necessarily leads to the others. Consequently, I suggest that because the crises requires that we rethink our relationship with the environment and with one another, we have no choice but to see our current crises as an opportunity to develop a new understanding of nature and to transform our economic and political systems to reflect the need to provide for the common good.

If we are to accomplish these goals, we need to transform our educational system so that students, teachers, and community members ask the essential question of our time: How are we to create a world that is environmentally and economically sustainable? Responding to this question will require us to rethink the nature of the curriculum and process of learning. We need to admit that the answers to these questions do not exist in textbooks but, instead, students and teachers must be involved in seeking answers to questions that have no one answer, but are open to debate and discussion. Furthermore, schools must play an active role in solving these problems. Fortunately, many students have become interested in food, nutrition and gardening, the risks posed to their families and community from toxins such as pesticides and lead, and proposed and argued for policies that would create a more sustainable community (for examples, see: Hursh, Martina, & Fantauzzo, 2009; Pollan, 2006, 2008; Stone, 2009).

THE LONG EMERGENCY

David Orr (2009) adopts the phrase, "the long emergency," first used by William Howard Kunstler (2005), to argue that even the most optimistic scenarios regarding global warming and its impact on the environment will be catastrophic. Because of nature's positive feedback loops, such as how the warming atmosphere increases melting of the permafrost, thereby releasing increased amounts of methane gas, which adds to global warming, even if we were to immediately eliminate producing green house gases, the effects from our past activities will be with us for centuries (see Archer, 2009). Consequently, writes Orr (2009),

> even if we stop emitting heat-trapping gases quickly; we will still experience centuries of bigger storms, large and more frequent floods, massive heat waves, and prolonged drought, along with rising sea levels, disappearing species, changing diseases, decline of oceans, and radically altered ecosystems. (xii–xiii)

Orr argues that these current and ongoing environmental catastrophes require that we confront not only the question of our relationship to the earth, but also the question of on what basis and process do we make (or avoid) societal and economic decisions. What kind of governing and economic system do we need if we are to live on the earth in way that is sustainable? These two crises—one environmental and one political—compose "the long emergency," an emergency that we cannot eliminate but, at best, only remediate by changing the way we live.

To complicate matters, at the same time that the developed world needs to reduce the amount of green house gases it produces, the developing world needs to shift from its reliance on biomass and coal. A recent United Nations report, Energy Access Situation in Developing Countries (Legros, Havet, Bruce, and Bonjour, 2009), reminds us that two billion people in the developing world still lack natural gas, propane or other modern fuels used for cooking or heating their homes, and 1.5 billion people live entirely without electricity. Those without modern fuels rely typically on wood or dung for fuel, which are often used in unventilated indoor cook stoves that produce smoke and gases that result in numerous illnesses. The same U.N. report notes "two million people die every year from causes associated with exposures to smoke from cooking with biomass and coal." Furthermore, children and adults who rely on biomass are much more likely to die from pneumonia and chronic lung diseases. Consequently, we face the problem of reducing oil and gas use in the developed world while at the same time producing reliable sources of fuel in the developing world.

We also confront an environmental disaster of another kind, one already occurring in cites. Mike Davis, in *Planet of Slums* (2006), describes how more than half the world's population now lives in cities and the poor are concentrated in vast slums on the edge of those cities. The lack of clean water and proper waste disposal is responsible for most of the diseases. Davis quotes public-health expert Eileen Stillwaggon (1998) as stating, "Every day, around the world, illnesses related to water supply, waste disposal, and garbage kill 30,000 people and constitute 75 percent of the illnesses that afflict humanity." (p. 95) Davis adds, "Digestive-tract diseases arising from poor sanitation and the pollution of drinking water—including diarrhea, enteritis, colitis, typhoid, and paratyphoid fevers—are the leading cause of death in the world, affecting mainly infants and small children" (p. 142–143). These diseases are preventable, if we only provided the world's poor with clean water and an effective way of disposing of their waste.

The second crisis, which is political and exacerbates the environmental crises, results from the rise and dominance of neoliberal approaches to politics and economic policies. Neoliberal policies elevate commodities and various markets above all other concerns, thereby making it difficult to consider non-market considerations such as global warming or the common good. The desire for profit dominates all social and economic interactions. Neoliberal policies, which gained global dominance in the 1980s, have, therefore, radically transformed societal institutions, and our economic and interpersonal relationships. Yet, particularly in the United States, the public in general and students in particular are largely unaware of the term neoliberalism, its characteristics, and the consequences neoliberal policies for out own and the planet's welfare.[1]

If we are to understand the dire consequences resulting from neoliberal policies, we need to understand what neoliberalism replaced and its effects on both political and economic decision-making and the way in which people conceive of themselves as individuals and members of society. In the section that follows, then, I briefly describe how neoliberalism replaced social democratic policies and the implications that neoliberalism has for both human welfare and environmental sustainability. And while the social democratic, like neoliberal policies, promoted consumption as a measure of economic health, at least questions regarding the common good and equality could enter the conversation. Under neoliberalism, the pursuit of profit within free markets takes precedence over all other goals.

Neoliberalism has largely replaced social democratic policies, begun in the United States during the administration of Franklin Delano Roosevelt. Social democratic policies, which is what many in the United States think of when hearing the word 'liberal,' built on Keynesian economic policies in which the government shared some responsibility for safeguarding the material conditions—such as welfare, financial regulations, health care, and education—that could enable people to flourish. During the Great Depression, President Roosevelt implemented government spending, taxation, and welfare policies to rebuild the country and to support the military effort in World War II. In 1944 Roosevelt called for a Second Bill of Rights, arguing that freedom demanded that individuals be provided with such basic human needs as a "useful and remunerative job ... a decent home ... medical care ... a good education ... and social security" (Sunstein, 2004, p. 13). The U.S. emerged from the war victorious, but corporations resisted Roosevelt's Second Bill of Rights.

It was never implemented. Nonetheless, after the war, workers, women, and people of color struggled for and were able to extend their personal and political rights to education, housing, healthcare, workplace safety, and the ballot box (Bowles & Gintis, 1986, pp. 57–59).

The early post-war decades were marked by the "historic compromise" between capital and labor by which, in exchange for improving wages, labor consented to capital's right not only to control the workplace but also to capitalist control of investment and growth, primarily through multinational corporations. In part fueled by workers' growing wages, the period was marked by unusually rapid and stable economic growth. The majority of Americans experienced improved standards of living as the middle class expanded and race and gender inequalities decreased (see Hacker, 1993). School desegregation proceeded (*de jure* desegregation, if not always de facto), states expanded public post-secondary education, and workplace safety regulations and welfare benefits improved.

Corporate profits began to fall in the late 1960s due to deficit spending by the federal government (to fund the Vietnam War), the formation of OPEC and rising oil prices (Faux, 2006, p. 82), and the inability of corporations to pass the cost of wage increases on to consumers in the increasingly competitive and open world economy (Parenti, 1999). To restore higher rates of profit, the United States and other developed countries implemented monetarist and neoliberal policies that supported corporations over workers (Gill, 2003). In the United States, monetarist policies restored the power of capital by raising interest rates. This produced a recession that increased job scarcity and deflated wage demands, and reversed gains in social spending. These policies were designed to reduce the standard of living of all but wealthy Americans. Paul Volcker, Federal Reserve Board Chairman in 1979, pushed for a recession, asserting: "The standard of living of the average American has to decline. I don't think you can escape that" (Parenti, 1999, p. 119). Such monetarist policies were soon linked with neoliberal policies such as deregulation, repealing social democratic controls, and elevating the free market above the public interest.

Neoliberalism transforms how we conceptualize the role of government and the relationship between the individual and society. Neoliberalism denounces social democratic liberalism as a recipe for an interventionist government that threatens individual liberty through taxes and other regulations and, instead, neoliberalism promotes personal responsibility through individual choice within markets. Under neoliberalism, the individual is conceived as an autonomous entrepreneur who can always take care of his or her own needs. Lemke (2002) describes neoliberalism as seeking

> to unite a responsible and moral individual and an economic- rational individual. It aspires to construct responsible subjects whose moral quality is based on the fact that they rationally assess the costs and benefits of a certain act as opposed to other alternative acts. (p. 59)

For neoliberals, those who do not succeed are held to have made bad choices. Personal responsibility means nothing is society's fault. People have only themselves to blame. Moreover, the market becomes central within such a conception of the individual.

> Every social transaction is conceptualized as entrepreneurial, to be carried out purely for personal gain. The market introduces competition as the structuring mechanism through which resources and status are allocated efficiently and fairly. The 'invisible hand' of the market is thought to be the most efficient way of sorting out which competing individuals get what. (Olssen et al., 2004, p. 137–138)

Neoliberalism, writes Leitner, Sheppard, Sziarto & Maringanti (2007), replaces the common good and state concern for public welfare with the entrepreneurial individual aiming to succeed within competitive markets. Neoliberal policies favor

> supply-side innovation and competitiveness; decentralization, devolution, and attrition of political governance, deregulation and privatization of industry, land and public services [including schools]; and replacing welfare with 'workfarist' social policies ... A neoliberal subjectivity has emerged that normalizes the logic of individualism and entrepreneurialism, equating individual freedom with self-interested choices, making individuals responsible for their own well-being, and redefining citizens as consumers and clients. (p. 1–2)

Neoliberalism expands on classic liberalism's faith in individual's pursuing their self-interest within markets by reconceptualizing the individual as not merely making choices but as an autonomous entrepreneur responsible for his or her own self, progress and position, responsible for their own success and failure. However, while Thatcher and others, such as the journalist Thomas Friedman (2005; for a critique of Friedman, see Hursh, 2010) claimed that we have no choice but to embrace neoliberalism, neoliberalism has failed to achieve its stated goals of increasing corporate profits, and reducing inequality both within and between countries (Faux, 2006), in addition, neoliberalism has irreparably damaged the environment.

As Robert Brenner (interviewed in Seong-jin, 2009) describes, because little effort has been given to improving most families' income, other than through "trickle-down economics," family incomes failed to increase during the 1980s, therefore dampening demand for consumer products, and, consequently, curbing corporate profits. In an effort to increase profits, the 1990s, the Federal Reserve, lowered interest rates to encourage investments in financial assets and, subsequently, consumers increased their investment in both the stock market and real estate (Seong-jin, 2009). Brenner (Seong-jin, 2009) notes that "housing by itself accounted for one-third of the growth in GDP and close to half of the increase in employment in the years 2001–2005."

Unfortunately, because banks could borrow money so cheaply, "banks were willing to extend loans to speculators, whose investments drove the prices of assets of every type ever higher [and] housing prices soared" (Seong-jin, 2009). At the same time, the profits that could be made on guaranteed loans, such as U.S. treasury bonds, plunged, leading an increasing number of lending institutions to turn to "investments in dubious sub-prime mortgages. The housing bubble reached historic proportions, and the economic expansion was allowed to continue" (Seong-jin, 2009). The ongoing effort to make money readily available for investment in either real estate or stocks led to a rise in housing values and stock prices that could not be sustained. "When housing prices fell, the real economy went into recession and the financial sectors experienced a meltdown" (Seong-jin, 2009). Under neoliberalism, the relentless pursuit for profits ultimately undermined common sense and the economy, resulting in many losing their jobs and/or homes.

The federal government has responded to the financial crisis by providing funds to bail out financial institutions such as Citi Bank and the Bank of America and insurance companies such as AIG that also sought to make money through speculative investments. In response to the significant increase in unemployment, the federal government has also increased funding for projects that will build the infrastructure (roads, railroads, and utilities) and institutions such as schools. Such policies reflect a recognition that implementing some Keynesian democratic economic policies is necessary for the economic system to survive. Brenner (Seong-jin, 2009) remarks that

> Governments today really have no choice but to turn to Keynesianism and the state to try to save the economy. After all, the free market has shown itself totally incapable of preventing or coping with economic catastrophe, let alone securing stability and growth. That's why the world's political elites, who only yesterday were celebrating deregulated financial markets, are suddenly now all Keynesian. But there is reason to doubt that Keynesianism in the sense of huge governmental deficits and easy credit to pump up demand can have the same impact that many expect. (Seong-jin, 2009)

However, Brenner's optimism regarding governments' willingness to replace neoliberalism with social democratic policies may be misplaced. Given that, for example, many of President Obama's financial advisors (Lawrence Summers, Timothy Geithner) are the same individuals whose policies contributed to our current financial collapse, they may well be temporarily adopting some Keynesian polices as a stopgap measure to save major corporations from collapse and capitalism from itself.

Instead, I want to suggest that neoliberal economic policies are dangerous both in terms of their goals—expanding the economy as measured by the gross domestic product and increasing corporate profits—and their process—free markets with an emphasis on individual choice—have damaged the environment, the common good, and the democratic process. We must, therefore find alternative economic and social goals and more democratic decision making processes.

Because neoliberalism prioritizes markets, economic growth, and profit, all other values, such as the environment, are slighted. Moreover, because its only concern is the corporate balance sheet and corporations desire to externalize any environmental costs, such as pollution, to the public, neoliberalism excludes from its calculations damage to ecosystems and the biosphere, and destabilization of the environment.

Such principles are evident when President George W. Bush argued against environmental policies that might limit corporate profits or infringe on corporate prerogatives. Bush, in defending his veto of the Kyoto protocols that would limit carbon emissions, claimed: "I will explain as clear as I can, today and every other chance I get, that we will not do anything that harms the economy ... That's my priority. I'm worried about the economy" (Bush, cited in McKibben, 2006, p. 18). The supposed costs to corporate growth continue to be one of the arguments against policies that may reduce global warming. Furthermore, as I described above, neoliberalism replaces concern for the common good with the entrepreneurial individual aiming to succeed within competitive markets. In the same way that environmental conditions are externalized from economic and political decisions, so are questions regarding the general welfare of society. Problems are to be solved, if they are to be faced at all, through the magic of the marketplace. Deliberation over our values and societal goals are replaced by voting with our dollars.

Consequently, neoliberalism cannot not solve but only exacerbate the environmental and economic problems we face and must be replaced with policies that situate people within the larger environmental system and aim to promote the common good. We need to reinvent democracy so that we deliberate over the issues, educate one another, and develop ways of interacting that result in a fair and sustainable society. We also must create an economic system that focuses not on creating more of the same but, instead, on improving people's quality of life and fairness. If we are to develop a new relationship with nature Bill McKibben, in *Deep Economy: The Wealth of Communities and the Durable Future* (2007), pushes us to rethink our economic principles so that rather than focusing on growth and increasing the Gross Domestic Product, we, instead, focus on improving the quality of our lives, our local communities. How do we measure people's quality of life and how do we develop economies that work towards improving the well being of everyone? What would a different economic system look like?

James Speth, former Dean of Forestry and Environmental Sustainability at Yale, argues that we need "a postgrowth society where what you really want is to grow very specific things that are desperately needed in a very targeted way—you know, care for the mentally ill, health-care accessibility, high-tech green-collar industries" (Goodell, 2008). We will need to substantially rethink democracy, economics, justice, and the very purpose of society, and incorporate new decision-making processes that work toward those goals. While the changes required will ultimately transform how we live in the world, doing any less is likely to result to a degraded society that we all should want to avoid. Therefore, in the remainder of this chapter I suggest that we need to transform our educational system so that students, teachers, and community members ask the essential question of our time: How are we to create a world that is environmentally and economically sustainable?

THE ENVIRONMENTAL CRISIS: THE CHALLENGES OF SUSTAINABILITY

Our educational system currently focuses on preparing students to become economically productive individuals and aims to hold them accountable through high-stakes standardized tests (Hursh, 2008). Consequently, teaching and learning is often reduced to what can be measured on a standardized test, typically in the form of multiple- choice questions. Furthermore, the curriculum has been narrowed, with subjects other than math and English marginalized. Lessons that would teach students to think across disciplines have been largely eliminated (Martina, Hursh, & Moskowitz, 2009).

In contrast, David Orr (1994, 2002) and Bill McKibben (2007) argue that environmental sustainability requires rethinking the purposes of education and society and suggest that our current environmental crisis poses the essential questions of our time. Orr (2002) began a recent book by asking,

> How do we reimagine and remake the human presence on earth in ways that work over the long haul? Such questions are the heart of what theologian Thomas Berry (1999) calls "the Great Work" of our age. This effort is nothing less than the effort to harmonize the human enterprise with how the world works as a physical system and how it ought to work as a moral system. (p. 3)

As Orr suggests, this great work requires that we improve our understanding of our relationship and dependence on nature and, at the same time, grapple with questions regarding the nature of justice and how to transform the political and economic system to create a socially just world. We need to ask: How do we develop a just sustainable world? How we are to live on this planet in a way in which we meet "the needs of the present without compromising the ability of future generations to meet their own needs" (World Commission on Environment and Development, 1987, p. 8)? Moreover, it is not enough to develop a world that is environmental sustainable if most in the global north live comfortably and most in the global south live in poverty (Bello, 2004). We also need ask is how do we create a "just sustainable world." Orr, then, situates environmental studies within ethical, economic, and political contexts and criticizes our current approach to education and politics for failing to take on the "great issues" of our age. Orr quotes Vaclav Havel (1992), the Czech playwright, writer, and politician, who stated that "Genuine politics—politics worthy of the name ... is simply a matter of serving those around us: serving the community, and serving those who will come after us." (p. 6)

We need, then, to engage our students in education in the sense that Havel describes, asking what we need to know if we are to live together, and how can we create political and economic structures that will enable more people to enjoy the rights Roosevelt proposed; healthy neighborhoods, homes, schooling, and meaningful work. Rather than avoiding global warming because it may cause children to be pessimistic about the future, we need to involve students in participating in making the future better, whether it be by recycling, limiting their energy usage, or actively working for change, so that they have a sense of what they can do to shape the future, rather than ignore or fear it.

Michael Stone, in *Smart by Nature: Schooling for Sustainability* (2009), reminds us that:

> young people in school today will inherit a host of pressing—-and escalating—environmental threats of climate change; loss of biodiversity; the

end of cheap energy; depletion of resources; environmental degradation; gross inequities of standards of living; obesity, diabetes, asthma, and other environmentally linked illness. The generation will require leaders and citizens who can think ecologically, understand the interconnected ness between human and natural systems, and have the will, ability, and courage to act. (p. 4)

Figuring out how to develop such a sustainable and just world requires that we develop an interdisciplinary understanding that incorporates global politics and local initiatives, science and ethics, history and technology. Almost every question that we might ask about working towards environmental sustainability connects to other issues: climate, food, energy, diversity, and health are intertwined.

A good example of the interrelatedness of seemingly disparate issues is Michael Pollan's (the author of *The Omnivore's Dilemma* and *In Defense of Food*) argument that if we in the U.S. are to decrease the amount of energy we use, improve people's health, reduce our reliance on fossil fuels, and combat global warming, we need to rethink what we eat. A month before the last presidential election, Pollan's (2008b) open letter to the incoming "Farmer in Chief" outlined his proposal for a new food policy to whomever would be the incoming president. In the article, he argued that because our current agriculture policies subsidize growing corn, soy, wheat, and rice (most of the corn is turned into corn syrup for our soft drinks or feed for livestock) the subsidies make fast food burgers and soft drinks cheap but vegetables and fruit expensive. Consequently, people are more likely to be obese and suffer from illnesses, such as adult onset diabetes. In fact "four of the top killers in America today are chronic diseases linked to diet: heart disease, stroke, Type 2 diabetes, and cancer." Therefore, while our fast food may be cheap, we pay for it with our health and rising medical costs.

In addition, the amount of energy necessary to plant, fertilize, harvest, and ship these crops so that they can be made into foods is significant. In the U.S., the food industry uses more energy than used by people to commute to and from work. Moreover, by subsidizing crops that are grown not for human consumption but for cattle, and are shipped long distances contributes significantly to global warming. In writing about food policy, Pollan interweaves what he has learned about agricultural policies and practices, nutrition, diseases, health care, energy use and global warming and concludes that we must change our food policies if we are to reduce energy use, slow global warming, and improve nutrition and people's health. In fact, he argues that we cannot solve the problem of global warming and our worsening health without confronting our abysmal agricultural policies and developing a new food (rather than agricultural) policy.

Other sustainability issues, such as global warming, energy, and toxins in our environment, require that we develop an interdisciplinary approach that includes rethinking governance and economics. For example, we need to find alternatives to oil, gas, and coal not only because they contribute to global warming, but they also add toxins to the atmosphere. The burning of coal to generate electricity, for example, adds mercury and fine particulates to the atmosphere and contributes in acid rain. Gasoline powered vehicles not only contributes to global warming but add toxins to the air.

Furthermore, while supplies of oil, gas, and coal will not be eliminated in the near future, and "peak oil" may not occur for another decade or two, we face the eminent crisis of demand exceeding supply. We need to figure out how to supply energy through more sustainable resources, how to conserve, and how to organize our society so that we use less energy. We need to rethink out cities, suburbs, and exurbs, and our transportations systems. Solving sustainability issues will require technological, economic, political, and cultural solutions.

EDUCATING FOR AN ECONOMICALLY AND ENVIRONMENTALLY SUSTAINABLE WORLD

The essential question that should be part of the curriculum focuses on how we develop an environmentally sustainable world that is also socially just. How do we create a world in which we meet the needs of the present generation without compromising the needs of the future, in which humans and other living things continue to flourish? If we fail to answer this question, human civilization and the global environment will decline. Consequently, how we develop an environmentally sustainable world that is also just, that treats fairly people, is *the* essential question of our time.

Answering this essential question requires that we take an interdisciplinary approach to examining a wide range of complicated questions that will require our best scientific, philosophical, political, and economic thinking. As I have suggested above, responding to sustainability issues such as global warming, energy use, and food requires rethinking governance, economics, and ethics, including critiquing neoliberalism for the ways in which it diverts us from and undermines our ability to answer these questions. Furthermore, focusing on these questions will require that we rethink our educational systems away from one in which teachers deposit knowledge in students heads while teaching an artificially segregated subject area to one in which students, teachers, and community members actively work to answer questions that are important to both individuals and communities. Students can and must become community resources.

As essential questions, there is no one agreed upon answer to how we develop a just sustainable world (or even whether this is the question we should be asking). What makes sense for one community will be different for another. What makes sense at one time will be different from another. Moreover, there will be differences of opinion in what counts as fair. Such questions promote dialogue between communities and countries and a greater understanding of what people face in order to live healthy and safe lives.

Lastly, I suggest that we are unethical if we are not assisting students in asking and answering questions like these. Rather than thinking about how our students have performed on a standardized test, or whether they have memorized their textbook sufficiently in order to pass an exam, we need to ask whether our students are gaining the skills needed to survive and perhaps prosper during "the long emergency." Students, teachers, and community members can together learn how to pose questions, collect and analyze data, and make decisions for themselves and their community.

In the end we need a new social studies in which students and teachers focus on what they can accomplish together rather than competing as individuals. We need a new social studies in which the status quo is unacceptable and new ways of being in the world are envisioned. In short, we need to rethink social studies so that we can ask the questions necessary to develop a post neoliberal society, one in which we all share in developing and being part of the common good.[2]

NOTES

[1] Recent work on examining the impact of neoliberalism on education includes: Kumar and Hill (2009), Porfilio and Malott (2008), and Ross and Gibson (2007).

[2] The author would like to thank Joe Henderson, Elaina Stover and the students in my doctoral class on teaching environmental sustainability for their assistance on this chapter.

REFERENCES

Archer, D. (2009). *The long thaw: How humans are changing the next 100,000 years of earth's climate*. Princeton, NJ: Princeton University Press.

Bello, W. (2004). *Deglobalization: Ideas for a new world economy*. New York: Zed Books.

Berry, T. (1999). *The great work*. New York: Bell Tower.

Bowles, S., & Gintis, H. (1986). *Democracy and capitalism: Property, community and the contradictions of modern thought*. New York: Basic Books.

Broder, J. M. (2009. December 8). Climate deal likely to bear big price tag. *The New York Times*. Retrieved March 16, 2010, from http://www.nytimes.com/2009/12/09/science/earth/09cost.html

Center for Ecoliteracy. (2009). *Food, Inc. discussion guide*. Retrieved March 16, 2010, from http://www.ecoliteracy.org/ publications/food_inc.html

Davis, M. (2006). *Planet of slums*. New York: Verso.

Faux, J. (2006). *The global class war: How America's bipartisan elite lost our future – and what it will take to win it back*. New York: Wiley.

Friedman, T. L. (2005). *The world is flat: A brief history of the twenty-first century*. New York: Farrar, Straus & Giroux.

Gill, S. (2003). *Power and resistance in the new world order*. New York: Palgrave Macmillan.

Goodell, J. (2008, September/October). Change Everything Now: One of the nation's most mainstream environmentalists says it's time to get a lot more radical. Interview with Gus Speth. *Orion Magazine*. Retrieved March 16, 2010, from http://www.orionmagazine.org/index.php/articles/article/3222/

Hacker, A. (1993). *Two nations: Black and white, separate, hostile*. New York: Ballantine Books.

Hansen, J. (2007, July 28). Climate Catastrophe, *New Scientist, 195*(2614), 30–34.

Harvey, D. (2005). *A brief history of neoliberalism*. Oxford: Oxford University.

Havel, V. (1992). *Summer meditations*. New York: Knopf.

Hursh, D. (2008). *High-stakes testing and the decline of teaching and learning: The real crisis in education*. Latham, MD: Rowman and Littlefield.

Hursh. D. (2010). The world is not flat: Thomas Friedman and neoliberal governmentality. In S. Macrine, P. McLaren, & D. Hill (Eds.), *Critical pedagogy: In search of democracy, liberation and socialism*. New York: Routledge.

Hursh, D., Martina, C. A., & Fantauzzo, M. (2009). Toxins in our environment: health and civic responsibility. In E. Heilman (Ed.), *Social studies and diversity education: What we do and why we do it*. New York: Routledge.

Intergovernmental Panel on Climate Change. (2007). *Intergovernmental panel on climate change fourth assessment report: Summary for policy makers*. Retrieved March 16, 2010, from http://www.ipcc-wg2.org

Kumar, R., & Hill, D. (2009). *Global neoliberalism and education and its consequences*. New York: Routledge.

Legros, G., Havet, I., Bruce, N., & Bonjour, S. (2009). *The energy access situation in developing countries: A review focusing on the least developed countries and Sub-Saharan Africa. UNDP-WHO.* Retrieved March 16, 2010, from http://content.undp.org/go/newsroom/publications/environment-energy/www-ee-library/sustainable-energy/undp-who-report-on-energy-access-in-developing-countries-review-of-ldcs—ssas.en

Leitner, H., Sheppard, E. S., Sziarto, K., & Maringanti, A. (2007). Contesting urban futures: Decentering neoliberalism. In H. Leitner, E. S. Sheppard, & J. Peck (Eds.), *Contesting neoliberalism: Urban frontiers.* New York: Guilford Press.

Lemke, T. (2002). Foucault, governmentality, and critique. *Rethinking Marxism, 14*(3), 49–64.

Martina, C. A., Hursh, D., & Markowitz, D. (2009). Contradictions in educational policy: Implementing integrated problem-based curriculum in a high stakes environment. *Environmental Education Research, 15*(3), 279–297.

McKibben, B. (2006, January 12). The coming meltdown. *New York Review of Books, 53*(1), 16–18.

McKibben, B. (2007). *Deep economy: The wealth of communities and the durable future.* New York: Times Books.

Kunstler, J. H. (2005). *The long emergency: Surviving the end of oil, climate change, and other converging catastrophes of the twenty-first century.* New York: Grove Press.

Olssen, M., Codd, J., & O'Neill, A. M. (2004). *Education policy: Globalization, citizenship and democracy.* Thousand Oaks, CA: Sage.

Orr, D. (1994). *Earth in mind.* Washington, DC: Island Press.

Orr, D. (2002). *The nature of design: Ecology, culture and human intention.* Oxford: Oxford University Press.

Orr, D. (2009). *Down to the wire: Confronting climate collapse.* Oxford: Oxford University Press.

Parenti, C. (1999). Atlas finally shrugged: Us against them in the me decade. *The Baffler, 13*, 108–120.

Pollan, M. (2006). *The omnivore's dilemma: A natural history of four meals.* New York: Penguin.

Pollan, M. (2008). *In defense of food: An eater's manifesto.* New York: Penguin.

Pollan, M. (2008, October 12). An open letter to the farmer in chief. *The New York Times Magazine.* Retrieved March 16, 2010, from http://www.nytimes.com/2008/10/12/magazine/12policy-t.html

Porfilio, B., & Malott, C. (2008). *The destructive path of neoliberalism.* Rotterdam: Sense Publishers.

Ross, E. W., & Gibson, R. (Eds.). (2007). *Neoliberalism and education reform.* Cresskill, NJ: Hampton Press.

Seong-jin, J. (2009, Februrary 7). Overproduction not financial collapse is the Heart of the Crisis: The US. East Asia and the world: Interview with Robert P. Brenner. *The Asia-Pacific Journal.* Available at http://www.japanfocus.org/-Robert-Brenner/3043.

Speth, J.G. (2008). *The bridge at the end of the world: Capitalism, the environment, and crossing from crisis to sustainability.* New Haven, CT: Yale University Press.

Stillwaggon, E. (1998). *Stunted lives, stagnant economies: Poverty, disease and underdevelopment.* New Brunswick, NJ: Rutgers University Press.

Stone, M. K. (2009). *Smart by nature: Schooling for sustainability.* Berkeley, CA: University of California Press.

Sunstein, C. (2004). *The second Bill of Rights: FDR's unfinished revolution and why we need it more than ever.* New York: Basic Books.

World Commission on Environment and Development: *Our Common Future.* (1987). *Our common future.* Retrieved March 16, 2010, from http://www.un-documents.net/wced-ocf.htm

David Hursh
University of Rochester

WILLIAM T. ARMALINE

9. BUILDING DEMOCRACY THROUGH EDUCATION

Human Rights and Civic Engagement

INTRODUCTION

This essay is admittedly written from a particular, though widely shared, subjective standpoint characterized by two fundamental assumptions. First, the US is not, and has never been a truly democratic society, where the needs and desires of everyday people (regardless of race, class, gender, sexuality, and so forth) are reflected ("represented") in and by the state, where most people enjoy equal opportunity to meaningfully participate in the major decisions that will shape their lives and communities. Where the notion of democracy in the US has been handily critiqued elsewhere (see, for example, Parenti, 2007; Domhoff, 2009), I will instead demonstrate the salience of this critique in a brief discussion of the recent (roughly, 2008) economic recession. If nothing else, the recession and state responses to it highlight the inability of everyday people to meaningfully participate in the major political economic decisions that shape their lives. How might education and educators have some role or agency in changing this historically dominant dynamic in the US and elsewhere?

Secondly, in order to build sustainable democratic societies and communities, pedagogical space must be created and protected where students and teachers might safely engage with democratic concepts and praxis. As even Max Weber (Andreski, 2008) warned in his work pointing out the fundamental differences between bureaucratic and democratic forms of human organization at the onset of industrial capitalism, democratic societies cannot flourish and reproduce themselves if people have no experience in or significant exposure to democratic organizations and the "doing" of democracy. In terms of classic theory at the core of critical pedagogy, this fundamental assumption is easily identifiable in the works of Dewey (1938, 1944), and Freire (1970), who conceptualized pedagogical space as having the capacity for horizontal democratic organization, and for "students" and "teachers" (to the extent these should be exclusive categories at all) to develop together as active subjects and agents of fundamental social change. Where theoretical discussions on the socially transformative possibilities of education and educators for various aims of social justice is taken up at length elsewhere (for several examples, see: Darder, Baltodano, & Torres, 2003), this chapter will explore new strategies and inspirations for building and utilizing democratic pedagogical space, namely through re-centering social studies education around human rights praxis.

From a policy perspective, this essay is written in response to continued trends in US public education that simultaneously marginalize public civic education, civic engagement, and space for critical discourse on the *fundamental* assumptions upon which US (and hegemonic global, in terms of political economy) ideologies and social structures are based. Such trends are manifest in the historical corporatization of public schools and in the contemporary standardization movement marked by *No Child Left Behind* legislation (Bowles & Gintis, 1976; Callahan, 1962; Armaline & Levy, 2004), likely to continue relatively unchanged and unchallenged under the Obama Administration and Education Secretary Arne Duncan (Department of Education, "Reauthorization Can't Wait," 9/24/09). We might begin to reclaim social studies for the purpose of popular civic engagement through the employment of human rights as a central subject and object of critical inquiry in public schooling. Specifically, a human rights framework might provide the following in the interest of fundamental reform: (1) a venue through which the substantive nature of "human rights"—invoking critical reflection on the concepts of (for example) humanity, community, and justice can be critically explored as a terrain of political and cultural conflict; (2) via study of the "rights of the child" (for example) students might realize and grapple with their position as plausibly the agents and claimants of inalienable rights, and potentially see themselves as invested in civic engagement and the making of history; (3) as demonstrated in the movement for "human rights cities," human rights discourse is a useful tool to empower local communities to define themselves with some level of autonomy from and resistance to dominant political economic forces and players. Such movements might prove necessary, if not just well received, as local communities all over the country struggle with the effects of the global recession: massive unemployment, persistently high rates of home foreclosure and bankruptcy filings, skyrocketing poverty rates, restricted access to credit, and widespread local and state budget shortfalls—often resulting in massive cuts to public education and social services.

LESSONS FROM THE RECESSION AND BANK BAILOUT

One of the most interesting aspects of the recent credit and mortgage crises, and resulting global recession, is the extent to which many people are confused about the processes through which their own homes, retirement, employment, and life savings instantly vanished. In fact, in April of 2009 on NBC's *Meet the Press*, NPR's *Money Matters* contributors, Adam Davidson and Alex Blumberg discussed how the causes of the crises were particularly complicated, even for trained economic "experts" such as themselves. More importantly, they suggested that there is a certain connection between the inability to explain a Credit Default Swap in under an hour, and the "don't ask don't tell" approach to the bank bailout. Since the public has been essentially excluded from the investigation of large financial firms, and the dialogue over the resultant public welfare payments to failing banks, insurance firms, and large corporations, the state has the option of saying, "just leave it to us, you wouldn't understand."

Of course, we *can* understand—at least some of the important parts. Elements of the story reflect an historical pattern—a land (or other central resource) owning ruling class with control over centralized capital (banks) using their position to maximize, even at the cost of potential system collapse, their political economic exploitation of everyone else. (Sweet!). The collapse of the mortgage market in the US, largely due to aggressive predatory lending in the subprime market and the selling and re-selling of Credit Default Swaps [CDS] to "insure" the risk represented by subprime investments, sent shock-waves throughout global markets. As we now know all too well, the financial products division of American International Group [AIG] and other similar firms claiming to insure volatile financial products had no capital to cover the impossibly risky investments of clients such as Goldman Sachs and similarly large US and EU firms. As one result, global credit came to a halt, and stock prices plummeted for companies across the global landscape that were directly or indirectly financed through big banks, who placed themselves on the hook for massive uninsured debt. As another, banks cut off access to credit for working people, manifesting most obviously in the mafia-inspired rates of return for credit cards. In order to save or salvage their bottom lines, corporations immediately decimated labor through all the typical channels: layoffs, furloughs, gutting benefits and retirement, aggressive attacks on unions and union negotiated contracts, and so forth.

The working and un/underemployed majority are now intimately familiar with the effects of the recession, as banking executives—even those who accepted corporate welfare—continue to receive massive bonuses based on record, tax-payer subsidized (directly or indirectly), quarterly gains. Speaking particularly of the American Midwest, Roger Bybee (2009) describes three notable effects of the recession on American workers (or would-be workers). First, after already suffering a drop in real wages by 18% since 1973, "working families are being hit with the greatest wage-slashing wave since the 1930's" (Bybee, 2009, p. 1). In fact the combination of lost employment, lost income, and increased debt loads has resulted in a surge of personal bankruptcy filings—up one third in 2009 from the previous year. The massive rise in bankruptcies is all the more meaningful when one considers that a significant portion of the surge are Chapter 7 filings (Chapter 7 requires a "means test" post-2005 reforms—so successful Chapter 7 applications indicate serious financial burdens), and filings from those previously earning $100–$300K per year (Murray & Dougherty, 2010). Second, the shift away from a productive base has, to a great extent, cut out the American worker. As production is moved elsewhere, traditionally stable jobs have evaporated, and as capital growth initiatives moved increasingly to the mystical financial sector, workers are implicitly excluded from Wall Street's new casino style methods of wealth production. Third, record housing foreclosure rates continue to decimate the working class, particularly in cities like Pontiac, Michigan where "some 700 families lost their homes to foreclosures in 2008 and the median income for a family is now $31,207 [the national median is $44,334] … The current unemployment rate is 35.2 percent" (Bybee, 2009, p. 2).

Certainly there are many other variables that have, and continue to contribute to our current economic crises: "excessive financialization" following massive bank deregulation over the past 30 years, allowing for capitalists to construct virtual investments rather than produce actual goods for profit (the financial sector represented

2% of corporate profit in 1950, and 27.4% in 2008) (Bybee, 2009; Glasberg & Skidmore, 1997); the exportation of jobs to foreign communities with cheaper labor, little or no regulations or tax, and little union presence; and the marked shift away from the productive base, to a "post-Fordist" service economy. But as previously suggested, we have the ability to understand our current political economic situation, so to speak, as something beyond a "crisis" that connotes something akin to a natural disaster (similarly, see Naomi Klein's (2007) work on "shock doctrine capitalism"). We can reasonably explain a chain of events that reflect tangible decisions made by tangible actors in conceivable contexts.

The state response by the late-term Bush, and Obama Administration is also quite clear: "bail out" the massive banks, insurance firms, and corporations whose risky business threatened their own existence, and the broader neoliberal, supposed "free-market." To date, via TARP, the Fed, and via the Treasury department, the "bail-out" of these financial and corporate organizations have cost the taxpayers an amount estimated in the trillions (Prins, 2009; Bybee, 2009). Though some recipients of bail out funds have repaid portions of their aid, none of the regained wealth seems to be "trickling down" to the general public—as previously demonstrated. In a functional democracy the state, that in theory represents the public electorate, would act in the defense and interest of the lives and rights of the public constituency. The exact opposite is demonstrated in recent policy decisions concerning the bailout and health care reform. Researcher and journalist/author Paul Street (2009) recently compiled a number of public polls that might indicate some level of public interest on these issues: (1) two-thirds of respondents to a 2009 Rasmussen poll thought that "big business and big government work together against the people's interests;" (2) 62% in a 2004 Pew survey believed corporations made too much profit; (3) 64% of those who responded to a CNN poll said they would pay higher taxes to provide for universal health coverage. Though these are anecdotal data, it is worth mentioning this indication of state misrepresentation. How is the state acting in the interest of everyday people on these policy issues? To what extent did people have any say in (or knowledge of) such political economic decisions that went on to affect populations all over the world? Here we should return to the public interpretation of the "crises" and state responses.

Like many teachers, I make every attempt to bring the outside world into the classroom. However, in trying to discuss the economic crises, it becomes immediately apparent that my undergraduate students are completely intimidated by the subject, and lack the "background knowledge" (in their own words) to engage the topic. A majority of those who would speak, often repeated, uncritically, media sound-bites that blamed the crisis on "stupid" or "greedy" consumers who tried to borrow more than they could afford (see, for example, Leonhardt, 2008; Carlson & Cox, 2009). The Wharton School of Business (2009) released a position paper directly contradicting this stance, placing the blame soundly on the practices of de-regulated banks and capital, who engaged in predatory lending and the (re)packaging of risky assets into large investment funds to make record profits in record time. Further, evidence is now relatively clear that banks such as Wells Fargo specifically targeted African Americans in the pushing of subprime mortgages, called "ghetto loans" by bank insiders (Fowell, 2009; Reckard, 2009). Indeed, a great deal of the "subprime mortgage crisis" can be explained as relatively conscious decisions made by tangible actors.

However, it is no surprise that my students (1) believed what they were told by news media; and (2) reflected the understanding of a well socialized consumer: you shouldn't buy more than you can afford, unless it's the late 1990s and everyone on earth—including the state and your credit card companies—tells you to. This brings us back to the recession and bailout. In his colorful expose of the bailout of US banks, Matt Taibbi (2009) makes a crucial point:

> The real question from here is whether the Obama administration is going to move to bring the financial system back to a place where sanity is restored and the general public can have a say in things ... By creating an urgent crisis that can only be solved by those fluent in a language too complex for ordinary people to understand, the Wall Street crowd has turned the vast majority of Americans into non-participants in their own political future. There is a reason it used to be a crime in the Confederate states to teach a slave to read: Literacy is power. (paras. 90, 93)

The notion of using cultural capital as a method of exclusion should be familiar to most critical scholars. As Stanley Aronowitz (1992, 2008) points out in his work, formal public schooling takes on a primary function of class reproduction, where students are socialized, trained, and provided a credential to join the labor market, or move on for further credentials.

Similarly, Joel Spring (2001) refers to a global culture of education that abides by a "human capital" model, in the interest of reproducing laborers and consumers:

> There is a tendency for the world's school systems to embrace an educational model that emphasizes human capital accounting and economic development. This global model is a result of colonialism, global contacts, and international economic planning. It envisions schools educating workers for jobs created by economic development. (p. 10)

As he points out in an earlier work, Spring (1998) suggests that contemporary public schooling is constructed according to the needs of global capital expansion and "development" as defined by neoliberal capitalists. One goes to school such that they can get a job, and buy the things that supposedly define a successful and happy existence. Public education is driven by a limiting purpose; as long established by previous scholars (Bowles & Gintis, 1976; Carnoy & Levin, 1985) it amounts to the ability of students to sell their labor in return for the wages necessary to survive and consume.

But this training often fails to provide people the tools and access necessary to be aware of, or participate in the political economic decisions that shape their lives—such as the deregulation that allowed for the packaging, sale, and implosion of Credit Default Swaps leading up to the recession. It is hard to imagine a functional democracy under these conditions, where even the reasonable election of "representatives" would require the electorate understand the political economic decisions made at the hand of their elected officials. Perhaps a shift away from a training-for-labor model is necessary here to prepare students to meaningfully participate in their world, and begin to build more democratic communities—a topic I will return to shortly. This is not to say that a change in educational policy and curriculum would suddenly gain students access to the upper echelons of finance capital, or that we should seek to train the entire population as investment bankers. But it might be seen as a necessary step for shifting away from the dominant roles of public education (job training and class reproduction) that in part function to exclude the general public from infiltrating or resisting powerful or privileged circles. This ability necessarily involves critical understandings of capitalism, the state, and one's theoretical and actual position in relation to these systems and institutions.

Social studies education is arguably where this preparation could and should take place, and where students might be politically defined as critical subjects instead of objects of history and the needs of global capital. As I will suggest, social studies curricula and pedagogy might be re-oriented to have a central and explicit focus on the critical pursuit to define and realize "human rights." Such an orientation gives purpose to the pursuit of "social studies" and gaining the necessary tools for civic and political engagement beyond simply getting a credential for a job: to somehow realize agreed upon standards for fundamental human life and dignity. This orientation, or human rights framework, also constructs the student as an active political agent and the claimant of inalienable rights, and provides a useful discourse and model for local civic engagement. As a more obvious point, formal international human rights instruments[1] point to education and political participation as fundamental human rights—suggesting the legitimacy of creating educational space for democratic pursuits.

POTENTIALS AND POSSIBILITIES FOR HUMAN RIGHTS BASED SOCIAL STUDIES CURRICULA

Spring (2001) makes an interesting point concerning education as a widely recognized, fundamental human right. It is his contention that, "the growing uniformity of global culture involves an acceptance of definitions of equality and freedom that are, respectively, focused on equality of opportunity and freedom to consume. These concepts are basic to the human capital model" (p. 12). Spring offers this as simultaneously recognizing the possibilities of a human rights discourse—where it suggests that all people have the fundamental right to education, while warning that the emancipatory potential of this right depends heavily on how education and its provision are defined in interpretation and action. The re-centering of social studies education to reflect a critical human rights framework might provide epistemological tools to define public social studies education (and, ironically, one's universal right to it) as something beyond a training ground for wage work and relatively passive citizenship. How might a human rights framework in social studies education help to make active subjects (instead of passive objects) of students and teachers, in the social, cultural, economic, and political development of our communities and broader society?

The study of human rights conceptually, and the history of formal international human rights instruments and law, inevitably require one to address issues of "universality"—that is, the extent to which concepts of humanity, justice, and notions of "right" are, can, or should be defined for all human beings. Indeed, the universality or cultural relativism of any proposed fundamental human right is an issue of great contention in the applied and scholarly fields (Donnelly, 2003). This philosophical aspect to human rights provides at least two significant opportunities for critical social studies education. Students and teachers, from the beginning, have the opportunity to address the ultimate subjectivity of knowledge and Truth— particularly involving attempts to define central unifying concepts. A focus on exploring the ongoing contested terrain of human rights—a conversation that also potentially transcends and integrates national, ethnic, and cultural identities—could begin with critical reflection on and contributions to the conceptualization of justice, rights, and so forth, rather than the dominant, hegemonic, historical Truths about the inherent "good" and inevitability of our existing political economic system and governing state as reflected in dominant US social studies curricula. (Can you condense this sentence?) This focus can also contribute to the democratization of pedagogical space, where students and teachers might struggle with the initial questions of how one comes to conceptually or substantively define "human rights." Should it be done through a decree by the powerful, "well educated," or culturally dominant (such as "Western civilization")? Should it be done through democratic processes? How so? How does one establish democratic representation, through consensus or "majority rule"?

In other words, the opportunity is created for students and teachers to wrestle with the actual, complex doing of democracy and democratic decision-making. Further, these explorations allow for students and teachers to participate in the defining of socially constructed concepts, and critically evaluate the extent to which current policies, practices, and conditions reflect their interpretations of, for example, "justice." When negotiated standards of fundamental human dignity guide critical analysis (rather than the desirability and inevitability of capitalism, for example), how might working class students and teachers come to view the poverty, unemployment, home foreclosures, and cuts to public education and social services widely experienced in the recession?

As a second opportunity, the history of international human rights instruments and law is largely a history of conflict and constant (re)negotiation. The teaching of contemporary history with a focus on international human rights standards (conceptually and as formal international law) potentially presents the construction of governance and law (at national and international levels) as the result of extensive conflict and compromise, where relations of power (along lines of nationality, ethnicity, political economic philosophy, race, gender, sexuality, and so forth) are deeply influential (Lauren, 2003; Ishay, 2008). As students study the history of human rights, they are exposed to a history of global ideological conflict over, for example, the salience of citizenship, race, and gender in determining who has claim to fundamental human dignities, and who is responsible for protecting and providing these dignities. Paul Lauren's widely used work (2003) details the tumultuous history behind central human rights instruments, that serves simultaneously as a primer on international relations during much of the 19th and 20th centuries.

Ultimately, the history of formal human rights and international law is a history of global power struggles. Within this framework, in the study of history, substantive law, existing forms of governance, and dominant forms of social organization do not have to be presented as unquestionable and inevitable. Instead, they are seen to reflect the conflicts and negotiations—in particular contexts—that led to their design, interpretation, and employment. Such an ideological frame is arguably necessary for one to see other social phenomena, such as the economic recession and state responses to it, as reflecting relations of power in action, rather than obvious or inevitable effects of and responses to a naturally occurring crisis. The first frame invites the active participation of a democratic subject, the second inspires one to be the object of, or one simply subjected *to* somehow objective and alien conditions, to which one can only react and/or accept.

Of course, a functional democracy depends on the active engagement of its members. Human rights instruments, such as the Convention on the Rights of the Child (CRC), position young people as the agents and claimants of their own inalienable rights. This should be seen in direct contradiction to how legal minors are constructed in juvenile justice, "representative" democracy (complete formal exclusion), educational policy and schools, and the mass media. Young people, particularly teenagers, are commonly constructed as inherently risky, dangerous (especially for youth of color), and in need of protection—somehow unable to articulate or participate in the articulation of their own "best interests." Scholars such as Mike Males (2002; Youthfacts website, 2010) have done a great deal of work to illustrate a distinctly anti-youth culture in the US spanning scholarship, news media, and popular culture. To the contrary, Males empirically demonstrates how today's youth contribute far less to societal ills such as violence or drug addiction than commonly believed. His work points out that we should be at least as wary of the decision making capacity of adults as with their younger counterparts, suggesting also the capacity of young people to make reasonable decisions in defense of their own rights and self-interests.

Human rights scholars who focus on the CRC and the rights of youth such as Shareen Hertel (2006) have pointed to the importance of youth making their own decisions in practice, and their ability to represent their own rights and interests. In her research on anti-sweatshop campaigns, Hertel (2006) details the pitfalls of speaking for the interests of young sweatshop workers in the global "South" or "Third World." She finds that in many cases, well-intentioned adult activists moved to shut down abusive sweatshops, but failed to plan for economic alternatives for the young workers who now escaped exploitation, but had no economic means of survival. That is, she points out that activists *never spoke to the young workers*, who could have otherwise articulated their needs. Her work points to the importance of young peoples' voice and participation in their communities, and in the design of public policy and practice meant to contribute to their, and the collective "best interests." Introducing students to human rights instruments like the CRC, and their employment in various contexts where young populations and their allies draw upon a human rights discourse (such as anti-sweatshop, anti-child slavery, and anti-child prostitution campaigns), might help to engage students as full participants in communities. Civic and political engagement then becomes something immediately relevant, rather than an alien practice only understood and realized at adulthood. What tangible opportunities exist for students to practice civic and political engagement through a human rights framework?

As a first and obvious point, drawing again from classic educational theory, the social studies classroom (or less formal pedagogical space, in or outside of school) could, and arguably should be modeled democratically (Dewey, 1938, 1944). For example, students and teachers could go about the messy democratic process of conceptualizing relatively universal "rights" or dignities to guide their interactions and collective work. Where these are well-established pedagogical approaches in critical education, we might look beyond classroom models to see how young people might have the opportunity to have some meaningful participation in their broader communities.

Here we might turn to the emergent "Human Rights Cities" movement, as demonstrated in (for example) Eugene, Oregon (Human Rights City Project, 2010), Washington DC (Cities For Progress, 2010), and Chapel Hill/Carrboro, North Carolina (Chapel Hill and Carrboro Human Rights Center, 2010). In recognition that the realization of human rights practice is most likely achieved through grassroots action and bottom-up democratization (see also Armaline & Glasberg, 2009), the human rights cities movement takes seriously the call to "bring human rights home" in the US (and elsewhere). As defined by Cities for Progress (2010) in Washington DC, a human rights city is "one whose residents and local authorities, through learning about the relevance of human rights to their daily lives, guided by a steering committee, join in ongoing learning, discussions, systematic analysis and critical thinking at the community level, to pursue a creative exchange of ideas and the joint planning of actions to realize their economic, social, political, civil and cultural human rights." Though some human rights city projects have taken a more or less aggressive posture at the level of local/municipal governance, their ultimate goal is to have local policy decisions and city planning guided centrally by formal human rights instruments (however accepted and interpreted by that community/city).

Social studies curricula and pedagogy can be retooled with a human rights framework to foster a more democratic society that respects fundamental human dignities, the human rights cities movement retools cities to base policy decisions on realizing human rights practice, rather than meeting the limited goals of local elites, capital expansion, and so forth. The human rights cities movement provides an opportunity for young human rights scholars and activists to engage beyond the classroom, where they might participate on steering committees and otherwise politically engage local government to recognize (1) the legitimacy of human rights as defined in that community, and (2) public school students as legitimate political actors and claimants to inalienable rights. In so doing, a bridge is created between classroom and civic engagement around and through a human rights framework. More broadly, employing a critical human rights framework in social studies education might provide the necessary tools and democratic pedagogical space(s) to prepare students for civic and political participation in a more democratic society where they see themselves as having some significant stake, and meaningful voice.

NOTES

[1] For example, several rights associated with the right to political participation are articulated in both the Universal Declaration of Human Rights (UDHR) and International Covenant on Civil and Political Rights (ICCPR). The right to education, as discussed by Spring (2001), is also reflected in the UDHR and International Covenant on Economic, Social, and Cultural Rights (ICESCR).

REFERENCES

Andreski, S. (Ed.). (2008). *Max Weber on capitalism, bureaucracy and religion*. New York: Routledge.
Armaline, W. T., & Levy, D. (2004). No Child Left Behind: Flowers don't grow in the desert. *Race and Society, 7*(1), 31–62.
Aronowitz, S. ([1973]1992). *False promises: The shaping of American working class consciousness*. Durham, NC: Duke University Press.
Aronowitz, S. (2008). *Against schooling: For an education that matters*. Boulder, CO: Paradigm.
Bowles, S., & Gintis, H. (1976). *Schooling in capitalist America: Educational reform and the contradictions of economic life*. New York: Basic Books.
Bybee, R. (2009, December 3). Apocalypse now in the industrial midwest: The Katrina of all recessions, *ZNet*. Retrieved December 4, 2009, from www.zcommunications.org/zmag
Callahan, R. (1962). *Education and the cult of efficiency*. Chicago: University of Chicago Press.
Carlson, T., & Cox, A. (2009, March 3). Balance of power with Tucker Carlson and Ana Marie Cox. *The Washington Post*. Retrieved December 2, 2009, from www.washintonpost.com
Carnoy, M., & Levin, H. (1985). *Schooling and work in the democratic state*. Stanford, CA: Stanford University Press.
Chapel Hill & Carrboro Human Rights Center. (2010). Retrieved February 27, 2010, from www.humanrightscities.org
Cities for Progress. (2010). Institute for Policy Studies, Washington DC. Retrieved February 27, 2010, from http://citiesforprogress.org/index.php?option=com_content&task=view&id=780&Itemid=74
Darder, A., Baltodano, M., & Torres, R. (2003). *The critical pedagogy reader*. New York: Routledge.
Dewey, J. (1938). *Experience and education*. New York: Collier Books.
Dewey, J. (1944). *Democracy and education*. New York: Free Press.
Domhoff, W. (2009). *Who rules America? Challenges to corporate and class dominance*. Columbus, OH: McGraw-Hill.
Donnelly, J. (2003). *Universal human rights in theory and practice*. Ithaca, NY: Cornell University Press.
Freire, P. (1970). *Pedagogy of the oppressed*. New York: Continuum.
Glasberg, D. S., & Skidmore, D. L. (1997). *Corporate welfare policy and the welfare state*. New York: Aldine de Gruyter.
Human Rights City Project. (2010). Retrieved February 27, 2010, from www.humanrightscity.com
Ishay, M. (2008). *The history of human rights: From ancient times to the globalization era*. Berkeley, CA: University of California Press.
Klein, N. (2007). *The shock doctrine: The rise of disaster capitalism*. New York: Picador.
Lauren, P. G. (2003). *The evolution of international human rights: visions seen* (2nd ed.). Philadelphia: University of Pennsylvania Press.
Leonhardt, D. (2008, March 19). Can't grasp the credit crisis? Join the club. *The New York Times*. Retrieved December 2, 2009, from http://www.nytimes.com/2008/03/19/business/19leonhardt.html

Males, M. (2002). *Framing youth: 10 myths about the next generation.* Monroe, ME: Common Courage Press.

Murray, S., & Dougherty. C. (2010, January 7). Personal bankruptcy filings rising fast. *The Wall Street Journal*, p. A3.

Parenti, M. (2007). *Democracy for the few.* New York: Wadsworth.

Powel, M. (2009, June 6). Bank accused of pushing mortgage deals on Blacks. *The New York Times.* Retrieved August 1, 2009, from www.nytimes.com/2009/06/07/us/07baltimore.html

Prins, N. (2009). *It takes a pillage: Behind the bailouts, bonuses, and backroom deals from Washington to Wall Street.* Hoboken, NJ: Wiley and Sons.

Reckard, E. S. (2009). NAACP Suits claim African Americans were targeted for subprime mortgages. *The LA Times.* Retrieved October 15, 2009, from http://articles.latimes.com/2009/mar/14/business/fi-black-housing14

Street, P. (2009, December 5). To save the capitalist system: reflections on Orin Kramer's understanding of Barack Obama's duty to America. *ZMagazine, 22*(12). Retrieved December 4, 2009, from www.zcommunications.org/to-save-the-capitalist-system-by-paul-street

Spring, J. (2001). *Globalization and educational rights: An intercivilizational analysis.* Mahwah, NJ: Lawrence Erlbaum Associates.

Spring, J. (2000). *The universal right to education: Justification, definition, and guidelines.* Mahwah, NJ: Lawrence Erlbaum Associates.

Taibbi, M. (2009, March 19). The big takeover. *Rolling Stone, 1075.* Retrieved December 2, 2009, from www.rollingstone.com/politics/story/26793903/the_big_takeover

US Department of Education. (2009, September 24). Secretary Duncan says rewrite of 'No Child Left Behind' should start now; Reauthorization can't wait." Retrieved January 4, 2010, from http://www.ed.gov/news/pressreleases/2009/09/09242009.html

Wharton School, University of Pennsylvania. (2008). Victimizing the borrowers: Predatory lending's role in the subprime mortgage crisis." Retrieved February 20, 2009, from www.//knowledge.wharton.upenn.edu/artilce.cfm?articleid=1901

Youthfacts website. (2010). Retrieved February 27, 2010, from www.youthfacts.org

William T. Armaline
San Jose State University

WAYNE AU

10. CRITICAL REFLECTION IN THE CLASSROOM

Consciousness, Praxis, and Relative Autonomy in Social Studies Education

Only when we understand the "dialecticity" between consciousness and the world—that is, when we know that we don't have a consciousness here and the world there but, on the contrary, when both of them, the objectivity and the subjectivity, are incarnating dialectically, is it possible to understand what *conscientização* is, and to understand the role of consciousness in the liberation of humanity. (Freire in Davis & Freire, 1981, p. 62)

INTRODUCTION

There is a long history in critical education theory of trying to understand the relationship between schooling, capitalist society, and student consciousness (Au, 2006; Au & Apple, 2009). Different impulses within this strand of critical educational analysis, working from a more vulgar, non-dialectical, and deterministic interpretations of Marx and Marxism, for instance, have at times asserted that human consciousness mechanically corresponds to capitalist socioeconomic relations, leaving little room for resistance within the contexts of society, culture, and education (see, e.g., Bowles & Gintis, 1976). Other, more dialectical formulations of the interaction between education and capitalist socioeconomic relations have not only theorized the role of conscious human action and subjective agency in the learning process (see, e.g., Apple, 1995, 2004), but also pressed for an understanding of the ways in which humans actively seek to transform the world around them, with education playing a key role in setting the stage for such transformation to take place (see, e.g., Freire, 1974; Shor & Freire, 1987).

Given the increasing inequality and conservatism that is unfolding in both schools and society today, particularly the rise of neoliberalism and the ongoing attack on civil liberties and programs aimed at ameliorating inequities (Apple, 2006), the assertion that education can provide key, strategic interventions and resistance to status quo consciousness is paramount: It recognizes the power that educators and students have to change the world. Further, it is important to recognize that social studies classroom play a particular role in this process since, literally, one of the central purposes of the social studies is to study society. As such, social studies educators are in a particularly powerful position in which they can raise foundational questions about the organization of our society both historically and in contemporary times (Marker, 2000), and thus situate their classrooms as spaces of critical consciousness and resistance (Hursh & Ross, 2000).

AU

This chapter will take up these substantive issues in critical educational theory, with particular attention paid to the ways in which critical reflection in social studies education can contribute to both the development of critical student consciousness and the nurturing of students' visions of more equitable and just socioeconomic futures.

I begin here by framing out a dialectical conception of consciousness and its relation to praxis. This highly theoretical discussion is critical because it outlines the fundamental ways-of-knowing that contribute to understanding consciousness as a central part of the process of transformation. I then follow with a discussion of how these concepts connect with theories of relative autonomy and the social construction of consciousness—as part of a process of understanding the relationship between individual, conscious transformation and social transformation. This particular discussion further highlights the relative collectivity from within which we all "think," and thus cuts against much of the mainstream gravitation towards thinking as a product of autonomous individuality. I then address the implications of these ideas for education, the politics of knowledge, and critical consciousness, paying particular attention to social studies education. Finally, in an attempt to concretize the conceptual work done here, I analyze a social studies activity that both challenges and encourages students to seek out alternatives to dominant relations by fostering critical reflection on our current socioeconomic structures.

A DIALECTICAL CONCEPTION OF CONSCIOUSNESS

The Dialectics of Consciousness

While dialectics constitutes its own philosophical subfield with its own treatises and explications on dialectical logic, for the purposes of this discussion, I will mainly focus on how dialectics applies to our conscious understanding of the world. In short, at the heart of dialectics is the idea that all "things" are actually processes, that these processes are in constant motion, or development, and that this development is driven by the tension created by two interrelated and internally related opposites acting in contradiction with each other (Allman, 2007; Gadotti, 1996; Ollman, 2003; Woods & Grant, 2002). These two opposites require each other to exist, for together they make up a unified whole (Allman, 1999). Hence, unlike the positivist logics associated with Enlightenment rationality—which focuses on isolation of individual pieces or phenomenon as well as simple, linear cause and effect relationships (Benton & Craib, 2001), "opposites" in a dialectical relationships are actually deeply and intimately integrated with each other. Thus, a dialectical conception sees the world as a multilayered, interrelated system, a living totality, a complex of relationships and processes (Gadotti, 1996; Ollman, 2003; Sayers, 1990).

In a dialectical conception of consciousness, then, as Freire (1998) asserts, "Consciousness and the world cannot be understood separately, in a dichotomized fashion, but rather must be seen in their contradictory relations" (p. 19). Dialectically speaking, such "contradictory relations" mean that we have to envision human consciousness coming from an interrelated, non-dichotomized relationship *with* and *within* the material world, including the human capability to act back upon that very same world around. In this way consciousness must be understood as a process where the dialectical interaction between humans and their environments continually unfolds and develops, where "being" (ontology) in the world and our theory of knowledge (epistemology) of that world are dynamically connected (Allman, 1999) as we simultaneously react to and act upon the world in which we live.

Materialism and Consciousness

Fundamentally, a dialectical conception of consciousness is rooted in the idea that human understanding and knowledge of the world (epistemology) originates, develops, and grows from human interaction with the material world—a material world that includes humans and thus is constituted by physical reality as well as culture and society (Allman, 1999, 2007; Engels, 1940; Vygotsky, 1987). As Allman (1999) explains, from a dialectical view:

> [I]deas and concepts arise from the relations between people and from relations between people and their material world (the world created by human beings as well as the natural world) ... [where] we actively and sensuously experience these relations; therefore, our consciousness is actively produced within our experience of our social, material and natural existence. (p. 37)

This is the basis for a materialism in a dialectical conception of consciousness. Materialism, in a philosophical sense, is the idea that matter precedes consciousness, that the material world has existed and would exist regardless of whether or not any humans or divine beings conceived of such existence (Marx & Engels, 1978).[1] Relative to how we understand epistemology, how we "know" what we "know," a materialist conception is important because it recognizes that our consciousness of the world is in a sense fundamentally produced by the world itself, and not the other way around. Recognizing the material basis for consciousness is not enough, however, because it does not recognize the power of humans to not only understand the world, but also to transform the world (Au, 2006).

Praxis

The dialectical nature of this conception of consciousness thus leads to several important implications. The first is that consciousness is directly linked with action. Essentially, this implication is the extension of the dialectical link between "being" (ontology) and "knowing" (epistemology), discussed above. Because we are in constant, dialectical, interaction with the material world (a world that is also sociocultural since it also contains human relations), we come to know things vis-à-vis our inseparable relationships with the totality of our environments. Thus, our very existence means we "are not only *in* the world, but *with* the world" (Freire, 1982a, p. 3, original emphasis) at all times. However, to be *with* the world, to exist in this inseparable relationship, to be always interacting with our environment, is a process that requires constant activity, constant interchange, and constant reflection. Put more simply, "being" is in fact an activity, and in a dialectical conception of consciousness, that activity is being *in* and *with* the world.

This process of constant, simultaneous thinking and being in and with the world is called "praxis." Freire (1982b) explains that,

> [H]uman beings ... are beings of "praxis": of action and of reflection. Humans find themselves marked by the results of their own actions in their relations with the world, and through the action on it. By acting they transform; by transforming they create a reality which conditions their manner of acting. (p. 102)

Here Freire points to the dialectical link between reflection and action. While praxis is often defined as the application of theory to practice and is often illustrated as a step-by-step, linear process, praxis is more correctly conceived dialectically as the "inseparable unity of thought and practice" (Allman, 2007, p. 33). Indeed, we might even consider human *being* as the continuous, simultaneous and connected processes of *thinking* (reflection) and *doing* (action).

Social Consciousness

> To paraphrase a well-known position of Marx's, we could say that humans' psychological nature represents the aggregate of internalized social relations that have become functions for the individual and forms of his/her structure. (Vygotsky, 1981, p. 164)

Freire (Freire & Macedo, 1987, 1995) explains the social nature of consciousness where, through his literacy work in education, he concludes that because humans are part of the world, and that because our consciousness comes from dialectical interaction with that world, other humans included, ultimately our consciousness is both shaped by and shapes our physical and social worlds (Roberts, 2003). Thus, because we use language and communication in this relationship, for Freire (1982b) "Subjects cannot think alone" and there "is no longer an 'I think' but 'we think'" (p. 137).

Within a dialectical conception of consciousness our thinking is essentially and fundamentally social in origin, as Vygotsky (1929; 1981; 1987) argued in several different settings and studies. For instance, Vygotsky (1981) discusses the role of signs (language) as mediating tools in the cultural development of children:

> If it is correct that the sign initially is a means of social interaction and only later becomes a means of behavior for the individual, it is quite clear that the cultural development is based on the use of signs and their inclusion in a general system of behavior that initially was external and social. In general, we could say that the relations among higher mental functions were at some earlier time actual relations among people. (p. 158)

Thus, Vygotsky concludes, because we use socially constructed language systems to mediate our interactions with our social and physical contexts, ultimately our consciousness originates socially (Bakhurst, 1991).

Indeed, the dialectical conception of consciousness leads us to understand how the social nature of consciousness can be seen in our reliance upon language and sign systems for thinking and communication of ideas. The basic logic is this: All linguistic meaning is drawn from socio-linguistic and cultural contexts. Put slightly differently, we cannot make meaning of words unless we have a systematic, social, historical, and cultural context in which to make linguistic and conceptual sense of them in the first place (Gee, 2008). Hence, in a most basic sense, our consciousness is social and exhibits aspects of external social relations if for no other reason than the fact that our linguistic systems are also social and carry social relations in their structure and meaning (Volosinov, 1986).

Further, as Leont'ev (1981) discusses, the social nature of consciousness is not just about the content of our thinking. Rather, such social structuring runs beyond just our use of language, because, as he explains:

> Consciousness is not given from the beginning and is not produced by nature: consciousness is a product of society: it is *produced* ... Thus the process of internalization is not the *transferal* of an external activity to a pre-existing, internal 'plane of consciousness': it is the process in which this internal plane is *formed*. (pp. 56–57, original emphasis)

Leont'ev's point is particularly important because he reminds us that, in a dialectical conception of consciousness, consciousness does not just appear. Rather, if we are to understand consciousness in a materialist manner, we have to recognize that it is generated, not by nature but by the meanings humans develop vis-à-vis social interaction. Further still, as Leont'ev argues, the internal structure of our consciousness is itself formed by social production—which requires that we consider the possibility that the social basis of our consciousness runs so deep as to be embedded in how consciousness is structured and organized.

Being Conscious of Our Consciousness

However, for all of the aspects of a dialectical conception of consciousness I discussed thus far, the question of what "consciousness" is, still remains. What is key here, and runs as a strand among and within all of my above discussion, is the process of reflection (meant here in the sense of "consideration" or "thinking"). Our dialectical interactions with our environment are, in part, guided by our continual reflection and subsequent responses based on that same reflection. This is human ontology, the defining praxis of our being. Thus, fundamentally, "consciousness" requires active consideration of how one interacts with one's social, cultural, and material environment. In this sense we might say that, "*Consciousness is intentionality towards the world*" (Freire in Davis & Freire, 1981, p. 58, original emphasis), where we develop "the capacity to adapt ... to reality *plus* the critical capacity to make choices and transform ... reality" (Freire, 1982a, p. 4, original emphasis).

Dewey (1916) explains this aspect of consciousness in the following way:

> To identify acting with an aim and intelligent activity is enough to show its value—its function in experience ... To be conscious is to be aware of what we are about; conscious signifies the deliberate, observant, planning traits of activity. Consciousness is nothing which we have which gazes idly on the scene around one or which has impressions made upon it by physical things; it is a name for the purposeful quality of an activity, for the fact that it is directed by an aim. Put the other way about, to have an aim is to act with meaning, not like an automatic machine; it is to *mean* to do something and to perceive the meaning of things in light of that intent. (pp. 103–104, original emphasis)

The last part of Dewey's point here is particularly important, because acting consciously—with intent, also carries with it a reflection on the intent itself, what Dewey says is to "perceive the meaning of things in light of that intent." Thus we might conceive of consciousness as "consciousness *of* consciousness" (Freire, 1974, p. 107, original emphasis), where, in Vygotsky's (1987) words, "Conscious awareness is an act of consciousness whose object is the activity of consciousness itself" (p. 190). In this regard consciousness may be understood as a meta-awareness of the interplay of our thoughts and real-world actions, an awareness that develops through an active process of first decoding reality, only to recode through the envisioning of alternative structures (Au, 2009a).

Thinking about our thinking—being conscious of our consciousness—is thus an extension of the dialectical unity between reflection and action because of its relationship to volition and human activity in the world. If we are conscious about something, then our "doing" is guided by our "thinking," and vice versa. In this regard consciousness allows us to "become consciously aware of [our] context and [our] condition as a human being as Subject ... [and] become an instrument of choice" (Freire, 1982a, p. 56) because we can "... reflect critically about [our] conditioning process and go beyond it" (Freire, 1998, p. 20) in our actions.

Critical Consciousness

Despite my use of the above definitions, I want to emphasize that thinking about consciousness in terms of volition, intentionality, and/or meta-awareness is not precise enough if we are to take seriously the task of structural transformation for social justice: People can and do think quite "consciously" as they act in oppressive ways in our world on individual and institutional levels. For instance, historically the U.S. government has operated very strategically and with much forethought in its campaigns to undermine democratic movements domestically (Zinn, 1995) and internationally (see, e.g., Steenland, 1974). Similarly, neoliberals and policymakers have acted with intention and conscious awareness as they sought to dismantle New Orleans public schools by breaking the teachers' union, closing schools, and constructing the district along the lines of a free market system that is leading to massive educational inequalities (Buras, 2007; Dingerson, 2008).

Thus, we have to recognize that defining consciousness simply along the lines of active intent and volition falls short of progressive social change (Au, 2009a; Fine, 1997), and that a dialectical conception of consciousness necessarily requires an embrace of "criticality" (Allman, 2007; Freire, 1974). Consequently, the "critical" in critical reflection is central because to look at something critically requires that we become aware of our context to see how external relations impinge upon our praxis—our thinking and acting—and considering whether such relations contribute to or liberate us from forms of oppression.

Furthermore, given the social nature of consciousness, discussed above, critically reflecting on our own consciousness is simultaneously both an individual and social cognitive move because it necessitates a critical reflection on the social structures that shape our consciousness—it is both a reflection on our own thinking as well as a critical reflection on the structure of society itself. Subsequently, being critical also implies making "supra-empirical connections" (Vygotsky, 1987) in our cognitive and material relationship with the external world and using our understanding of such connections as a means to work more effectively for transformative social justice.

Freire (in Davis & Freire, 1981) explains the relationship between critical reflection and our contexts in terms of education for freedom (as opposed to education for oppression), where he observes:

> [E]ducation for freedom implies constantly, permanently, the exercise of consciousness turning in on itself in order to discover itself in the relationships with the world, trying to explain the reasons which can make clear the concrete situation people have in the world. (p. 59)

In discovering "the relationships with the world" and explaining the "reasons which can make clear the concrete situation people have in the world," through critical reflection we seek to develop more systematic analyses of these relationships—analyses whose point is to understand our world in ways that "exceed the limits of actual and or even potential experience" (Vygotsky, 1987, p. 180). Examining our relationships in a systematic way allows us to see things that we did not necessarily see before in the immediacy of our everyday experiences: We may learn something new about an object we've taken for granted on a day-to-day basis, or we may learn something new about an object that we have never actually physically experienced (Au, 2007).

Additionally, it is important in the context of the present discussion to recognize that reflection is always retrospective and introspective. There is no choice but for it to be retrospective since we cannot "reflect" into the future because time continues to move beyond the present moment into the past. Further, because of our individual consciousness, reflection is also introspective because we cannot reflect (nor think) for someone else—even if the social nature of conscious (and language) requires that we need other humans to systematically think about the world (Freire, 1974). Rather, we can only look within ourselves and consider our relationships with our external environments as we have experienced them.

Learning and developing critical consciousness thus require retrospection and introspection—looking backwards and inwards to consider how our experiences and the outward social structures shape our consciousness. All of which points to the power of the "critical" moment of reflection, because it is in that moment that we shift our understanding of whatever it is we are considering. This shift in perspective is important because, "To perceive something in a different way means to acquire new potentials for acting with respect to it ..." (Vygotsky, 1987, p. 190)— or "go beyond" our "conditioning process," as Freire (1998, p. 20) suggests above.

A central issue for us to consider relative to a dialectical conception of consciousness, then, is the politics that guide both our critical reflections and our actions, because these politics help dictate what new potentials for acting manifest in our consciousness. Allman (2007) talks about these politics in terms of "critical/revolutionary praxis" and "reproductive/uncritical praxis." Reproductive praxis, Allman explains, is a form of praxis where people "only engage in the social relations into which they are born, assuming all the while that these relations, or practices, are natural and inevitable" (p. 34). This type of engagement, Allman continues, "will serve only to reproduce the extant relations and conditions" (p. 34).

Conversely, in critical praxis people "choose to critically question the existing social relations and to engage in transforming, or abolishing, them whilst also developing new social relations and conditions aimed at creating a better existence for all human beings" (p. 34). It is this critical questioning of inequitable social relations and working towards their abolition, while simultaneously developing new, more equitable relations (including more equitable social, cultural, and material environments), that inhabits a dialectical conception of consciousness.

Consciousness, Education, and Relative Autonomy

Before continuing, it is important to enter into a particular argument within critical educational theory. If consciousness, as Allman (1999) suggests above, "... is actively produced within our experience of our social, material and cultural existence" (p. 37), is consciousness thus totally determined by external material and social factors, or do humans have the capability to determine how they think about and "know" the world around them?

This question correlates with a parallel question about the relationship between schools and consciousness more broadly, one that has been asked by many critical educational scholars with varying effect (see, e.g., Apple, 2004; Bernstein, 1996; Bourdieu & Passeron, 1977; Bowles & Gintis, 1976; Giroux, 1980). Mainly: Do schools simply reproduce the unequal social and economic relations associated with capitalism, or can they exist as sites of critical social and cultural resistance to status quo inequalities?

The parallel between these two questions can be found in their mutual interrogation of the relationship between ideas and material reality. In the case of human consciousness, we are dealing with how human thinking relates to and extends from interaction with the material world. In the case of education, we are dealing with how schools, as sites of knowledge construction/reconstruction and as sites of cultural production/reproduction, relate to and extend from the material social and economic relations that exist externally to schools themselves (Au, 2009c).

When we look at both consciousness and schools, we certainly see external relations impinging upon the structures of both. In terms of consciousness, for instance, work in the sociology of school knowledge outlines how pedagogic discourse—literally, the communicative discourse in classroom settings—functions to regulate how students see and understand the world through the regulation of the knowledge they interact with/are taught in that discourse (Au, 2008; Bernstein, 1996). In this regard, the external social, cultural, and material environment holds significant (but not total) power over how student consciousness is formed.

In terms of schools, nearly any statistic related to educational outcomes will bear out the ways external social and economic relations encroach: Students of color, as well as low-income students of all colors, have lower test scores, lower graduation rates, higher drop out rates, and higher disciplinary rates than their white, higher income counterparts (see, e.g., Ladson-Billings, 2006; Laird, Lew, DeBell, & Chapman, 2006; Nichols & Berliner, 2007; Sirin, 2005). Given such outcomes, it would seem that, generally speaking, schools structurally (and simply) reproduce the inequalities we see in society more broadly.

Other educational research, however, also challenges the idea that schools simply reproduce inequality. For instance, as Apple (1995; 2004) and Carnoy and Levin (1985) explain, despite reproducing socio-economic inequalities in a general sense, schools also play the somewhat contradictory role of legitimating ideologies of individual equality and meritocracy. Additionally, there is ample evidence that students (see, e.g., Dance, 2002; Shor, 1992; Willis, 1977) and teachers (see, e.g., Allman, McLaren, & Rikowski, 2000; Carlson, 1988) resist the structuring forces of schooling in both cultural and material ways. Indeed, significant portions of this resistance can be directly attributed to the ideology of equality that the schools themselves help maintain.

These seemingly contradictory relations embodied by schools—largely reproducing external socio-economic inequalities while simultaneously producing resistance to those very same inequalities—speak to the "relative autonomy" of the schools from capitalist socio-economic relations (Althusser, 1971). Thus, even though "in the last analysis" (Gramsci, 1971, p. 162) or "in the last instance" (Althusser, 1971, p. 135), the dominant economic relation may "finally asserts itself as necessary" (Engels, 1968, p. 692) and structures schooling in a broad sense, the relatively autonomous positioning of schools also means that they are not totally structured by outside forces: that sites of alternative relations and resistance functionally exist within schools as well (Bernstein, 1996).

A similar argument can and should be made regarding consciousness. Even while our consciousness of the world is in a sense produced by the world itself—produced vis-à-vis our relations with the social, cultural, and material world, there is a level of relative autonomy of consciousness from the structuring forces of that world. Put differently, consciousness is not only a product of our relationship with our external environments, it also contributes to the production of our external environments as well. As such, consciousness cannot be understood as linear, as a mechanical reflection of the material world, or as completely determined by external factors.

Rather, just as the relative autonomy of schools from economic relations must be understood in non-deterministic, non-mechanical ways (Au, 2006), the relationship between consciousness and our material environments must also be conceived of *dialectically* in that there exists interaction, unity, and dynamic fluidity in the connected interchange between humans and their social, cultural, and material environment. In this regard, we see the fundamental role that a dialectical conception plays in how we understand both consciousness and schooling within our current socio-economic context. It is this relative autonomy of schools and consciousness that creates the space for social studies education to take up a more critical stance and act as a conceptual tool in the praxis of working for social justice (Hursh & Ross, 2000).

CRITICAL CONSCIOUSNESS AND SOCIAL STUDIES EDUCATION

Having outlined a dialectical conception of consciousness, let us now turn its implications for social studies education. In what follows I will apply some of the key aspects of a dialectical conception of consciousness to social studies education in a general sense—fleshing out how we might think of the teaching of social studies within the conceptual milieu I've suggested here. I will then consider some specific social studies teaching ideas and texts, discussing how they work to develop critical consciousness within the framework taken up in this chapter.

A Consciousness Approach to the Social Studies

There are several implications for social studies education within the dialectical conception of consciousness:

– Because consciousness is essentially produced through human interaction with our environment (Allman, 1999; Marx & Engels, 1978), it is critical to consider both the types of classroom environments social studies curriculum create (Au, 2009b; Huebner, 1970) as well as the types of student consciousness said environments potentially foster;

– Because being and knowing are dynamically intertwined within the dialectical relationship between consciousness and our environment (Allman, 1999; Freire, 1998), the content of social studies education should relate to students' contexts, experiences, and identities (see, e.g., Ladson-Billings, 1997). Put differently, not relating social studies to students effectively alienates their knowing from their being, and turns social studies education into a key factor in producing that alienation;

– Because our consciousness is expressed through praxis—the dialectically unified process of thinking and doing (Allman, 2007; Freire, 1982a, 1982b), social studies education is powerful if it is linked to action in some form. For the social studies teacher this implies using pedagogy that actively engages students in learning and it implies that one of the objectives of social studies education is for students to take some form of action (in the present or future) in their own social, cultural, political, and economic contexts (see, e.g., Yang & Duncan-Andrade, 2005);

– Because we use tools in the development of consciousness (Vygotsky, 1987), then social studies teachers and students should consciously consider what tools they make use of in their classrooms and other environments. For the teacher, in this instance, the curriculum itself (including textbooks, films, or other artifacts that guide practice) is a tool that they are using to leverage certain forms of consciousness within their classroom environments (see, e.g., Stoddard & Marcus, 2006). Social studies teachers also make use of conceptual tools such as "historical thinking" (VanSledright, 2004), "controversial issues" (Hess, 2009), and/or specific explanatory theories (e.g., push-pull factors in immigration) in their instruction as a means to develop student consciousness about social studies itself;

– Because consciousness is fundamentally social in its development and structure (Leont'ev, 1981; Vygotsky, 1987), it is important for social studies teachers and students to not only recognize that social relations are present in every facet of social studies curriculum and instruction vis-à-vis the politics of knowledge of content (Apple, 2000; Ross, 2000) and classroom interactions (Freire, 1974; Shor & Freire, 1987), but also to recognize that social studies education needs to be connected to pressing social issues (Bigelow, 1990; Hursh & Ross, 2000);

– Because consciousness implies thinking about thinking, volitional action, and intentionality towards the world (Davis & Freire, 1981; Vygotsky, 1987), social studies education can enable teachers (through their practice) and students (through their learning) to become thoughtful and deliberate as they consider their own views of history and social relations, with the intent of carrying such thoughtfulness and deliberation into their daily lives (Parker, 2005).

– Because being critical in our reflection is central to developing consciousness that can challenge existing, unequal social relations and work towards more equitable and just social change (Allman, 2007; Freire, 1974), a critical social studies education seeks to foster systematic understandings of the social, cultural, and material world amongst students in order to establish the conditions for them to develop more complex and complete knowledge of themselves and their contexts (see, e.g., Bigelow, 2006). The development of such consciousness thus opens up the possibility for students to develop new potentials for acting relative to their contexts, which in turn creates potential for students to actively interrupt inequality as change agents working for social justice (see, e.g., Au, 2000);

– Finally, because of the relative autonomy of both schools and consciousness (Au, 2008; Bernstein, 1996), it is perhaps most important that social studies teachers and students understand that they have the capacity to think (and learn and teach) in ways that challenge the status quo socio-economic structures that broadly impinge on the process of schooling. Put differently, social studies education can only develop and maintain critical consciousness when teachers and students recognize that they actually have the power to do so (Counts, 1932).

AU

The Organic Goodie Machine

In order to more clearly illustrate how social studies education can foster critical consciousness in the classroom, I'd like to discuss a key example: "The Organic Goodie Simulation" (Bigelow & Diamond, 2007; Messner, 1976). This simulation was first created as part of a larger unit on labor history and relations in the United States, and it is premised on the teacher playing the role of factory owner relative to employed and unemployed students in the simulation. The activity begins with a teacher announcing the premise that all students and the teacher are to be trapped in their classroom forever. Fortunately for all, the teacher has an Organic Goodie Machine, which with proper labor produces the perfect food: organic goodies (no waste, no soil needed, no sunlight needed, no emissions).

Working on the machine for the teacher allows students to make money to buy goodies to live. Not working on the machine means starving. After explaining these relationships to the class, the teacher-owner asks for volunteers to work the machine. Generally, most if not all students want to work on the machine. The teacher-owner, however, only chooses half of the class to work. The other half remains unemployed. After separating the students into two large groups – employed and unemployed – the teacher displays and explains the "Organic Goodie Economy" (Bigelow & Diamond, 2007, p. 101) where workers earn a subsistence wage of $6/day (minus $1 to support the unemployed), the unemployed receive a small, unsustainable subsidy of $2/day, and the teacher-owner gets to consume $6/day worth of goodies while earning a surplus of $4 per worker and paying out $1 per unemployed.

If students complain about the inequity of this economy, the justification for the teacher-owner surplus is the simple fact that the teacher's ownership of the machine "benefits" the whole group (e.g., "We" are lucky "we" have this machine so "we" can survive …). In broad strokes, then, "The Organic Goodie Simulation" creates a three-tiered society with half the students being workers, the other half being unemployed, and the teacher being the owner of the machine. Worker-students make enough money to survive producing organic goodies for the owner-teacher while unemployed-students slowly starve on their portion of state supplied "welfare" goodies.

The friction that drives the simulation is the owner-teacher's goal to increase profits by any means necessary, and there are several techniques the owner-teacher can use to increase profits. The first technique is to start a wage battle between employed and unemployed students, firing any employee who does not take a wage cut and replacing them with someone from the ranks of the unemployed who are slowly starving and are willing to work for less than $6 a day. Having taught this lesson many times myself, I have found this technique to be alarmingly successful. Students, in their individual interest, have generally been quick to take lower pay than their peers (My personal record is driving wages down to less than $3 a day).

Other techniques suggested in the lesson plan include: asking workers to repeat the phrase "I am a happy worker" and firing any who do not comply; making derogatory comments about the unemployed students; firing anyone who even mentions the word "union" or is disruptive in any way; forcing workers to sign "yellow dog" contracts promising they'll never join a union; hiring a foreman, spy, or security guard for slightly higher pay than the workers; having unemployed students "die" of starvation at regular intervals (Bigelow & Diamond, 2007).

The teacher ultimately plays two contradictory roles within the simulation. As the teacher-owner in the context of the simulation, the teacher wants to fight student-worker organization and promote selfish individualism at all costs. However, outside of the simulation, the teacher hopes for the students to successfully organize and perhaps collectively take the machine over. In the end, students may or may not be successful at taking over the Organic Goodie Machine from their teacher for a variety of reasons. Or, even if they do take it over, sometimes another student or small group of students simply reclaims the machine in their name alone, and tries to force everyone else to work for the new owners instead. The closing of the lesson then revolves around students' critical reflections on their experience, and questions are raised about its implication for the classroom community and society at large (see Au, 2009b for further discussion).

As an example of social studies education that promotes critical consciousness, "The Organic Goodie Simulation" embodies many aspects of the dialectical conception of consciousness, discussed above. As a simulation, it is an activity that literally creates a classroom environment that requires students to contend with a particular set of socio-economic relations (albeit simplified ones), and it uses a physical tool (the Organic Goodie Machine) as well as several conceptual tools (the Goodie economy and concepts of employment and competition, among others) to get students to actively relate to each other and the classroom environment. Further, the simulation asks students to not only be introspective as they make decisions regarding their survival, but it explicitly relates those decisions to the simulation's socio-economic relations in a way where they can't help but see how the social structures are influencing their thinking and acting. Consequently, and perhaps most importantly, within the context of the simulation, students are asked to make conscious, volitional choices regarding their immediate individual survival and acting collectively in solidarity with others for long term group survival. Indeed, in this regard "The Organic Goodie Simulation" requires students to intentionally choose between a simulation-based reproductive praxis or a simulation-based critical praxis.

Outside of the simulation, as a learning experience that students reflect upon both introspectively and retrospectively, is where this simulation contributes significantly to student critical consciousness. Here, students are asked to consider the choices they made during the simulation and reflect upon the implications of those choices. Did they sell out their fellow workers? Did they stand their ground and try find solidarity with both the employed and unemployed? Did they try to organize their peers to change the socio-economic structure within the simulation? The key follow-up questions for individual reflection and group discussion on all of these questions is simple: Why or why not? And in answering this one simple follow-up, students interrogate the simulation-structured motivations behind their decision-making.

Similarly, students not only get to consider what kept them from uniting and organizing against the teacher/owner of the Organic Goodie Machine, they also get to reflect upon what they might do if they had the chance to do it all over again. This deliberation is important because it directly links critical reflection with a new way of perceiving their simulation experience, and thus also links with new possibilities for action relative to that same (or a similar) experience. Indeed, in the experience of Bigelow and Diamond (2007), as well as in my own experience, students have in fact asked to repeat the simulation to attempt to improve the outcome. Most times students are more successful in organizing against the teacher/owner in the repeated simulation, however, there have been times when individual students, despite the critical reflection of the class, have still chosen to undermine the collective good of the group—leading to yet another victory on behalf of the teacher/owner.

The simulation also works on other levels of meta-awareness. One of the central issues students have to wrestle with is whether or not they have the collective authority to take control of the Organic Goodie Machine. While contemplating this issue happens within the immediate context of the simulation, students also have to struggle with whether or not they have the democratic authority to take the machine (and authority) away from *their teacher*—a serious and sometimes scary proposition within any classroom setting. But, in even considering the radical idea of removing teacher authority in the classroom experience, they automatically raise the possibility of making such a removal a reality in their consciousness (Bernstein, 1996)—and this, in turn, opens up the potential for students to take on more authority and empowerment in their education.

We can also see the ways that "The Organic Goodie Simulation" (Bigelow & Diamond, 2007) fosters the making of "supra-empirical connections" (Vygotsky, 1987) between society and student consciousness. This takes place on two levels. On one level, in reflecting on their simulation experience students are asked to think about the social origins of extreme individualism, particularly if they or their peers placed individual self interest above the survival and good of the group. On another level, they are also encouraged to consider not only the social implications of extreme individualism, but also how similar class relations play out amongst and between groups in society at large. Further, and perhaps most importantly, at each and every step along the way, students use critical reflection to actively and intentionally consider how their thoughts are connected to their actions, how they embodied particularly kinds of praxis. Indeed, within context of state budget crises, the tumultuous gains and losses in the stock market, rising unemployment, and the housing crash, an activity such as the Organic Goodie certainly pushes students to consider contemporary problems in particularly powerful ways.

Finally, it is important to recognize the ways the "Organic Goodie Simulation" (Bigelow & Diamond, 2007) represents a critical pedagogic praxis on the part of teachers. First and foremost, we can see the ways the simulation promotes critical reflection and provides the opportunity for students to take action in the classroom. Additionally, the simulation very consciously brings society into the social studies, raising important issues of income distribution, socio-economic relations, and labor organizing for students to consider. In doing so, pedagogically the simulation asks students to think about how they might challenge the inequalities associated with these issues. Further, the simulation also asks students to consider power inequalities in their own classroom environments since, pedagogically, it invites them to challenge teacherly authority in a constructive and potentially liberatory way. There is no "banking education" (Freire, 1974) to be had in the pedagogy of this activity. Rather, there is critical reflection, dynamic interaction, and an active consideration of how social relations affect our thoughts and actions.

CONCLUSION: CRITICAL REFLECTION IN SOCIAL STUDIES EDUCATION

In this chapter I have attempted to outline a dialectical conception of consciousness, one that is materialist, critical, dynamic, and built around praxis. The overall purpose of this conception has been for educators to better and more clearly understand how our practice relates to the types of consciousness we foster in students. More specifically, however, I have been interested in how this conception might inform the teaching of social studies. As such I've tried to connect some central aspects of this conception with social studies education, using "The Organic Goodie Simulation" (Bigelow & Diamond, 2007) as just one example of how critical consciousness (and, by extension, critical praxis) can be nurtured in our classrooms.

It is important, however, to recognize that there are many other examples of social studies education that also develop critical consciousness in students, and do so without requiring the dynamism of a simulation to be effective (see, e.g., Bigelow, 2006; Bigelow & Peterson, 1998, 2002; Chen & Omastu, 2006; Lee, Menkhart, & Okazawa-Rey, 1998; Menkhart, Murray, & View, 2004; Wei & Kamel, 1998). Thus we see the potential power of social studies education to promote critical reflection in the classroom with the specific intent of also promoting a critical consciousness amongst students that seeks to challenge inequitable social relations and build a more just society (Bigelow, 1990; Segall, 1999). However, this potentiality can only be reached if social studies teachers and teacher educators themselves critically reflect on their own conditions, recognize their own relative autonomy, embrace the power they have, and engage in critical praxis in their own classrooms, institutions, and communities.

NOTES

[1] "Materialism" and "materialist" used here should not be confused with the popular usage of the terms, which often refer to the accumulation of material goods. Here I am using them specifically in reference to philosophical materialism, discussed in the chapter.

REFERENCES

Allman, P. (1999). *Revolutionary social transformation: Democratic hopes, political possibilities and critical education* (1st ed.). Westport, CT: Bergin & Garvey.
Allman, P. (2007). *On Marx: An introduction to the revolutionary intellect of Karl Marx*. Rotterdam, The Netherlands: Sense Publishers.

Allman, P., McLaren, P., & Rikowski, G. (2000). *After the box people: The labour-capital relation as class constitution – and its consequences for Marxist educational theory and human resistance.* Retrieved May 1, 2004, from http://www.ieps.org.uk.cwc.net/afterthebox.pdf

Althusser, L. (1971). *Lenin and philosophy and other essays* (B. Brewster, Trans.). New York: Monthly Review Books.

Apple, M. W. (1995). *Education and power* (2nd ed.). New York: Routledge.

Apple, M. W. (2000). *Official knowledge: Democratic education in a conservative age* (2nd ed.). New York: Routledge.

Apple, M. W. (2004). *Ideology and curriculum* (3rd ed.). New York: RoutledgeFalmer.

Apple, M. W. (2006). *Educating the "right" way: Markets, standards, god, and inequality* (2nd ed.). New York: Routledge.

Au, W. (2000). Teaching about the WTO. *Rethinking Schools, 14*(3), 4–5.

Au, W. (2006). Against economic determinism: Revisiting the roots of neo-Marxism in critical educational theory. *Journal for Critical Education Policy Studies, 4*(2). Retrieved December 12, 2006, from http://www.jceps.com/?pageID=article&articleID=66

Au, W. (2007). Vygotsky and Lenin on learning: The parallel structures of individual and social development. *Science & Society, 71*(3), 273–298.

Au, W. (2008). Devising inequality: A Bernsteinian analysis of high-stakes testing and social reproduction in education. *British Journal of Sociology of Education, 29*(6), 639–651.

Au, W. (2009a). Fighting with the text: Critical issues in the development of Freirian pedagogy. In M. W. Apple, W. Au, & L. A. Gandin (Eds.), *The Routledge handbook of critical education* (pp. 83–95). New York: Routledge.

Au, W. (2009b). The 'building tasks' of critical history: Structuring social studies for social justice. *Social Studies Research and Practice, 4*(2).

Au, W. (2009c). *Unequal by design: High-stakes testing and the standardization of inequality.* New York: Routledge.

Au, W., & Apple, M. W. (2009). Neo-Marxism in critical educational theory. In M. W. Apple, W. Au, & L. A. Gandin (Eds.), *The Routledge handbook of critical education* (pp. 83–95). New York: Routledge.

Bakhurst, D. (1991). *Consciousness and revolution in soviet philosophy: From the Bolsheviks to Evald Ilyenkov.* New York: Cambridge University Press.

Benton, T., & Craib, I. (2001). *Philosophy of social science: The philosophical foundations of social thought.* New York: Palgrave.

Bernstein, B. B. (1996). *Pedagogy, symbolic control, and identity: Theory, research, critique.* London: Taylor & Francis.

Bigelow, B. (1990). Inside the classroom: Social vision and critical pedagogy. *Teachers College Record, 91*(3), 437–448.

Bigelow, B. (2006). *The line between us: Teaching about the border and Mexican immigration.* Milwaukee, WI: Rethinking Schools Ltd.

Bigelow, B., & Diamond, N. (2007). The Organic Goodie Simulation. In W. Au, B. Bigelow, & S. Karp (Eds.), *Rethinking our classrooms: Teaching for equity and justice* (2nd Rev. ed., Vol. 1, pp. 100–102). Milwaukee, WI: Rethinking Schools.

Bigelow, B., & Peterson, B. (Eds.). (1998). *Rethinking Columbus: The next 500 years* (2nd ed.). Milwaukee, WI: Rethinking Schools, Ltd.

Bigelow, B., & Peterson, B. (Eds.). (2002). *Rethinking globalization: Teaching for justice in an unjust world* (1st ed.). Milwaukee, WI: Rethinking Schools Ltd.

Bourdieu, P., & Passeron, J. (1977). Reproduction in education, society, and culture. Beverly Hills, CA: Sage.

Bowles, S., & Gintis, H. (1976). *Schooling in capitalist America: Educational reform and the contradictions of economic life* (1st ed.). New York: Basic Books.

Buras, K. L. (2007). Benign neglect? Drowning yellow buses, racism, and disinvestment in the city that Bush forgot. In K. J. Saltman (Ed.), *Schooling and the politics of disaster* (pp. 103–122). New York: Routledge.

Carlson, D. L. (1988). Beyond the reproductive theory of teaching. In M. Cole (Ed.), *Bowles and Gintis revisited: Correspondence and contradiction in educational theory* (pp. 158–173). New York: The Falmer Press.

Carnoy, M., & Levin, H. M. (1985). *Schooling and work in the democratic state*. Stanford, CA: Stanford University Press.

Chen, E., & Omastu, G. (Eds.). (2006). *Teaching about Asian Pacific Americans*. New York: Rowman & Littlefield.

Counts, G. S. (1932). *Dare the schools build a new social order?* New York: John Day.

Dance, J. L. (2002). *Tough fronts: The impact of street culture on schooling* (1st ed.). New York: Routledge Farmer.

Davis, R., & Freire, P. (1981). Education for awareness: A talk with Paulo Freire. In R. Mackie (Ed.), *Literacy and revolution: The pedagogy of Paulo Freire* (pp. 57–69). New York: The Continuum Publishing Company.

Dewey, J. (1916). *Democracy and education* (Free Press Paperback, 1966 ed.). New York: The Free Press, a division of Macmillan Publishing Co., Inc.

Dingerson, L. (2008). Unlovely: How the market is failing the children of New Orleans. In L. Dingerson, B. Miner, B. Peterson, & S. Walters (Eds.), *Keeping the promise? The debate over charter schools* (pp. 17–34). Milwaukee, WI: Rethinking Schools.

Engels, F. (1940). Dialectics of nature (C. Dutt, Trans., 1st ed.). New York: International Publishers.

Engels, F. (1968). Engels to J. Bloch in Konigsberg. In *Karl Marx & Frederick Engels: Their selected works* (pp. 692–693). New York: International Publishers.

Fine, M. (1997). A letter to Paulo. In P. Freire, J. W. with Fraser, D. Macedo, T. McKinnon, & W. T. Stokes (Eds.), *Mentoring the mentor: a critical dialogue with Paulo Freire* (pp. 89–97). New York: Peter Lang.

Freire, P. (1974). *Pedagogy of the oppressed* (M. B. Ramos, Trans.). New York: Seabury Press.

Freire, P. (1982a). Education as the practice of freedom (M. B. Ramos, Trans.). In *Education for critical consciousness* (pp. 1–84). New York: The Continuum Publishing Company.

Freire, P. (1982b). Extension or communication (L. Bigwood & M. Marshall, Trans.). In *Education for critical consciousness* (pp. 93–164). New York: Continuum.

Freire, P. (1998). Politics and education (P. L. Wong, Trans.). Los Angeles: UCLA Latin American Center Publications.

Freire, P., & Macedo, D. (1987). *Literacy: Reading the word and the world* (D. Macedo, Trans.). Westport, CT: Bergin & Garvey.

Freire, P., & Macedo, D. (1995). A dialogue: Culture, language, and race. *Harvard Educational Review, 65*(3), 377–402.

Gadotti, M. (1996). *Pedagogy of praxis: A dialectical philosophy of education* (J. Milton, Trans., 1st ed.). Albany, NY: State University of New York Press.

Gee, J. P. (2008). *Social linguistics and literacies: Ideology in discourses* (3rd ed.). New York: Routledge/Falmer.

Giroux, H. A. (1980). Beyond the correspondence theory: Notes on the dynamics of educational reproduction and transformation. *Curriculum Inquiry, 10*(3), 225–247.

Gramsci, A. (1971). *Selections from the prison notebooks* (Q. Hoare & G. N. Smith, Trans.). New York: International Publishers.

Hess, D. (2009). *Controversy in the classroom: The democratic power of discussion*. New York: Routledge.

Huebner, D. E. (1970, March 2). *Curriculum as the accessibility of knowledge*. Paper presented at the Curriculum Theory Study Group, Minneapolis, MN.

Hursh, D. W., & Ross, E. W. (2000). Democratic social education: Social studies for social change. In D. W. Hursh & E. W. Ross (Eds.), *Democratic social education: Social studies for social change* (pp. 1–22). New York: Falmer Press.

Ladson-Billings, G. (1997). Crafting a culturally relevant social studies approach. In E. W. Ross (Ed.), *The social studies curriculum: purposes, problems, and possibilities* (pp. 121–136). Albany, NY: State University of New York Press.

Ladson-Billings, G. (2006). From the achievement gap to the education debt: Understanding achievement in U.S. schools. *Educational Researcher, 35*(7), 3–12.

Laird, J., Lew, S., DeBell, M., & Chapman, C. (2006). *Dropout rates in the United States: 2002 and 2003 (No. NCES 2006-062)*. Washington, DC: U.S. Department of Education: National Center for Education Statistics.

Lee, E., Menkhart, D., & Okazawa-Rey, M. (Eds.). (1998). *Beyond heroes and holidays*. Washington, DC: Network of Educators on the Americas.

Leont'ev, A. N. (1981). The problem of activity in psychology. In J. V. Wertsch (Ed.), *The concept of activity in Soviet psychology* (pp. 37–71). New York: M.E. Sharpe Inc.

Marker, P. (2000). Not only by our words: Connecting the pedagogy of Paulo Freire with the social studies classroom. In D. W. Hursh & E. W. Ross (Eds.), *Democratic social education: social studies for social change* (pp. 135–148). New York: Falmer Press.

Marx, K., & Engels, F. (1978). The German ideology: Part I. In R. C. Tucker (Ed.), *The Marx-Engels reader* (pp. 146–200). New York: W.W. Norton & Company.

Menkhart, D., Murray, A. D., & View, J. L. (Eds.). (2004). *Putting the movement back into civil rights teaching*. Washington, DC: Teaching for Change.

Messner, M. (1976). Bubblegum and surplus value. *The Insurgent Sociologist, 6*(4), 51–56.

Nichols, S. L., & Berliner, D. C. (2007). *Collateral damage: How high-stakes testing corrupts America's schools*. Cambridge, MA: Harvard Education Press.

Ollman, B. (2003). *Dance of the dialectic: Steps in Marx's method* (1st ed.). Chicago: University of Illinois Press.

Parker, W. (2005). Teaching against idiocy. *Phi Delta Kappan*, 344–351.

Roberts, P. (2003). Knowledge, dialogue, and humanization: Exploring Freire's philosophy. In M. Peters, C. Lankshear, & M. Olssen (Eds.), *Critical theory and the human condition: Founders and praxis* (pp. 169–183). New York: Peter Lang.

Ross, E. W. (2000). Diverting democracy: The curriculum standards movement and social studies education. In D. W. Hursh & E. W. Ross (Eds.), *Democratic social education: social studies for social change* (pp. 203–228). New York: Falmer Press.

Sayers, S. (1990). Marxism and the dialectical method: A critique of G.A. Cohen. In S. Sayers & P. Osborne (Eds.), *Socialism, feminism, and philosophy: A radical philosophy reader* (pp. 140–168). New York: Routledge.

Segall, A. (1999). Critical history: Implications for history/social studies education. *Theory and Research in Social Education, 27*(3), 358–374.

Shor, I. (1992). *Empowering education: Critical teaching for social change* (1st ed.). Chicago: The University of Chicago Press.

Shor, I., & Freire, P. (1987). *A pedagogy for liberation: Dialogues on transforming education*. South Hadley, MA: Bergin & Garvey Publishers.

Sirin, S. R. (2005). Socioeconomic status and student achievement: A meta-analytic review of research. *Review of Educational Research, 75*(3), 417–453.

Steenland, K. (1974). The coup in Chile. *Latin American Perspectives, 1*(2), 9–29.

Stoddard, J. D., & Marcus, A. S. (2006). The burden of historical representation: Race, freedom, and "educational" Hollywood film. *Film & History, 36*(2), 26–35.

VanSledright, B. A. (2004). What does it mean to think historically ... and how do you teach it? *Social Education, 68*(3), 230–233.

Volosinov, V. N. (1986). *Marxism and the philosophy of language* (L. Matejka & I. R. Titunik, Trans.). Cambridge, MA: Harvard University Press.

Vygotsky, L. S. (1929). The problem of the cultural development of the child. *Journal of genetic psychology: child behavior, animal behavior, and comparative psychology, XXXVI*(1), 415–434.

Vygotsky, L. S. (1981). The genesis of higher mental functions (J. V. Wertsch, Trans.). In J. V. Wertsch (Ed.), *The Concept of activity in Soviet psychology* (pp. 144–188). Armonk, NY: M.E. Sharpe.

Vygotsky, L. S. (1987). Thinking and speech (N. Minick, Trans.). In R. W. Rieber & A. Carton (Eds.), *The collected works of L.S. Vygotsky: Problems of general psychology including the volume thinking and speech* (Vol. 1, pp. 37–285). New York: Plenum Press.

Wei, D., & Kamel, R. (Eds.). (1998). *Resistance in paradise: Rethinking 100 years of U.S. involvement in the Caribbean and the Pacific.* Philadelphia: American Friends Service Committee.

Willis, P. (1977). *Learning to labor: How working class kids get working class jobs.* New York: Columbia University Press.

Woods, A., & Grant, T. (2002). *Reason in revolt: Dialectical philosophy and modern science* (North American Edition ed., Vol. 1). New York: Algora Publishing.

Yang, K. W., & Duncan-Andrade, J. (2005). *Doc Ur Block.* Retrieved June 26, 2009, from http://www.edliberation.org/resources/records/doc-ur-block

Zinn, H. (1995). *A people's history of the United States: 1492-present* (Rev. & updated ed.). New York: HarperPerennial.

Wayne Au
University of Washington, Bothell

STEPHEN C. FLEURY

11. THE RADICAL AND THEORETICAL IN SOCIAL STUDIES

Each day seems like a natural fact/And what we think changes how we act.

Gill & King (1981)

Everything comes from somewhere, exists, and functions in a particular context or set of contexts; there's no such thing as a 'natural fact.'

Nealon & Searls Giroux (2003)

INTRODUCTION

This concluding essay asks the reader to consider the project of this book as both *less* radical and *more* radical than what its editors planned. It is less radical when viewed as "challenge[ing] the limits of ... the tradition of 'informed social criticism' within social studies education" (DeLeon & Ross, 2010, p. 4). Traditions, as socially learned habits and behaviors, enact personal preferences that may hardly be receptive to challenges in thinking from anyone outside of a respective cultural context. But when viewed through the lenses of theory—itself an activity of knowledge that strives for more thoughtful explanations and whose very rules compel the consideration of alternative ideas—this book is very radical indeed. "Radical" is an evocative term, often intentionally so, but its meaning becomes more extensive and gripping when one considers its etymological origins in the Greek *radicus*, or "with roots." Something radical—an idea, an action, a movement, a theory—can be startling, not because of being far removed from the normal, but because of having a deeper claim to the logic at hand, and for assuming the normal.

Much less evocative sounding, "theory" is frequently used so loosely and so ambiguously as to go unnoticed. But being unnoticed is not a good thing, especially in an institution that formally sets out to improve thinking. Nealon and Searls Giroux (2003), responding to the playfully serious lyrics of "Why Theory" by Gang of Four, explain that we *need* theory in life, especially in the socially deliberated activity called education. Theory can do work for us, as well as works on us, offering "angles of intervention" that are otherwise unavailable (p. 6). This is what the writings in this book provide. While no chapter is a self-standing theory (we might be wary of any that claimed to be one), each can be read as part of a theoretical arc of reflection and action, radical, also, because of being *rooted* in a social studies theory that has been muted and silenced in social studies discussions for a long time.

NOT ATTENDING TO THEORY

Social studies is a field long bereft of theory. At the forefront of discussions in the literature over the past half-century are terms like "camps" and "battles" and "wars" and "traditions." More recently, accounts have been framed in terms of "ideologies" and "cultures."

While useful metaphorical tools for categorizing a variety of different instructional ends, means, objectives, content, and teaching approaches, none of these constructions come close to the synthesizing and explanatory potential of an educational theory.

Educational theory—to be useful—needs to be deliberately prescriptive in practice as well as consonant with socially determined ends-in-view. Egan (1983) argues that this implicitly unique social policy function distinguishes the important role theory plays in education from the purely descriptive role it serves in other disciplines, i.e., disciplines that generate knowledge, such as the natural or social sciences. For sure, educational theories do well to draw upon the theoretical findings from these other fields, but such findings or theories by themselves do not constitute a sufficient basis for an "educational theory" and, with deleterious results, its underlying assumptive values may divert the intended educational goals. In fact, the tendency to allow theories wholesale from other disciplines to direct the purposes of social studies accounts, in large measure, for the curricular phenomenon identified by DeLeon and Ross in the Introduction to this book, that is, while appearing to involve a wide diversity of aims and approaches, the social studies is marked by an amazing uniformity in its actual delivery in the classroom.

How so?

The case at hand is the perplexing endurance of what has come to be called "traditional social studies," whose chronological framework of deliberately selected events and people amounts to a *de facto* theory of social knowledge that subtly inculcates a fateful sense of causality and inevitability—the vestige and secular manifestation of the Western cultural belief that history, properly recorded and told, is a revelation of "God's will unfolding" (Jackson, 2006, p. 80). From this deeply embedded cultural basis, the uncritical presentation in social studies classrooms of the Protestant Work Ethic, American Exceptionalism, Manifest Destiny, and Supply Side Economics is purely and theoretically deductive, albeit not consciously. Or as George Carlin (personal memory, circa late 20th Century) sardonically remarked, once you have the kids believing in the Easter Bunny and the Big Man in the Sky, you get the whole sha-bang—obedience, conformity, dogmatism, patriotism, the Fourth of July, and the Super Bowl!

Complementing this implicit social theory, the teaching methods of social studies are themselves unduly influenced by the nearly wholesale adoption of psychologically oriented findings as the foundations of pedagogy in general, but whose effect in social studies is even more invidious. The culturally embedded preference for "fate" that seems to underlay the disciplinary emphasis on "development" in educational psychology trumps the emancipatory potential of social studies, making the possibility of critical thinking seem contradictory. For example, Piaget's work has been interpreted to support and promote an age-bound accretion model of natural development—a model that, now promulgated by textbook companies as a description of thinking, becomes a *prescription* for teaching thinking, mitigating or even displacing one's rationale for teaching conceptually (for deliberately intervening to enhance a student's ability for thinking).

Allied in support of natural development, Bloom's Taxonomy is commonly perceived in many quarters of education as a scientifically-derived tool for teaching "higher order thinking," yet Bloom and his colleagues (1956, 1971) fully disclose in the first chapter of their book that the empirical basis for the taxonomy was limited to asking each other how they thought the categories should be organized. In other words, a group of psychometricians "thought up" the taxonomy for greater ease in organizing test items and objectives—face validity for sure, but arguably not qualifiable as a theoretical sound foundation for teaching. Despite its specious origins, Bloom's category system continues to import a linear theory of thinking into teaching that implicitly becomes a constraining order on the value of teaching conceptually for any but those students who already think well.

Research on "historical understanding" is one of the most prominent and high-status scholarly areas in social studies today. Primarily in the domain of psychological research, it emanates from the body of work developed by Lee Shulman on pedagogical content knowledge in the 1980s (Wineburg, 2001). One might hope that the previous misapplications of psychological research and theories to education would alert social studies educators to be more cautious about the tacit social and political values and objectives that are imported by focusing on "understanding" instead of on theoretical analysis, prediction, and explanation. But, alas, the prescriptions emanating from the work of historical understanding (at least as these can be observed on the posters of classroom walls) are laced with guidelines for helping students develop "perspective" about "occasions," "identifying motivation," "determining cause and effect," and concluding with "proof."

Speaking strictly from a knowledge generating perspective, history is not an inherently theory-bound activity (one needs to bring a theory to account for change in structures and social dynamics, i.e., "history"), and, lacking an epistemological structure for equitably negotiating and arriving at joint understandings (other than to argue over perspectives), a better historical understanding does not necessarily lead a student into being more self aware of the limitations of what they think they know, nor guide them in more equitably negotiating joint understandings, and may, at worse, sharpen their ideologies. While appropriate for generating imaginative personal perspectives and opinions of literary characters and events, the pedagogical results of this research seem far too cognitively ambiguous and analytically insufficient to represent that a useful social studies theory is either *at work* or working *for* students. As a nod to C. Wright Mills' (1959) concern in the late 1950s that "abstract empiricism" was erroneously displacing theorizing in the social sciences, there is still no reason today to believe that an aggregation of all the empirical findings on how students develop "historical understanding" leads to a social studies theory, nor that the findings alone provide sufficient evidence that its development makes any significant difference in the citizenship thinking and behavior of students. For this, we would need to begin with asking what *kind* of history and what kind of *understanding* is most desirable—an inherently value-laden, prescriptive inquiry.

CRITICAL ROOTS

Based on the case made above, the search for an independent social studies theory does not look very promising when examining contemporary practices. This was not the case nearly a half-century ago, when Lawrence Metcalf provided a comprehensive review and analysis of social studies research in the first *Handbook of Research on Teaching* (Gage, 1963). Drawing extensively from three contemporary review summaries (McLendon, 1960; McPhie, 1959; Gross & Badger, 1960), Metcalf reports disappointingly that most of the research in social studies was "broadly and vaguely defined" (p. 929) and that even the summaries themselves lacked a "framework or theory that would make possible a distinction between basic and trivial investigations" (p. 933).

Calling McLendon (1960) "at his best" in his "accounting" of research on social studies objectives (finding them "excessive" and "nebulous"), Metcalf makes an even stronger point of noting that McLendon's review of critical thinking fails to question "what it is, or how it might be taught, or even, indeed, whether it can be taught ... leav(ing) one with the unhappy impression that social studies research may have nothing to say on a matter as crucial as the teaching of critical thinking" (p. 931).

McPhie's (1959) attempt at summarizing all of the social studies dissertations of the previous twenty five years was apparently successful, but "listing and annotating everything of significance that has ever come to his attention, and much that had not" left both McPhie and the research open to Metcalf's criticism for lacking any "sustained concern with building and clarifying theory for teaching the social studies" (p. 931).

With a pattern now becoming familiar, Metcalf's pat description of Gross and Badger's (1960) review of 274 studies as a "competent history," and his gratuitous complement that their bibliography was the "most complete this writer has ever seen," barely conceals his frustration with their "objective" approach that lacked interpretive value, treatment of "technique without reference to a guiding theoretical framework," and equivocation between controversial social issues and personal problems when discussing the "problem-solving method"—supposedly, an area Gross championed (pp. 932–933). But most remissive in Metcalf's mind was their failure to reference Alan Griffin (1942), whose dissertation was "among the most significant studies of the past 20 years" (p. 932).

Tracing the theoretical trajectory of reflective thinking and conceptual teaching from Dewey (1910–1933) to Bayles (1950) and Hullfish and Smith (1961), Metcalf credits Griffin (1942) for "standing almost alone in his attempt to elaborate in practical and theoretical terms what reflective theory means for teaching history and for the subject matter preparation of high school history teachers" (p. 934). The importance and value Metcalf places on this social studies theory can be measured in his allocation of a majority of his review (29 of 35 pages) to describing its main theoretical principles, reviewing those studies that attempted to test some aspect of these principles, and outlining a number of theoretical and research issues regarding its implementation and implications for social studies education. Although likely familiar to the reader, some of the main propositions are highlighted here as examples of theoretically oriented, empirically testable, prescriptive propositions that relate a theory of knowledge and education with citizenship ends. In many ways, each is as current today as in 1963, potentially "falsifiable" through research and modifiable on the basis of further empirical and theoretical research—keeping in mind desired social ends, whether some form of reflective citizenship, social justice, human rights, or anarchy:

> Reflective thought is the active, careful and persistent examination of any belief or purported form of knowledge, in the light of the grounds that support it and the further conclusions toward which it ends. (p. 934)

> The survival of democracy in present times depends upon our recognition of reflection as THE method of determining truth. (p. 934)

> Societies are democratic in the degree to which they refrain from setting limits upon matters that may be thought about. (p. 934)

> Democracies have order and stability not by instilling beliefs, but rather through a reliance on knowledge. They must encourage occasions for doubt. (p. 934)

> Reflection, as the only means of ascertaining belief, becomes the central all embracing value (of a democracy). (p. 934)
>
> The development of children into adults who can steadily modify their beliefs in terms of their adequacy for explaining a widening range of experience requires two things: (1) improving and refining the reflective capacities of children, and (2) breaking through the hard shell of tradition which encases many deeply rooted and emotionally charged beliefs. (p. 935)
>
> Many areas of belief in American culture are not subject to reflective examination. Our beliefs about race and sex are more open to study than they once were. Religion and economics remain particularly difficult ... (p. 935)
>
> Students taught by the reflective method become more conscious of their attitudes, what they mean, and their interrelationships in a field of consequences. (p. 933)

One should carefully note that these principles are not simply calls for more enlightened self awareness or "informed social criticism"—a phrase that conceals the depths of reflective theory for "carefully examining beliefs" by confusing an informative stance about ontology (questioning *knowing that*) with an epistemological predisposition and ability to manipulate and challenge one's own knowledge (questioning *knowing how*). The theoretical principles outlined by Metcalf are tantamount to those of critical theory applied to social studies, albeit anachronistically. Or, critical theory, as it has developed, is in large part tantamount to reflective theory outside of the subject matter domain of social studies.

THE THOUGHTFUL DIFFERENCE

Metcalf recognized a social studies theory that challenged common beliefs would always be susceptible to criticism and resistance by individuals and groups in society who felt their way of life threatened. Cautioning teachers to be fully aware of the risks for being misunderstood or considered subversive, Metcalf also reminded readers of the much larger risk to the survival of democracy if social studies educators did *not* act on this theory. These risks are real. Popper (Miller, 1985) reminds us that this was the case in pre-Socratic Greece, and largely the context for the writing of the *Republic*, Plato's educational prescription to bring the spread of democracy under control. The Ionian School's creation of the pedagogical method of inquiry, and its related forays into science and democracy, had spread too rapidly and too widely for the comfort of the societal elite. Popper's homily on early democracy and critical thinking should prompt a slightly more alarming perspective about Alfred North Whitehead's (Griffin & Sherburne, 1979) observation that the philosophical tradition of Western civilization "consists of a series of footnotes to Plato" (p. 39).

Disappointed with the paucity of attention among his colleagues to significant questions of social studies research, Metcalf's concern for the role of theory was further prodded by the surge of federal funding for social studies reform in the early 1960s. He was critical in his review of Gross and Badger (1960) for not taking "to task those who label the social studies 'social slush,' without making it clear whether they oppose those who would substitute courses in history, political science, geography, economics, and sociology for various fused or correlated offerings" (p. 932). In retrospect, Metcalf rightly perceived that well-funded "experts" from the academic disciplines might hijack educational theory, or at the very least, displace it with the only type of theory they understood, that of their own disciplinary structures. This turned out to be true, for while the new social studies projects offered a great opportunity for theorizing in education (Schwab, 1978), an ironclad rationality and philosophy of positivist science predominated the language and materials of most efforts, turning the role of concepts, conceptual teaching, and inquiry into a veneered version of traditional social studies. Instead of experiencing genuine inquiry, discussion, and the challenges of theorizing, in most situations, students 'discovered' reified concepts and structures that had been identified by experts of each social science discipline (resulting in a continuation of the uniformity of social studies instruction of which DeLeon and Ross refer in the Introduction).

This is why, on the cusp of the second decade of the 21st century, a book on radical pedagogies and alternative perspectives on critical social studies theories is important. It offers to bring back the language of social studies theory and provides a rich offering of social studies concepts ranging from those probing a deeper and more contextual meaning of citizenship to different people and groups over time and place, to those concerning the inextricable political, economic and cultural relationships between our social and physical worlds, to those that challenge our very basis for thinking about thinking, knowing, seeing and understanding itself. The emphasis on concepts is important, and also important is that, like Griffin (1942), no distinction be made between concepts and generalizations. Generalizations are testable propositions (we may debate theories of testing as well), the starting point for analysis, and the method for bringing subject matter to bear on challenging student beliefs. It remains useful to keep in mind Metcalf's point (or was it Griffin's or Dewey's?) that no matter what the teacher is doing, the "task is largely conceptual in nature and will only be successful if rooted in sound theory."

A TENTATIVE SUMMARY

The creeping authoritarianism, militarism, and fascism in our major institutions signals danger to our relatively short experiment in democracy (about as long as the Ionians endured). No armies can protect a society against itself, and the only effective resistance is a heightened awareness of how we think, and so how we educate is more important than ever before. For those of us who teach social studies teachers, "critical" theory can be an elixir for some, and a torture for others. Attracted to the abstracting comforts of "grand theory," the former may have a tendency to become "drunk on syntax and blind to semantics" (to use the words of C. Wright Mills' (1961). The latter group, sensing that close attention to abstractions may lead to something concretely uncomfortable, may embrace a self-righteous temperance that repels the need for further thinking. The chapters in this book, engagingly conceptual and concretely applicable to both the means and ends of social studies education, avoid both dysfunctions, and return the radical potency of theory to social studies discussions.

REFERENCES

Bloom, B. S. (Ed.). (1971). *Taxonomy of educational objectives: The classification of education goals, handbook I: Cognitive domain*. New York: David McKay. (Original publication 1956)

Egan, K. (1983). *Education and psychology*. New York: Teachers College Press.

Gill, A., King, J., & Gang of Four. (1995). Why theory? [Recorded by Gang of Four]. *On Solid Gold* [CD]. New York: EMI. (Original recording 1981).

Griffin, A. F. (1942). *A philosophical approach to the subject-matter preparation of teachers of history*. Unpublished dissertation, The Ohio State University, Columbus, Ohio. (Reprinted by the National Council for the Social Studies, 1992)

Griffin, D. R., & Sherburne, D. W. (Eds.). (1979). *Process and reality* (Gifford lectures delivered in the university of Edinburgh during the session 1927–28). New York: Free Press.

Gross, R. E., & Badger, W. V. (1960). Social studies. In C. W. Harris (Ed.), *Encyclopedia of educational research* (3rd Ed., pp. 1296–1319.). New York: Macmillan.

Hullfish, G. H., & Smith, P. G. (1961). *Reflective thinking: The method of education*. New York: Dodd, Mead.

Jackson, P. T. (2006). *Civilizing the enemy: German Reconstruction and the invention of the West*. Ann Arbor, MI: University of Michigan Press.

Metcalf, L. E. (1963). Research on teaching the social studies. In N. L. Gage (Ed.), *Handbook of research on teaching* (pp. 929-965). Chicago: Rand McNally.

Mills, C. W. (1961). *The sociological imagination*. New York: Oxford University Press.

McPhie, W. (1959). *A comprehensive bibliographic guide to doctoral dissertations in social studies education*. Washington, DC: Research Committee, National Council for the Social Studies.

McLendon, J. C. (1960). *Teaching the social studies*. Washington DC: American Educational Research Association, National Education Association.

Miller, D. (Ed.). (1985). *Popper selections*. Princeton, NJ: Princeton University Press.

Nealon, J., & Searls Giroux, S. (2003). *The theory toolbox: Critical concepts for the humanities, arts, and social sciences*. New York: Rowman & Littlefield.

Wineburg, S. (2001). *Historical thinking and other unnatural acts: Charting the future of teaching the past*. Philadelphia: Temple University Press.

Stephen C. Fleury
Le Moyne College

CPSIA information can be obtained at www.ICGtesting.com
Printed in the USA
LVOW091437310712

292376LV00002B/21/P